Beyond Vienna:
Contemporary Literature
from the Austrian Provinces

Studies in Austrian Literature, Culture and Thought

General Editors:

Jorun B. Johns
Richard H. Lawson

Beyond Vienna

Contemporary Literature from the
Austrian Provinces

Edited by

Todd C. Hanlin

ARIADNE PRESS
Riverside, California

Ariadne Press would like to express its appreciation to the Bundesministerium für Wissenschaft und Forschung, Vienna for assistance in publishing this book.

Library of Congress Cataloging-in-Publication Data

Beyond Vienna : contemporary literature from the Austrian provinces / edited and with an introduction by Todd C. Hanlin.
   p. cm.
   Includes bibliographical references.
   ISBN 978-1-57241-163-0 (alk. paper)
   1. Austrian literature—20th century—History and criticism.
2. Austrian literature—Austria—States. 3. Rural conditions in literature.
I. Hanlin, Todd C.

PT3818.B47 2008
830.9'9436--dc22

                                                        2008037935

Cover Design
Art Director: George McGinnis

Copyright 2008
by Ariadne Press
270 Goins Court
Riverside, CA 92507

All rights reserved.
No part of this publication may be reproduced or transmitted
in any form or by any means without formal permission.
Printed in the United States of America.
ISBN 978-1-57241-163-0

CONTENTS

Introduction   5
    Todd C. Hanlin

FRIEDRICH CH. ZAUNER   24
Heaven and Hell: Friedrich Ch. Zauner's
Heimat Tetralogy 'The End of Eternity'
    by Jörg Thunecke

ALOIS BRANDSTETTER   60
"Vienna is far away": Alois Brandstetter's
Proclivity to the Provinces
    by Paul F. Dvorak

ANNA MITGUTSCH   84
Landscapes of Suffering: The Depiction of Rural
Austria in Anna Mitgutsch's *Punishment*
    by Kathleen Condray

CHRISTINE LAVANT   112
Madness in the Landscape: Christine Lavant's
Provincial Modernism
    by Geoffrey C. Howes

4 *Beyond Vienna*

FELIX MITTERER 144
Felix Mitterer: An Attorney of the Weak and
Suffering
    by Gerlinde Ulm Sanford

GLORIA KAISER 178
Gloria Kaiser: From Provincial to International
Author
    by Donald G. Daviau

ELISABETH REICHART 208
Elisabeth Reichart's *Komm über den See*:
Upper Austria and the Excavation of Its History
    by Felix W. Tweraser

VLADIMIR VERTLIB 230
Vladimir Vertlib, a Global Intellectual: Exile,
Migration, and Individualism in the Narratives
of a Russian Jewish Author in Austria
    by Dagmar C. G. Lorenz

XAVER BAYER 262
Virtual Reality: The Internalization of External
Reality in Xaver Bayer's Novel *Weiter*
    by Renate Posthofen and Jörg Thunecke

Contributors 291

Introduction

> "Let us suppose for instance that a child endowed with the talent of a Mozart were born among some savage nation such as the Samoans before they were influenced by European civilization. Would such a child, after reaching maturity, compose stringed quartettes and symphonies? Certainly not."
>
> August Weismann[1]

Thus the remarkable influences of civilization upon our primeval talents, according to the eminent German biologist Weismann (1834-1914). For not only does community provide protection for the individual, it also allows a possible division of labor, permitting specialization, ultimately leisure time, and the opportunity to explore "impractical" talents, such as the arts. If these are the broad benefits of community, they can conceivably be multiplied if we organize into larger units such as towns and cities that act as a basis for the organization of government, commerce, even a social and spiritual life. Indeed, national capitals function as a focal point, a magnet for finance, political power, individual ability, and even beauty, such as occurred in England, France, Holland, and Spain. Fortunately for world culture, Mozart was able to spend much of his short-lived adulthood amidst a tradition of brilliant music, a sophisticated audience, and a covey of generous benefactors... in Vienna.

Vienna, the city of dreams, is just such a place where political, economic, and social currents meet. It has long been an inhabited site, first by the Celts, then as the Roman settlement

6   Beyond Vienna

Vindobona; after the disappearance of the original Roman encampment, an "Austrian" Vienna is first noted in 1137.[2] By 1440 it had become an imperial city, the residence of Habsburg emperors.

At the beginning of the 19th century, Vienna had become the undisputed cultural center of the sprawling Habsburg Empire as well, rivaling other major European centers such as London, Paris, Amsterdam, and Madrid. One hundred years later, the city was simply exploding with culture, as Janik and Toulmin point out:

> ... if we look on early-twentieth-century Viennese architecture and art, journalism and jurisprudence, philosophy and poetry, music, drama and sculpture as so many parallel and independent activities which just happened to be going on in the same place at the same time, we shall once again end by accumulating vast amounts of detailed technical information in each separate field, while shutting our eyes to the most significant fact about all of them—namely, that they *were* all going on in this same place at this same time.[3]

Nothing could compare with the bright lights, the sheer number and variety of sophisticated entertainments, the prestige of seeing and being seen with the best and the brightest of a multi-national empire.

It used to be said that a Viennese identity can be acquired. How else would it have been possible for members of all kinds of nations and mother tongues to assemble in this city over many centuries and, without shedding much of their outward and inner make-up, be integrated completely into a very specific community?

Most of them were newcomers at one time or another.[4]

Indeed, though Hofmannsthal, Altenberg, Broch, von Doderer, Zweig, and Schnitzler were actually born in Vienna, other notable writers of the time, such as Kraus, Trakl, Musil, Roth, Lenau, Bahr, and the Prague natives Kafka and Werfel were drawn to the city for greater or lesser parts of their lives. Conversely, a civil servant, employee, or soldier posted to the provinces, say, Galicia or Dalmatia, would consider himself expelled from heaven or, at the very least, banished for an indeterminate period of time from the radiance of the "imperial sun," to employ Kafka's analogy.[5]

This widely held belief in Vienna's cultural superiority persists to the present day. Felix Mitterer, responding to the question of his contact with dramatist-colleagues, is quoted as saying:

> In general I would say that the writers here in Austria are pretty individualistic in their approach; each lives and works for and by him- or herself. And then too, I'm a bit isolated, geographically speaking, since I choose to live here in Innsbruck, while almost all of the others, even those who came from the country, have moved to Vienna. There are some in Graz, too, but most of them live in Vienna. Also, I have opted to not have much to do with the business side of literature and literary circles, and this of course takes place in Vienna.[6]

Nevertheless, the dynamic relationship between writer and readership has changed drastically over the last century. Whereas there were previously a cluster of prestigious publishers in Vienna (today Böhlau, Braumüller, Zsolnay/Deuticke, Kaiser-verlag are esteemed houses) with less prominent publishers in

8 Beyond Vienna

secondary cities (current regional examples would be Edition va bene in Klosterneuburg, Haymon-Verlag in Innsbruck, Jung und Jung or Otto Müller in Salzburg, and Residenz Verlag in St. Pölten), regional writers and publishers had little realistic hope of attracting a larger market; rarely would a regional author attract a major Austrian publisher—much less a larger audience in Germany. Consequently, a more realistic goal would be to target a local reading public. Each larger town or provincial capital would thus hope to cultivate a literary circle of writers and readers as proof of their indigenous "culture" and social worth. Moreover, in 1900 there were a finite number of publishers with finite budgets, and a limited number of booksellers, reviewers (as well as readers!); today the venues for books have expanded exponentially: with the Internet, publishers large and small, regardless of location or budget, can make their books and authors available to a global audience through on-line marketing and sales; ultimately, each and every book will conceivably be available through digital downloads, on computer as well as digital reading devices such as the Kindle e-book reader. And on a more personal level: at the beginning of the 21st century with scientific and technological advancements in transportation and communication (with satellite television and the Internet, for example), is there any longer a socio-political or cultural advantage to residing in Vienna? With instant communication, has it become irrelevant where (or even how) an author lives? And are life experiences noticeably different, whether a person resides in the capital or in any other city, large or small, near or far from Kafka's "Imperial sun"?

Certainly national or even international literary movements or affiliated groups (such as "Young Vienna" or *Jung-Wien* around 1900 or, later, the "Viennese Group" or *Wiener Gruppe,* the more recent *Neue Wiener Gruppe,* or movements such as Post-modernism) would more naturally find a home in the capital as a result of the urban concentration of both artists and a cosmopolitan audience; provincial cities were left to become imitators or competitors, such as with the "Graz Group" (*Grazer Gruppe*). As one scholar has indicated, a postwar attempt to bridge the gap between Vienna and the provinces met with little resonance:

> ... and the situation today remains as problematical as it always has been in Austria. The antagonism between the P.E.N. Club in Vienna and the "*Forum Stadtpark*" in Graz is as strong today as ever... A gulf now exists not only between Vienna and the provinces, but also between the older and younger generation of writers.[7]

It is curious that today's Austrians should question the very existence of a distinctly "Austrian" literature, as formulated in the two questions: Is there an Austrian literature? And, if so, what is its nature? This uncertainty is likely the result of their country's labyrinthian journey through the Twentieth Century: torn from the security of the Habsburg womb which had endured for more than 600 years, the people suffered the isolation and loss of 1918 that basically estranged them from their centuries'-old traditions and history. The defeat in World War I brought about a troubled republic and soon a desperate marriage with Nazi Germany, followed by yet another defeat in World War II, a humiliating occupation, and eventually humble neutrality within a second republic. Austria's erstwhile international influence has been reduced to housing functions of the United Nations, an ironic reminder of actual bygone importance of hosting the Congress of Vienna almost two hundred years prior. Simultaneously, its landmarks and landscapes have since been developed for the pleasure (and currency) of foreign tourists, even as their currency was being exchanged for a multinational standard which more easily enables Austrians to replace their distinctive customs and costumes with internationally imported fads and fancies of an unparalleled blandness. Ergo, a loss of national identity.

In the debate over the presence or absence of a distinctly Austrian literature, several of our contributors may write of a literature promoting rural values, customs, landmarks, dialect, even local historical dates or sites, representing a pastoral, paradisiacal milieu, all under the rubric of a *Heimatliteratur*, a "native literature" that signifies a certain beloved town or region or language area—often as an alternative to an inter- or supranational culture that bears no relationship to Austria or to the Austrians. One variation of this rural literature is its antithesis, an *Anti-Heimatliteratur* that exposes the harsh living conditions, the ignorance or cruelty of the rural inhabitants. But our question today is somewhat different: What is the contribution of the provinces? Is it to provide fresh inspiration and new vigor, unsophisticated yet unadulterated ideas, an uncorrupted and non-cynical view of life? Or should a relationship with the countryside emphasize our lost ties to Nature by fostering an insistence on the healthy rather than dwelling on the sick or demented, the decadent or degenerate within the urban setting? Some of the so-called provincial literature or *Heimatliteratur* is a result of talented writers being born in cities outside Vienna; in other instances, it is a resistance to or even a revolt against contemporary trends of inter-nationalization, where regional or even national characteristics are ignored or sacrificed to global trends in business, technology, and popular culture. As in most advanced societies, consumerism has become a dominant force, a force characterized by acquisition without appreciation. All too often rural areas are developed for tourist-intended amusements and rapidly become asphalt roadways, golf courses, and ski resorts—to the detriment of the environment as well as to the Austrian psyche.

As to the genesis of this book: I have long been aware of the stereotypical image of Habsburg Austria as top-heavy with

Vienna as its prestigious hub, especially at the turn of the 20th century. However, it is self-evident that not everyone could or should reside in the capital, and that many talented authors lived outside that glamorous residential city, either by choice or by circumstance. Thus, to me, the idea of "Beyond Vienna" became an expansive, fascinating, irresistible topic—and one that I could not hope to engage alone. Lacking the necessary research materials, the time, as well as the intestinal fortitude to complete this endeavor by myself, I turned to a thoroughly modern solution for productivity… outsourcing: I invited over a dozen scholars whose work I know and appreciate, whose writings and presentations I have admired over the years, and asked them to join in this project. Happily, enough complied to bring this book to fruition. I am indebted to them for making my idea a reality. Though I may have suggested a name here or there, the contributors themselves determined which authors were to be included in our book. Furthermore, the contributors were encouraged to incorporate extended passages from the works under consideration to give the reader, both in the original German and in English, a feeling for the unique flavor and style of each individual writer; they were also asked to provide a select bibliography of each particular author's works in the original and in translation for the curious reader.

The writers under discussion represent a mere sampling—there are many others who could as easily have been included, were it not for space limitations. Nevertheless, I am fascinated by the final outcome: men and women of all ages (including one deceased) and backgrounds, writers of poetry, drama, novels and short stories, of various approaches and subjects. The list of authors is admittedly not exhaustive, but does approximate a cross-section of Austrian writers, unintentionally representing several of the nine provinces: three are from Upper Austria, one from Styria, another from Carinthia, yet another from Tyrol, while a seventh writer lives in Salzburg; for balance, there is even a dyed-in-the-wool Viennese, because even for those authors who are not truly "provincial," a trip to the provinces can often lead to insights not available to them in their familiar surroundings in the capital. And, finally, writers nowadays don't even have to be committed patriots—Gloria Kaiser has spent half of her career writing about Brazilian history, while Felix Mitterer has moved his family to Ireland—indeed far "beyond Vienna"!

Since the primary focus of the project was literature outside Vienna, there was no inherent order of presentation. It was not my original intent to have one writer represent each of the different provinces or to present them according to style, genre, or any other categorization. But once the final selection had taken shape, I was struck by a quote from the Austrian Klaus Zeyringer (as cited in Kathleen Condray's article) to the effect that "a whole generation of Austrian authors who came of age from the 1960s to the 1980s did so in rural provinces and that their experiences are reflected in their work."[8] With this perspective in mind, I reconsidered the order of arrangement and settled on a generational approach, hoping that it might shed some light on the different generations' perceptions and attitudes toward provincial Austria and thus, indirectly, toward Vienna as well.

The two "elder statesmen" of our group, Friedrich Ch. Zauner and Alois Brandstetter, were both born in Upper Austria in the late 1930s; thus through their parents and grandparents, their neighbors and contemporaries, both have had contact with the "old Austria," with its traditions and values well before modernization, urban sprawl, and the accompanying erosion of indigenous customs and folk culture. Contributor Jörg Thunecke characterizes **FRIEDRICH CH. ZAUNER** (*1936) and his work —in particular a tetralogy spanning the years from approximately 1900 to the annexation of Austria in 1938—as "a fictional account of the effects of the outside world on a village community that, up to that point, had been hermetically cut off both socially and economically"(32). The novels are set in four rural villages rather than in the capital, all the better for Zauner to resurrect the lost world of his provinces through his fictional portrayal. Thuneke acknowledges the purpose of Zauner's work is neither to praise nor to condemn the *Heimat,* but "to (re-) discover it... based on an overwhelming amount of details founded in reality, stupendous quantities of established historical data and verifiable facts"(26). As a writer, Zauner is determined to present the local language, its vocabulary, including the terminology for institutions, implements, and customs that have become extinct in a rapidly evolving world. In strikingly visual terms, Zauner revives a lost world of "local customs, tools and work routines, the enumerations and descriptions of which are often more extensive than those in local history museums"(34). Through Zauner's eyes, we can recognize that change can be seen as a threat to this precious yet fragile environment.

If, at the outset, we sought the antithesis of a *"Heimatdichter,"* someone who defies the preconception of a petulant, outdated, reactionary Luddite curmudgeon, **ALOIS BRANDSTETTER** (*1938) would be an ideal candidate: he is a thoroughly modern man, at once an intellectual and a thoughtful citizen who recognizes qualities that should be preserved in the broader Austrian milieu. A native of Upper Austria, Brandstetter now lives in Klagenfurt, Carinthia. For this son of the provinces, Vienna (and, indeed, the rest of the modern world) represents the artificiality and shortcomings that pervade present-day consumer society, threatening the essential uniqueness and individuality of everything in its shadow. As Paul F. Dvorak succinctly notes, prized remnants of Brandstetter's youth include "father and family, home and mill, church, bible and religious devotions, local farmers and neighborliness, postmen (who brought more than the mail), unpaved roads, Greek, Latin, and local dialect, familial Habsburg loyalty, and Roman ruins and remnants"(66), in short, our Western cultural heritage, including its decimation by a post-modern society with its paved roads and modernization, its industrialization, technology, and consumerism. Brandstetter's affinity to the land, its traditions and its language, convince us that something substantial can be irretrievably lost, and we ignore our past at our own peril. The dilemma represents the specifically Austrian challenge of a modern society precariously balanced atop a centuries'-old cultural landscape. Brandstetter does not promulgate a return to the Middle Ages, but he is equally unwilling to sacrifice his substantial cultural heritage. The variations of his provincial writings, or *Heimatdichtung*, embody the richness of Austrian culture—at once, timeless and yet distinctly Austrian—tinged with a baroque melancholy.

Born a decade later than Zauner and Brandstetter, **ANNA MITGUTSCH** (*1948) is a child of the Second Republic, coming of age in the late 1960s. Mitgutsch was raised in Upper Austria, and in her first major novel *Punishment* (*Die Züchtigung,* 1985), the rural setting is synonymous with violence. It is reminiscent of Franz Innerhofer's shocking 1973 bestseller *Beautiful Days* (*Schöne Tage*), a chronicle of abuse and cruelty that instantly destroyed any preconceived ideas of a bucolic harmonious world (*heile Welt*). Moreover, Mitgutsch condemns not simply the countryside, but in broader terms her Austrian homeland as well. The rural setting is much more than a backdrop for the events of the novel; it plays a central role in the narrative itself, as the protagonist is both drawn to ownership of the land for the power it represents and repelled by the violence inherent in the agrarian society. The female protagonist Marie juggles a complicated dual relationship: on the one hand, she wants to belong to the farming community, however violent and flawed, because she understands the basic social principles behind it—foremost is that those who have land belong to the privileged class, as she did before her marriage to a man of lesser standing. At the same time, she is contemptuous of the backward rural ways and thus continuously attempts to depict herself as a city dweller upon returning to her farm. As Kathleen Condray writes: "At her core, Marie [the main character] remains a farmer's daughter which is why she is not accepted in the city, no matter how well she is able to fool the residents of the country with the trappings of urban society"(96). In Mitgutsch's view, the challenge of gaining respect as an individual, whether in an urban or rural social setting, is complicated by the unwritten rules that silently govern both societies—for someone from the lower middle-class, especially a woman, the goal may simply be unattainable.

CHRISTINE LAVANT (1915-1973) does not strictly meet our criteria for "living" authors, since she passed on almost two generations ago. Nevertheless, she represents a faith (or should we say, an obsessive piety) that could only be nurtured in the provinces where there is sufficient time and space for faith or its correlative, doubt. A native of Carinthia who lived exclusively in the village of St. Stefan, Lavant wrote poetry drawn mainly from four familiar and basic spheres: her rural Carinthian landscape, the Catholic Church, the skies, and the human body. As if to frustrate our expectations of a wholesome provincial upbringing, she destroyed every scrap of paper that she had written before the end of the Second World War, and all that remains is the poetry published since 1948. First and foremost, Lavant was definitely not a "primitive" artist, some Grandma Moses whose quaint portraits enchant us with their simplicity and naiveté. As a result of severe disabilities originating in childhood, she was faced with overcoming isolation, loneliness, and an overwhelming feeling of being deserted by her God. The resulting poetry may be described as 'provincial modernism,' for according to Geoffrey C. Howes: "Lavant's lyrical alter ego yearns to go mad, for this would mean a loss of painful individuation and isolation" (120). Her poetry, taken in this light, can perhaps be seen as a provocation, an attempt to so enrage her deity that He would be angered into a response, thus proving His existence and, more importantly, His concern for Lavant as an individual sufferer. Does she therefore feign madness as an excuse for provoking her God, or is this her fallback position if He doesn't respond? The larger question for Howes, however, is: how could "an apparent naïf who suffered chronic and serious childhood illnesses, which left her partly blind and deaf, blossom in spite of geographical, social, physical, and gender-related limitations into a recognized poetic talent who contributed some of the finest German-language lyric poetry of the twentieth century"(116)?

As Gerlinde Ulm Sanford writes so perceptively of **FELIX MITTERER** (*1948): "one could maintain that most of Mitterer's works are, in one way or another, variations on the topic of 'homeland'"(148). And, indeed, the rural and regional influences on this dramatist are especially significant, perhaps even more so than on a novelist or poet: his early theatrical training in the Tyrolean provinces, both as an actor and as a dramatist on small local or portable stages (so-called *Wanderbühnen*), brought him in close contact with his audiences and thus had a direct influence on his dramatic works. The intimate contact encouraged his humanistic approach while at the same time sharpening the theatrical impact of his writing. With his breakthrough play *Kein Platz für Idioten* in 1970, Mitterer's works have been, in the main, serious, problematic pieces, characterized by minimalist staging and costumes, a consequence of his provincial apprenticeship. With few exceptions, he writes in the tradition of bourgeois theater (often with small-town or rural lower-class protagonists as well), with dramatic emphasis on innocent victims—the elderly, the infirm, the displaced, the disadvantaged, and the disenfranchised—in Sanford's own words, "the weak and the suffering."

A native of Styria, **GLORIA KAISER** (*1950) had become a successful businesswoman as an accountant, but decided to forego her profession to become a freelance writer. With her first publications in 1980, short stories based on personal experience, she betrayed a keen eye and a good sense of the people and their lives in small-town Austria. However, a pleasure trip to Brazil allowed her a broader, international perspective. From this point on, Kaiser was no longer interested in dwelling on her hometown Vienna; she had grown away from the capital and, indeed, from the country itself. To some degree her initial interest in Brazil was fostered by her desire to redeem the debilitating influence of the Habsburgs on 19th-century Brazil. As Donald G. Daviau writes, her prose work presents a "detailed and insightful examination of the life and times of Brazil and Portugal from the 17th to the end of the 19th century"(209). Kaiser's literature certainly goes "beyond Vienna," focusing on third-world Brazil in an attempt at mutual Austro-Brazilian understanding, partially to offset the Austrian exploitation of Brazil. A realist who often depicts the decrepit conditions in disadvantaged small towns, Kaiser has written six novels to date, contrasting an ageing, dying Europe with a young, developing Brazil, while concurrently focusing on depicting intelligent women and their achievements in humanizing Brazilian culture. In subtle psychological ways, we could consider Kaiser's literary depictions of Brazil and the Brazilians as a form of *Heimatliteratur*, both for the indigenous portrait of a country and its people, but also since they represent much of intrinsic value that has disappeared from Austrian life during Kaiser's lifetime.

ELISABETH REICHART (*1953) was born in a small-town in Upper Austria, studied history and German literature in Salzburg and Vienna, and wrote a doctoral dissertation on the resistance to National Socialism in the Salzburg region. Since 1982 she has been a professional writer, with her first literary success in 1984, the novel *February Shadows* (*Februarschatten*).

She also edited an anthology on 'Austrian Women Writers' (*Österreichische Dichterinnen*) in 1993, and presently lives in Vienna. Since Reichart has lived both in the provinces and now in Vienna, her relationship to both is of great interest to our topic, in a personal and artistic vein. We might be intrigued, for example, whether she praises or criticizes Upper Austria, and whether she could be considered a writer of *Anti-Heimatliteratur*? In her short novel 'Come Across the Lake' (*Komm über den See*, 1988), the main character, Ruth, leaves Vienna with unanswered questions that are only resolved in the provinces (albeit in the presence of uncooperative attitudes). Reichart's protagonist finds "truth," unpleasant and threatening truth, in the provinces; the author admits that similar, intimidating circumstances also existed in Vienna, that reflections on her Viennese experience are clarified by the distance, in time and space, which the provincial vantage point provides. According to Felix W. Tweraser, Reichart's purpose in writing this novel was to create or reawaken memory through an aesthetic experience on the 50th anniversary of Austria's annexation or *Anschluss* at the hands of the Nazis. While Vienna, as the capital, may exhibit public displays to the past, the decision to erect such monuments is made, not by the public at large, but by government bodies, either local or national, thus the number and anonymity of its inhabitants may ironically minimize the monuments' impact—while in the provinces, in smaller towns, face-to-face encounters with townspeople and neighbors may keep history alive on a personal level. Ironically, it is only after the protagonist has departed from Vienna's "comfort zone," that she is able to empathize and understand the historical resistance to Nazi inhumanity, suggesting that Viennese "civilization" and "culture" are so thick that reality cannot penetrate and that truth may effectively be buried under lovely monuments—whereas provincials have no such pretensions or facades, or simply don't take the effort to hide their prejudices.

VLADIMIR VERTLIB (*1966) was born in Leningrad in the former USSR. As a Jewish émigré and outsider, he originally settled with his family in Austria in 1981, initially in Vienna; but he then married an Austrian woman, moved to Salzburg, and in retrospect must confess: "I have truly become an Austrian, or more precisely, Viennese. I have to leave Vienna in order to understand that, over the years, I have assumed all the prejudices of this city—the smugness, arrogance, egocentricity, narcissistic love-hate, contempt for the 'provinces,' an inferiority complex toward foreign countries, and a nostalgic transfiguration of our former significance as a metropolis"(238). Vertlib's personal odyssey is dizzying: he is not considered Jewish enough in Israel because he comes from secular Russia, is not circumcised, has no Jewish education, and is not an observant Jew. In Germany, Austria, and the United States, on the other hand, he and his parents suffer abuse precisely because they are considered Jews and foreigners. As Dagmar C. G. Lorenz concludes: "It is nonetheless ironic that Germany and Austria, the countries most closely associated with the Nazi atrocities, are the most accessible fifty-some years after the Shoah"(248).

Fittingly, in his novel 'Deportation' (*Abschiebung*, 1995), the author depicts the central issue of Jews in Austria dating back to the early 20th century and Vertlib's counterpart, the Jewish writer Jakob Wassermann. As victims of global persecution, the Jews in Vertlib's works themselves become prejudiced out of self-protection, frequently disparaging others whom they deem to be inferior: thus prejudice and persecution beget further prejudice and persecution. Yet to settle outside Vienna poses another dilemma: precisely because the provincial town was not Vienna—it wasn't even Graz, Czernowitz, or Brünn, and "has played virtually no role in Jewish history"(256-257)—the author identifies it as a neutral space in which to construct a new identity. Therefore the province, or at least certain insignificant parts of the province that have no discernable Jewish past, can represent a curiously ahistorical *tabula rasa* for Vertlib and may thus be acceptable as a substitute *Heimat* for Vienna.

The final author in our anthology is the youngest and, in many ways, the most problematic. **XAVER BAYER** (*1977) was born and currently resides in Vienna and, as a result, would not appear to belong within the parameters of our discussion. But, as Renate Posthofen and Jörg Thuneke point out, for Bayer all larger cities on this planet have become internationalized, thus similar in their amenities as well as in the appearance of their inhabitants—unique or individualized aspects no longer exist, especially in densely-populated urban environments like Vienna. As depicted in his novel 'Onward' (*Weiter*, 2006), the "monotony and uniformity of modern existence"(277) are emphasized. In contemporary urban environments, regardless of the country or even the continent, emptiness—whether a space or a silence—cannot be tolerated and must be filled. Thus the narrator feels strange in this all-too familiar "global village" and would feel more "at home" in a totally unfamiliar setting, such as Antarctica. He yearns for his lost youth and the excitement when all was new and unexpected. The emptiness of life in an urban environment like Vienna is contrasted with a childhood journey to his grandparents' home in Lower Austria. In the provinces, even in winter with its loss of color and vitality, the author sees and appreciates everything in black and white, in a heightened "color." Nevertheless, Bayer questions whether life in today's provinces is any better, or if it merely reminds us of what we have lost through its remaining ruins. He concludes that we cannot experience anything new or unexpected in reality anymore, perhaps only in the virtual reality of computer games which have become strikingly similar to the "lost provincial reality of his childhood." It is truly ironic that Bayer yearns for an erstwhile reality that can only be re-created today by the very symbol of modern universal ennui that afflicts him... the ubiquitous computer.

Compared with the other authors in our anthology, Bayer represents a generational shift in his preoccupation with virtual reality—an innovation that allows a younger generation to experience the past (here: World War II) or even the provinces in a way that was not previously possible, except as fantasy; indeed, we can now not only physically escape Vienna and its present reality, but escape it virtually as well! Computer games thus have the potential to supplant contemporary reality (which is increasingly international, like life in today's Vienna) with an unfamiliar environment similar to the lost provincial life of Bayer's—and Zauner's and Brandstetter's—childhood.

Editorial Note

The original German titles of works are given in italics. If the work has been published in an English translation, the official title is also presented in italics; if the work has not appeared in English, an approximate title and related translations are offered in normal typescript and single quotation marks.

NOTES

[1] August Weismann, "Thoughts Upon the Musical Sense in Animals and Man," in *Essays upon Heredity and Kindred Biological Problems*, Vol. II, translated by Frau Lüroth (Oxford: Clarendon Press, 1892), 42.

[2] For a detailed account of the city's development over the centuries, I recommend Karl Mayreder's chapter on "Stadtentwicklung," in *Wien: Am Anfang des XX. Jahrhunderts: Ein Führer in technischer und künstlerischer Richtung*, hrsg. Vom österreichischen Ingenieur- und Architekten-Verein, Bd. 1 (Wien: Verlag von Gerlach & Wiedling, 1905), 49-79.

[3] Allan Janik and Stephen Toulmin, *Wittgenstein's Vienna* (New York: Simon and Schuster, 1973), 18.

[4] Hilde Spiel, *Vienna's Golden Autumn, 1866-1938* (New York: Weidenfeld and Nicolson, 1987), 26.

[5] "The Emperor, so it runs, has sent a message to you, the humble subject, the insignificant shadow cowering in the remotest distance before the imperial sun...." From "An Imperial Message" [*"Eine kaiserliche Botschaft"*], translated

by Willa and Edwin Muir, in Franz Kafka, *Parables and Paradoxes* (New York: Schocken Books, 1961), 13-15.

[6] As quoted in "An Interview with Felix Mitterer," by Nicholas J. Meyerhofer and Karl E. Webb, in *Felix Mitterer: A Critical Introduction*, edited by Meyerhofer and Webb (Riverside, CA: Ariadne Press, 1995), 37.

[7] Donald G. Daviau, "Introduction," to *Major Figures of Contemporary Austrian Literature*, ed. Daviau (New York: Peter Lang, 1987), 10-11.

[8] Klaus Zeyringer, *Österreichische Literatur 1945-1998: Überblicke, Einschnitte, Wegmarken* (Innsbruck: Haymon-Verlag, 1999), 106.

FRIEDRICH CH. ZAUNER
Courtesy of the Author

Heaven and Hell: Friedrich Ch. Zauner's *Heimat* Tetralogy 'The End of Eternity'[1]

by Jörg Thunecke

This is neither the time nor the place to discuss, once again, at great length the pros and cons of *Heimat* and anti-*Heimat* literature. Merely the main points of an extensive debate shall be briefly outlined so that Friedrich Ch. Zauner's (*1936) tetralogy *Das Ende der Ewigkeit* ('The End of Eternity'),[2] the work of one of Austria's most important contemporary authors, may be placed in its proper literary context, as Karl-Markus Gauß attempted some years ago: "The tradition which he [Zauner] rejects," he wrote in the mid-1990s, "is that of mendacious Austrian *Heimat* literature; the cliché which he takes objection to is based on the assumption that during the past thirty years anti-*Heimat* literature has almost become the standard of Austrian literature."[3] Thus this tetralogy reflects on the one hand Zauner's opposition to a tradition as practiced by authors from Rosegger to Waggerl,[4] establishing, parallel to the traditional *Heimat* novel, a 'corrective'[5] to help 'rehabilitate' this literary genre;[6] on the other hand, Zauner's tetralogy must also be regarded as a response to the anti-*Heimat* literature of the 1970s, i.e. to a kind of 'opposition' literature, meant to lay open the mendacity of traditional *Heimat* literature.[7] For anti-*Heimat*, in an attempt to expose a supposedly wholesome world as oppressive and restrictive,[8] had itself deteriorated into a kind of ideology, a literary lie by the time the first volume of Zauner's 'The End of Eternity' was published.[9] These four volumes therefore have to be seen in this dual context.[10] It is paramount, however, to bear in mind that "a genre, which does not see the world simply in terms of heaven or hell, but prefers to explore it by literary means, always had a difficult stand against two kinds of falsification, the ideology of the secluded retreat, as well as the dictate of the idiocy of rural life."[11] Such an approach, neither praising nor condemning the *Heimat* but setting out to (re-) discover it, is the purpose of Zauner's work, based on an overwhelming amount of details founded in reality, stupendous quantities of established historical data and verifiable facts.[12]

Strictly speaking the above claim is not as novel as it may at first seem; for the problems associated with *Heimatromane*[13] were already subject to critical debate in the 1960s, leading to new theoretical initiatives, such as those promulgated by Martin Walser.[14] And in the 1980s the view gained ground that radical anti-*Heimat* literature[15] was merely the very antithesis of traditional *Heimat* literature: "In the final analysis the authors of anti-*Heimat* literature made the same mistakes which they blamed on traditional *Heimat* literature. For they also used clichés, albeit the other way around."[16]

A critical analysis of core features of the two established types of *Heimat* literature shows how Zauner's tetralogy manoeuvres adroitly between two extremes—the Scylla of traditional *Heimatromane* and the Charybdis of anti-*Heimatromane*—and takes a stand.[17] According to Josef Donnenberg, true *Heimat* literature, like e.g. Rosegger's novel *Jacob the Last* (*Jakob der Letzte*, 1888) and Waggerl's *Bread* (*Brot*, 1930), adopts a conservative and reactionary stance, opposing scholarly and experimental approaches in literature, as well as decadent and 'aestheticizing' trends, while promoting popular, native, traditional presentations.[18] It furthermore tries to find an ideologically motivated response to the socio-cultural challenges of its era: opposing modernism, industrialization, urbanization, intellectualism, internationalism, new social developments, while promoting healthy, nature-orientated, rural forms of life, the preservation of the countryside, of national traditions, of pure ethnic origin, of 'legitimate' ownership, and of religious beliefs handed down by generations.

The 1960s phase, during which problems associated with *Heimatromane* came to the forefront of attention, Hans Lebert's novel *Die Wolfshaut* ('Wolfskin,' 1960) and Gerhard Fritsch's *Fasching* ('Fasching,' 1967), for example, were superseded in the 1970s by new approaches towards *Heimat* literature (including some radical ones). These were directed on the one hand at a cultural and linguistic revaluation of *Heimat*, aiming at either enlightenment by rejuvenating individuals' memory in a critical, realistic way or by ironic and sarcastic portrayals of conditions in the provinces (such as Peter Handke's novel *A Sorrow Beyond Dreams* (*Wunschloses Unglück*, 1972), Reinhard P. Gruber's *Aus dem Leben Hödlmosers* ('From the Life of Hödlmoser,' 1973), or short stories in *Daheim ist Daheim* ('Home is Home,' 1973), edited by Alois Brandstetter). On the other hand, such new initiatives were directed at social criticism of the political and economic conditions in the homeland, intended to affect changes in society, either by means of historical-materialistic analysis or by unearthing the causes of alienation and class conflicts – as in Elfried Jelinek's novel *Women as Lovers* (*Die Liebhaberinnen*, 1975, Michael Scharang's *Der Sohn eines Landarbeiters* ('Son of a Farm Worker,' 1976), Franz Innerhofer's *Beautiful Days* (*Schöne Tage*, 1977), as well as Gernot Wolfgruber's *Herrenjahre* ('Master Years,' 1976) and *Niemandsland* ('No-man's Land,' 1978).[19]

In 1981, some ten years prior to *Im Schatten der Maulwurfhügel* ('In the Shadow of the Molehills'), part one of 'The End of Eternity,' Zauner published a precursor to his *Heimatroman* tetralogy, entitled *Dort oben im Wald bei diesen Leuten* ('Up There in the Woods among these People').[20] 'Up There in the Woods' is a detective novel; but that concerns the current discussion only in so far as the protagonist, inspector Obermann of the Viennese police force, en route to a spa in Upper Austria, gets lost in the *Roßwald*, one of the most remote areas of Austria. He ends up in a village called Recheuz and gets involved in the investigation of a local crime. What matters in this context is not so much the crime *per se*—though Obermann solves the case, and yet considers himself a failure (cf. 215-17)—but the countryside where it was committed; for even prior to ever setting foot in the *Roßwald*, Obermann fantasized about this area, "which is extremely hard to imagine, a place about which one dreams somehow, and which nonetheless is quite different, much less romantic, not half as idyllic."[21] Or, as the first-person narrator puts it on another occasion: "Recheuz...This indescribable austere tranquillity, which only exists where countryside is still truly countryside."[22] In fact, outsiders, especially those from big cities like inspector Obermann, never come face to face with Recheuz, for "things are happening behind the scenes; it is a kind of façade, and the real Recheuz is hidden behind it."[23] A glimpse of the 'true' village can only be gathered indirectly, as e.g. in the cat-and-mouse scene (60-65) and in that of the pig slaughter (102-08), both symbolic of the murder that overshadows Obermann's arrival and abruptly ends the love affair between a local girl—Regine Jodok, the daughter of the village policeman—and a young Yugoslav guest worker, Petar Babić.

Recheuz is a village reinvented by Zauner a decade later in his tetralogy 'The End of Eternity'; for the information about the remote *Roßwald* hamlet applies equally to Oed, Thal, and Fegfeuer in the *Innviertel*:

'We haven't got the faintest idea these days of what countryside is really like. Thick layers of concrete and asphalt have cut us off from the soil, we have coerced this world into grids of horizontal and vertical lines and despoiled it with right angles. Ever since then the view prevails that countryside is a piece of nature devoid of towns—what a misconception! Tourism has turned parts of the country into a rustic Disneyland. Here, however, the ground still smells like soil, the houses still smell like soil, the people still smell like soil, not withstanding the clothes they wear, and none of those idyllic aromas prevail, none of those pine-needle sprays, none of those charming dirndl-type blouses, and none of the rural hullabaloo behind the facades of those holiday villages.'[24]

The ensuing discussions in 'Up There in the Woods' of what constitutes "nature" and "naturalness," follow Obermann's confrontation with various Recheuz individuals: Jodok, the policeman; Regine, his daughter; Jodok, the innkeeper, his brother; Ambros, the latter's son; Lercht, the farmer; Baldur, a handyman, his brother; the Yugoslavs, above all Petar Babić, Regine's lover, and Stojak, the leader of the itinerant workers—these discussions become the theoretical foundation for 'The End of Eternity' a decade later. One of the highlights of this debate is the following excerpt from 'Up There in the Woods,' in which the protagonist's inner monologue gives vent to the core issues at stake both here and in the tetralogy some ten years later:

> 'Undoubtedly, Obermann admires all things genuine, everything simple, he has a great yearning for nature, for the countryside, for he hopes to find something there which is part of himself... However, Obermann realizes that this longing has been the cause of a conflict. What does nature really stand for? Or natural? We constantly use the word, meaning: self-evident. If we claim that a person behaves naturally we consider him affable, casual, uncomplicated. But is being natural really the same as being uncomplicated or congenial? Obermann watches the tomcat in the armchair opposite him, sleepy, lazy, self-confident and attractive; and then he remembers how it tortured the mouse. Why does it do that? Why this way? According to what rules? Why does this magnificent, indolent animal acquire its food this way? Unnaturally, one feels inclined to say! And if we have such a biased view of animals, how much more slanted

must our view be of plants? Let alone of human beings! Maybe even our descent from apes is merely the outflow of our arrogance—who knows if monkeys wish to be related to us?!'[25]

Another theoretical analysis of *Heimat* unfolds near the end of 'Up There in the Woods,' when Obermann is about to leave the *Roßwald* for a spa to recuperate from the stress of city life. Just before the onset of a frightening thunderstorm, on the verge of exiting the *Roßwald*, the inspector meditates—in the form of an inner monologue—why he, the city-dweller, seems cut off from the wholesomeness of provincial life, and why the area makes him feel like a being from outer space:

'Only a few more hours, a few dozen kilometers, and then he will have left the forest behind him, and he'll probably feel as if he's just left a ghost train. Except that these grimacing sprites and gnomes, these imps, these fairies, these murderous deeds made him think. Why? He, a townsman for generations, whose roots to the countryside were cut off a long time ago, is unable to reestablish the link. He feels ashamed and guilty, disgusted and dismayed; he knows that this Roßwald means something to him, but he's forgotten what it is. Deep down everything is alien to him and alarming. He doesn't really know how a tree grows and dies, how strong the power of the wind is, how the air tastes, or how one defends oneself against the mighty forest. He doesn't know how the tomcat feeds itself, wait, he does, but it is only book knowledge, and he is frightened when he experienced it firsthand....'[26]

There is currently nothing comparable in contemporary German-speaking literature to this unassuming detective story, with the odd title of 'Up There in the Woods among these

People,' let alone Zauner's literary chronicle of the *Innviertel*, one of the most fascinating undertakings in modern literature, as pointed out by Gauß in the mid-1990s following the publication of the third volume of the tetralogy.[27] By locating a tale in a remote area and basing the plot in an era long gone, the author ventured to create what is nowadays considered an outmoded approach in fiction.

Two aspects of Zauner's tetralogy elevate it above the great mass of *Heimat* literature: on the one hand the way the author describes—not unlike Theodor Fontane in *Der Stechlin* (1899) just about a hundred years earlier vis-à-vis the Mark Brandenburg—how world historical events during a period of roughly forty years (1900-1938) produce an echo even in one of the remotest parts of Austria. On the other hand, trivial occurrences in this isolated region create a sense of anticipation of future events in the world at large: "The history of this region," Gauß wrote, "is insignificant and exciting at the same time," for "whatever happens in the big wide world... finds an echo in this impoverished area between Thal and Oed; conversely though, the epochal changes, which alter whole continents, can be anticipated like distant thunder in the petty activities and events which make up the everyday life of this forlorn province."[28] At the same time, however, Zauner has a knack of portraying the extraordinary mundaneness of ordinary people and a gift for "precise observation from *below*, baffling the reader with textbook-like exactitude of customs and habits, work routines and natural phenomena that seldom seem artificial and in most instances are neatly integrated into the narrative."[29]

The main narrative strand of the four novels 'In the Shadow of the Molehills,' 'And the Fish are Mute,' 'Fruit of Pine Trees,' and 'Hoarse like Jackdaws,'[30] a sociologically accurate peasants' chronicle,[31] deals with the life and love of Theres and Maurits beginning on New Year's Eve 1899, when both are catapulted into the new century, until the *Anschluß* of Austria in 1938—a plot which guides the reader through a *different* Austria, a doomed era[32] of fundamental changes:[33] "In the beginning this world seems totally rigid. However, even prior to World War

One, the customs and habits, practiced by generations, are gradually undermined, and the Great War completely shatters the once solid order of things."[34]

Zauner's rural study[35] is "a microcosm that compresses *en miniature* everything that takes place in the world at large."[36] The author, contrary to other representatives of the anti-*Heimatroman*, "does not adopt the stance of those directly affected but maintains historical distance."[37] Thus the tetralogy—as mentioned above—is a fictional account of the effects of the outside world on a village community that, up to that point, had been hermetically cut off both socially and economically. The first volume deals with the period from the turn of the century till the start of World War One; the second with the war years proper; the third with the immediate post-war era; and the final one with the 1930s till the *Anschluß*. In view of such a historical scenario it stands to reason that the inhabitants of the three *Innviertel* villages—at least in the first two volumes—equate the Austro-Hungarian Empire with Franz Joseph I. After all, for them "the Emperor is a unique *Leitfigur* holding the country together..."[38] However, "they [i.e. the people of Thal, Oed, and Fegfeuer] consider anything out of the ordinary, all change, as a threat. Homesickness sets in the moment the steeple of the village church disappears from sight. Though they know they are citizens of a huge empire, they never lose track of their own small world."[39]

Nonetheless, the people of remote regions like the *Innviertel* villages Thal, Oed, and Fegfeuer—"similar to the citizens of big cities, and similar to the Austrian aristocracy, as ineluctably tied to local events as international developments ineluctably seem to be bypassing them... fear fundamental changes in the structure of the monarchy long before the turn of the century."[40] And historical upheavals, fittingly captured in metaphors like 'Shadow of the Molehills,' 'Muteness of Fish,' and 'Fruit of Pine Trees,'[41] eventually cast a shadow even in this ultra-remote area:

'... the effects of World War One do not touch Thal directly. The military actions happen far away.... All the same, no one is spared.... The newspapers continue to sound optimistic.... News reports of glorious victories come in from all over the world, but at home the list of soldiers missing in action, attached to the door of the post office, grows longer by the day. Hardly a week goes by that the death knell does not ring, hardly a family is spared.'[42]

In view of the contemporary background of 'The End of Eternity,' and contrary to traditional plots of *Heimatromane* and anti-*Heimatromane*, neither a rural kind of romanticism nor hatred of the local conditions have any bearing on Zauner's tetralogy. Instead, his fictional presentation of village life—though not totally neutral—lacks false illusions, an attitude, which is echoed e.g. in the reaction of the people of Thal to the conscription of its male citizens into the imperial army:

'Things are as usual in Thal. Schmied senior had given his son a farewell handshake, but now he returns to the forge, and the highway maintenance man clears horse droppings from the road. Cobbler Bartl negotiates wages in front of the fire station; the carpenter paints the box cart he just finished green.... The crowd in front of the fire station disperses, the peasants return to their farms taking shortcuts across the fields, checking whether the laborers are doing their work, whether the unsupervised maids are resting at the edge of the field.... With great satisfaction they notice how much fruit the apple and pear trees are bearing.... There will be enough cider for two winters.... Firm round turnips stick out above the ground... and the potatoes are also ready... the harvest can begin. Only the mothers whose sons have died in action run around like frightened chickens, and no consolation can placate them.'[43]

In passages like these, Zauner adopts traditional narrative techniques, but never a complacent, old-fashioned, conversational tone. Which is to say, he slows down the action and peppers the plot with dialogues enriched with vivid regional nuances. Precisely and patiently he revives details—previously hardly ever noticed—of everyday life in a society on the verge of disintegration. His extraordinary pictorial language[44] always remains completely factual, visualising local customs, tools and work routines, the enumerations and descriptions of which are often more extensive than those in local history museums.

According to Donnenberg, the main issues of the traditional *Heimatroman* are portrayals of sound, natural and rustic forms of life, the preservation of the environment, of local folklore, of an unadulterated genealogy, of legitimate property ownership and of religious beliefs handed down by generations. Zauner's tetralogy has no truck with any of these claims: neither are the people and their local customs idealized in his novels, nor do villages and countryside acquire a romantic hue, although they are not likened to hell on earth either, as in many anti-*Heimatromane*. On the contrary: the description of Fegfeuer— the most remote, most foreboding and poorest of the three villages in question—is typical of the local color deployed throughout Zauner's *Innviertel* tetralogy:

> 'It is a callous landscape... stolid, lazy hills, rising stubbornly, overlapping towards the horizon, and ostensibly giving cause, over and over again, for new ones. Meadows and fields have a chessboard pattern. The farmsteads nestle in valleys and hide behind hillcrests. The countryside looks uninhabited except for the odd red tiled roofs that suddenly emerge from a hollow and for columns of smoke rising from invisible chimneys. The meadows are still green, and here and there cows graze godforsaken; the fields are brown at this time of the year and plowed. And there are woods everywhere. They crawl across the hilltops, form small hollows, advance along

the ditches showing autumnal colors of deep
green, vermilion, while brown and bright yellow
leaves have fallen from birch trees. The more
remote the stretch of woodland, the more intense
the colors, turning gloomy and almost black...
The fact that the devil must have had a hand in
the creation of this landscape can be gathered
from the names of the localities... and they are
presumably also a sign for the hellishly tough
way the people of Fegfeuer must earn their daily
living.'[45]

Similarly, historical facts, carefully researched and accurate to the last detail, are presented here. For example, the first-person narrator[46] supplies a meticulous commentary[47] on the hierarchical structure of village life in this remote part of Austria, rich with allusions to contemporary social criticism,[48] although the historical backdrop—one of Zauner's forte—is generally unobtrusive and transparent,[49] contrary to the typical social critique in anti-*Heimatromane*:

'Hierarchy is the pillar of every society. Thus
the people of Thal feel superior to those of Oed
and Fegfeuer, who in turn feel above those of
Hintern Wald. Personal status counts. A farmer
is superior to a civil servant, who in turn ranks
above artisans, followed by servants and day
laborers, and the bottom is made up of ordinary
workers. Those earning their keep in quarries or
brickyards are considered to be mere riffraff.
The borderlines between the various groups are
tightly drawn. A good carpenter would have no
chance asking for the hand of a farmer's
daughter in marriage, even if considerably better
off financially than the latter. Children of artisans on the other hand rarely need to offer
themselves as servants. Also, within each group,
the lines are firmly drawn. Among farmers,

family background counts and the size of the farm.... Among artisans, those rank highest who—like blacksmiths or cartwrights—are engaged exclusively in their own workshops; tailors, cobblers, coopers, and all the rest of them on the other hand, who constantly seek employment away from home, count for less. This kind of ranking is also closely observed among servants, ranging from chief farmhand... to cowherd, from main maid... to lowest kitchen maid.... Only among ordinary laborers are such distinctions non-existent; their reputation is simply too low for any worthwhile ranking... Despite such a complex system, everybody knows his precise place within this hierarchy and is constantly reminded of it....'[50]

As mentioned earlier, Zauner's tetralogy 'The End of Eternity' neither idealizes nor romanticizes local situations. Instead, the author soberly and meticulously[51] makes extensive use of agrarian and rural history, with the result that the reader is subjected to a kind of village saga whose social structures unfold like a kaleidoscope. That is to say, in 'The End of Eternity,' Zauner conjures up a many-faceted, multidimensional document that recounts in a panorama-like fashion key events of the local Catholic population: births, baptisms, weddings, extreme unctions, deaths, and funerals. Annual village feasts are described at great length exactly the way they were celebrated in days gone by; numerous commercial activities, long since disappeared, are resurrected in great detail and with encyclopaedic precision, giving the novels an extraordinary air of authenticity. Quite apart from the simplicity of the narrative, the immediacy of the strictly rural idiom[52]—a key aspect of regional fiction or *"regionalistisches Erzählen"*—prevents a relapse into pseudo-regionalism.[53]

Zauner does not mince words when it comes to describing rural conditions in the *Innviertel* at the beginning of the 20th century, spelling out both negative and positive aspects of village life in those days. In fact, disasters as well as strokes of luck, joyous and sad events, spread over four volumes, find mention without ever being toned down or glossed over. Thus, right at the beginning of the first volume of the tetralogy, 'In the Shadow of the Molehills,' the reader is confronted with blunt details of a difficult childbirth (I, 28), the vividness of which is later surpassed in the description of the final stages of Theres' pregnancy in 'Fruit of Pine Trees':

'She is seven months pregnant and waddles about with a drum of a belly... During her third pregnancy she feels like she is bigger than ever. No dress fits her any longer. Her blouses are too tight across the breasts, the buttons threaten to give way at any moment. She keeps her skirt up with rubber bands, and still her underwear sticks slatternly out through gaps on each side. Although the days of morning sickness are over, she now has to frequent the outdoor toilet every five minutes since the belly puts pressure on her bladder. Her skin is pale like that of old women, her freckles have expanded to ugly brown blotches, her nose juts out of her haggard face, her lips are reduced to colorless, narrow, limp lines. At times she scarcely feels any younger than her own grandmother, the old farmer's wife.... Her hair... has thinned, is dull, straggly, shaggy, and hard to control. Unsightly. She hates to look at herself in the mirror. When she observes the watery, pale-blue eyes starring at her, she feels revolted.'[54]

Nonetheless, such descriptive details never create the impresssion as if—compared e.g. to Innerhofer's *Beautiful Days*, which has been considered by some an anti-*Heimatroman*[55]—the author is denouncing something fundamentally evil or that his observations are meant to be judgmental, trying to affect changes in society. His narrative guideline seems to be rather: that's what life was like in those days! And as a result Zauner does not permit his auctorial narrator any value judgments, an absolute key point in this tetralogy. Instead he simply lets him tell his tale, drawing on his vivid imagination and an inexhaustible supply of personal experiences. A perfect example of this approach is the description of Maurits' return to Thal, one year after the end of the war:

> 'He has become extremely skinny, emaciated, hollow-cheeked, with deep furrows round the nose. His head is shaven bald... causing his eyes to protrude even more, giving them the appearance of black holes surrounded by black rims, from which piercing glances dart. His once full lips are now two narrow, pale lines, his mustache has been shaved off, and he has stubble on chin and neck instead.... He, who always was so particular about his clothes, has worn nothing for years except his old soldier's uniform.... On the very first day his belt had been taken away, and soon afterwards his greatcoat. Meanwhile the green color of the uniform has assumed an indefinable, dirty-gray hue, the sleeves are worn, the edges of his pockets frayed.... At the knees and elbows bare skin shines through, his shirt consists of tattered rags barely holding together, his feet are stuck in his boots without socks. There had been no supply of clean underwear in the POW camp for the past two years, and in an emergency the men had made underpants out of foot cloths, similar to diapers wrapped round a baby's bottom.'[56]

Even assuming that the author had no intention of frightening his readers, it is still conceivable that those with weaker nerves may put down the book in disgust at this point, never to resume its perusal. But then again, Zauner being neither a supporter of traditional *Heimat*-literature nor of the anti-*Heimatroman*, not all sections of his tetralogy create such a gloomy impression. On the contrary, happy and sad sequences intermingle in 'The End of Eternity,' as they do in life generally. And there are even some positive things to report about village life in this remote Austrian province, abounding with adversities during the first decades of the 20th century.

Such a positive picture of village life can be gathered, for example, from the description of the celebration of Theres' and Maurits' wedding at the end of the third volume of Zauner's tetralogy. It shows the author to be an expert in such matters, right down to culinary details (III, 206-07), and the same goes for his knowledge in all those passages dealing with one of the most common alcoholic beverages in this part of Austria, cider:

> 'It is not sold in inns, for everybody owning a cellar and a few fruit trees distills it himself. It is made from a particular mixture of apples and pears and tastes different in each place, often even in each barrel. It all depends on the mixture and on the quality of the fruit, on the care that is taken to produce it, and on the cellar.... Pure pear cider is rare.... Cider made from pears is dry and rough and coats the gum, and since pears have a higher sugar content, it is more potent.'[57]

Schnapps, on the other hand, is considered an elixir of life:
> ‚It can... alleviate all kinds of ailments: stomach upsets, headaches, and toothaches. It is rubbed onto the skin in the case of rheumatism, put on chest compresses in the case of fever, it helps to offset the cold, and sometimes even anxiety.... *Obstler* is the main product, made from the wort of malaceous fruit, depending on how good the harvest turns out. Some peasants distill slivovitz; one can usually recognize them by their bluish noses. Damson schnapps is the champion among

hard liquors. Pure pear schnapps is rare, and juniper schnapps is even rarer. Schnapps can be made out of virtually every fruit... though grain is seldom used, it is not customary: barley is used for beer only.'[58]

As mentioned earlier, customs, work routines, nature and landscape descriptions, everyday events (including local disasters), are used *en masse* by Zauner, at times in deadly earnest, often humorously and wittily, as, generally speaking, the author's mania of accumulating factual details—similar to Günter Grass's approach in *Too Far Afield* (*Ein weites Feld, 1995*)[59]—shows nothing but positive results,[60] since his superior narrative technique never has a didactic ring or becomes tiresome for the reader. Examples, among many, are the pilgrimage to Passau (I, 172ff.), the so-called Whitsuntide pranks (II, 170ff.), the annual funfair (III, 71ff.), and the celebrations between Christmas and Twelfth Night (II, 227).

Having said all this, as in the case of the lyric poetry of Theodor Kramer (1898-1956) almost half a century earlier,[61] Friedrich Zauner's narrative technique is based on a special kind of aesthetics, an *Ästhetik des Besonderen*—a characteristic feature of regional literature,[62]—and a wealth of character portrayals, of narrative stances. A long list of peculiar items make up the corpus of Zauner's prose in 'The End of Eternity,' like, for example, the description of Maurits' apprenticeship as a cooper with Master Bednar in Hintern Wald:[63]

> 'Maurits never gets enough sleep, and the degree of tiredness is almost unbearable. At times awareness of life occurs like behind thick-frosted windowpanes. Half-asleep, he cuts grass for the cows at dawn, grooms the chestnut and gives it water. As if in a trance he arranges the oak blocks and instinctively places the axe on the spot where the wood would most easily split. As if in a trance he raises and lowers his arm when hollowing out raw staves, and, as if by a miracle, retrieves the support fingers just in time

before the axe severs them. After hours, hardly aware of what he is doing, he hones nicks on spigot drills and hoop binders, adjusts and, often lost in thought, sharpens the same saws twice. Dropping off at the rhythm of the hammer, eyelids almost shut, he squats at dusk on the bench outside and sharpens scythes.'[64]

Quite apart from the sheer variety of artisan tools mentioned here (mostly unknown to contemporary—and especially younger—readers such as anvil, clamp, winch, gauge, and adjustable wrench for the manufacture of buckets, basins, tubs, wooden containers and barrels,[65] quite apart therefore from Zauner's mania for objects (his *Dingversessenheit*) in almost all walks of life, it is essential that no real sadness, hopelessness, or desperation ever arises, however hopeless and wretched the outsider-hero's situation may seem. Zauner basically does not waste time on such a negative outlook. After all, his philosophy of life is fundamentally optimistic and finds stylistic expression in his "exciting use of language,"[66] i.e. in his adoption of rural idioms, already extinct, involving his readership in the resurrection of a lost world. That is to say, he encourages positive solutions, without ignoring or glossing over genuine social problems in Upper Austria (*Oberösterreich*) in the 1920s. Zauner—like Kramer before him in his poetry about rural life in the Burgenland and Lower Austria (*Niederösterreich*) during the same era—thus revived interest in aspects of local countryside, environment and industry in the *Innviertel* during the years between the wars, imbuing many local terms, barely known by the end of the 20th century, with a new lease on life.

But the author also succeeded in painting nature scenes without underwriting the concept of an 'intact world' or *heile Welt*, as claimed by traditional *Heimat* literature. Thus wonderful atmospheric landscape descriptions (cf. I, 78) are contrasted with those of natural disasters and devastation (IV, 198). At the same time the author shows restrained disapproval regarding the introduction of modern technology in rural Austria in the early part of the past century. Instead, once more he manoeuvres adroitly between two types of *Heimatliteratur*, resisting on the one hand outright condemnation of modern developments (a good example for this attitude is Findel's introduction of bicycles in that part of rural Austria), while on the other hand criticizing fashionable trends by exposing them to ridicule (such as farmer Hölzenreiter's purchase of a motorbike):

> 'Hölzenreiter alone, always eager to be someone special, acquired a motorbike for his trips to Thal.... In order to make it fit him, he had to adjust the seat to its maximum height. Once the fat man mounted the bike, the saddle completely vanished beneath his buttocks. The whole thing looked like an ox on a spit, as if an iron rod was pushed straight up the farmer's ass towards his paunch. Subjected to his weight, especially on the steep inclines towards Fegfeuer, the bike at times gave up the ghost. Thus the people from Thal occasionally witnessed him, flushed, panting and cursing, changing and cleaning spark plugs, manipulating the gas pump, impatiently working on the carburetor or the accelerator. For he never permitted anybody to give him a helping hand.'[67]

And at times Zauner shows himself also adept at adding humorous touches to his descriptions, repeatedly offering comic relief under dire circumstances, for example in the case of Findel and his family's plight during their stay in the Pirater Fronhäusl:

> 'As a bonus... the result of a strange kind of humor customary among the people of Hintern Wald, the bricklayers of Bettelhöhe... had built a stone toilet that soon became a sensation in Oed and the surrounding area. Churchgoers, children on their way to and from school, peddlers, beggars, and vagabonds all used it to relieve themselves. It was claimed that sitting on

it was like sitting on the Emperor's throne. For light, small windows had been fitted instead of the customary heart in the door, windows which could even be closed with shutters, something that especially pleased the womenfolk since they felt safe from unwanted observers. At times there was even a line in front of the outhouse since the people refused to relieve themselves in the bushes as they used to and preferred to wait, legs crossed, till it was their turn. All this greatly annoyed Theres; since it was still an uninhabited building, it was her job to empty the toilet every other month so that the level of thin and firm, light and dark-brown reeking sausages, interspersed with speckled newspaper used to wipe people's asses, would not reach the seat.'[68]

In conclusion it can therefore be said that Zauner's tetralogy 'The End of Eternity' is a perfect example of a debate, initiated some time ago by Norbert Mecklenburg, about 'open' and 'closed' types of regional literature.[69] According to this theory "there are regional novels whose closed spaces cause 'idyllization', while in others they provoke 'dramatization'." Or, to put it differently: whenever closed spaces happen to reduce or eliminate conflicts, narrative action is idyllicized, while a plot's growing intensity dramatizes regional spaces. Primarily, idyllization always creates unity of regional space in all those instances, when there happens to exist an autonomous, insular space or an anti-space. At the same time, alien issues, or individuals alien to a plot, often have a dramatic effect on the unity of regional spaces since their intrusion may call the latter into question. In the context of such a scenario, traditional *Heimatromane* are to be assigned to the first category (idyllization), anti-*Heimatromane* to the second (dramatization). Zauner's tetralogy—as I hope to have shown—is neither an idyll, limited to certain isolated "green" scenes, nor is it merely based on contrast. 'The End of Eternity' also avoids established patterns according to which provincial novels, wedged between idyllization and dramatization, either turn into idylls or tragedies, which is to say, heaven or hell; for traditionally problem zones, saturated with conflicts, can only be *ex*-cluded, in which case conflict-free spaces emerge, or *in*-cluded, leading to tragic inevitability.

According to Mecklenburg, attempts at "open" presentations of provincial literature are primarily found, "when the narrative horizon is extended, contrasting province and wider world, country and city, home and abroad, near and far...."[70] This is precisely what characterizes Zauner's narrative approach in 'The End of Eternity': for on the one hand an open version of '*Heimat* literature' materializes here,[71] i.e. province and world at large are constantly linked and, as a result, regularly penetrate and influence each other positively and negatively; on the other hand, even the slightest danger of idyllization is immediately quelled by the deliberate exploitation of a special kind of aesthetics (the aforementioned *Ästhetik des Besonderen*), particulary in all those instances when standard clichés would normally have prevailed.

There is no denying that even in provincial literature productive, forward-looking fissions (*Ungleichzeitigkeiten*) do occur; and Zauner's tetralogy proves that backward regions can be dealt with in fiction, even if they are not yet 'liberated'.[72] The key issue of this type of '*Heimat* literature' was succinctly summarized by Michael Scharang, one of the foremost theoreticians of the anti-*Heimatroman*, in a programmatic contribution to the literary journal *Kürbiskern*, stating: "To love one's country, to support one's country, amounts to nothing less than outlining one's relationship with that country, and to openly say so."[73] Consequently, "literature whose character portrayals adopt this line will be the best kind of counterpropaganda against a mythology-based vilification of *Heimat*, countryside, and nature."[74] Scharang's supplementary claim, though, that only *that* kind of literature can be true *Heimatdichtung*, which "gives the lie to [traditional] *Heimatdichter*... depicting a kind of countryside that frightens property owner and speculators"[75]—as in *Beautiful Days*—is nothing but self-deception and proves why

Zauner's middle-of-the-road approach between the heaven of *Heimatromane* and the hell of anti-*Heimatromane* does far greater justice to the genre of '*Heimat* literature.'

Notes

[1] This contribution is an extended version of: "*Weder Idylle noch Hölle: Friedrich Ch. Zauners Heimatroman-Zyklus Das Ende der Ewigkeit*," a paper originally delivered in April 1998 at the 13th Annual Symposium on Austrian Literature and Culture: "Austrian Literature in Transition" at the University of California/Riverside, and subsequently published in *Modern Austrian Literature*, 31 (1998), 252-277.

[2] Zauner's tetralogy *Das Ende der Ewigkeit* consists of *Im Schatten der Maulwurfshügel* ('In the Shadow of the Molehills,' 1992), *Und die Fische sind stumm* ('And the Fish are Mute,' 1993), *Früchte vom Taubenbaum* ('Fruit of Pine Trees,' 1994), and *Heiser wie Dohlen* ('Hoarse like Jackdaws,' 1996), all published in Edition Geschichte der Heimat (Grünbach/Austria); volume and page references from these four novels follow citations in the text.

[3] Karl-Markus Gauß, "Erkundung der Welt in der Provinz," in *Freitag* (Berlin: 13 October 1995), Suppl., 7.

[4] See Karl-Markus Gauß, "Zumpf aus dem Latz," in *Die Presse* (Vienna: 11/12 March 1995), Suppl., VII; also Peter Zimmermann, *Der Bauernroman: Antifeudalismus—Konservatismus—Faschismus* (Stuttgart: Metzler, 1975) and Uwe Baur, *Dorfgeschichte* (Munich: W. Fink, 1978).

[5] Cf. Franz Haas, "Im Schatten des Mostkrugs," in *Neue Zürcher Zeitung* (Zurich: 25 February 1994), 34.

[6] Reinhold Tauber, "Heimat Quadrologie," in *Oberösterreichische Nachrichten* (Linz: 17 July 1996), 16.

[7] Herbert Zand, "Elend und Glanz der Heimatliteratur," in *Träume im Spiegel: Essays*, ed. Herbert Zand (Vienna: Europaverlag, 1973), 93-99; Karlheinz Rossbacher, *Heimatkunstbewegung und Heimatroman: Zu einer Literatursoziologie der Jahrhundertwende* (Stuttgart: Klett, 1975); Jürgen Hein, "Heimat in der Literatur und Heimatliteratur," in

Identität und Entfremdung: Beiträge zum Literaturunterricht, ed. Josef Billen (Bochum: Kamp, 1979), 119ff.; Klaus Heydemann, "Jugend auf dem Lande: Zur Tradition des Heimatromans in Österreich," in *Traditionen in der neueren österreichischen Literatur: Zehn Vorträge*, ed. Friedbert Aspetsberger (Vienna: Österreichischer Bundesverlag, 1980), 83-97; Karlheinz Rossbacher, "Dorf und Landschaft in der Literatur nach 1945: Thesen zum Stellenwert des Regionalen und drei Beispiele aus der österreichischen Literatur," in *Modern Austrian Literature*, 15 (1982), 13-27.

[8] Cf. Albert Janetschek, "Friedrich Ch. Zauner: *Heiser wie Dohlen*," in *Literatur aus Österreich* (Vienna: August 1996).

[9] See Maria Luise Caputo-Mayr, "Überlieferung aus neuer Sicht: Zur jüngsten österreichischen Prosaliteratur," in *Perspectives and Personalities: Studies in Modern German Literature Honoring Claude Hill*, eds. Ralph Ley et al. (Heidelberg: C. Winter, 1978), 89-100; Ina-Maria Greverus, *Auf der Suche nach Heimat* (Munich: Beck, 1979); Jürgen Koppensteiner, "Das Leben auf dem Lande: Zu den Anti-Heimatromanen österreichischer Gegenwartsautoren," in *Akten des VI. Internationalen Germanisten Kongresses Basel 1980*, vol. 4, eds. Heinz Rupp and Hans-Gert Roloff (Bern: Lang, 1980), 545-549; Jürgen Koppensteiner, "Anti-Heimatliteratur: Ein Unterrichtsversuch mit Franz Innerhofers Roman *Schöne Tage*," in *Die Unterrichtspraxis* 14 (1981), 9-19; Willfried von Bredow and Hans-Friedrich Foltin, *Zwiespältige Zufluchten: Zur Renaissance des Heimatgefühls* (Berlin/Bonn: Dietz, 1981), 51-105; Horst Bienek, ed., *Heimat: Neue Erkundungen eines alten Themas* (Munich/Vienna: Hanser, 1985); Hans-Georg Pott, "Der 'neue' Heimatroman? Zum Konzept der 'Heimat' in der neueren Literatur," in *Literatur und Provinz: Das Konzept 'Heimat' in der neueren Literatur*, ed. Hans-Georg Pott (Paderborn: Schöningh, 1986), 7-21; Wilhelm Solms, "Zum Wandel der 'Anti-Heimatliteratur'," in *Wesen und Wandel der Heimatliteratur: Am Beispiel der österreichischen Literatur seit 1945*, ed. Karl Konrad Polheim (Bern: Lang, 1989), 173-189; Karl Markus Gauß, "Land und Liebe," in *Parnaß* (Vienna: November 1993), 112-113; Karl Markus

Gauß, "Heimat, Antiheimat und darüber hinaus," in *Das Magazin: Österreich Schwerpunkt zur Frankfurter Buchmesse 1995*, 30-31; Karl Markus Gauß, "Über Friedrich Ch. Zauner," in *Die Rampe. Hefte für Literatur: Porträt—Friedrich Ch. Zauner* (Linz: 1996), 39-42.
[10] Andrea Kunne, *Heimat im Roman: Last oder Lust? Transformation eines Genres in der österreichischen Nachkriegsliteratur* (Amsterdam: Rodopi, 1991), especially 1-20.
[11] Cf. Gauß, "Erkundung der Welt."
[12] Karl-Markus Gauß, "Kleine Welt, große Literatur," in *Literatur und Kritik* (Salzburg: September 1993), 3.
[13] Cf. Walter Weiß, "Österreichische Literatur—eine Gefangene des habsburgischen Mythos?" in *Deutsche Vierteljahrsschrift*, 43 (1969), 333-345; see also W.W., "Die Literatur der Gegenwart in Österreich," in *Die deutsche Literatur der Gegenwart: Aspekte und Tendenzen*, ed. Manfred Durzak (Stuttgart: Reclam, 1971), 386-397; W.W., "Literatur," in *Österreich: Die Zweite Republik*, vol. 2, eds. Erika Weinzierl and Kurt Skalnik (Graz: Styria, 1972), 439-476; W.W., "Zwischenbilanz: Österreichische Beiträge zur Gegenwartsliteratur," in *Zwischenbilanz: Eine Anthologie österreichischer Gegenwartsliteratur*, eds. Walter Weiß and Sigrid Schmid (Salzburg: Residenz, 1976), 11-29; furthermore Walter Hömberg and Karlheinz Rossbacher, *Lesen auf dem Lande* (Salzburg: Institut für Germanistik, 1977); Joseph McVeigh, "Das Fortleben der 'Ostmark'–Literatur in der zweiten Republik: Zur Identität der österreichischen Literatur zwischen 1945 und 1965," in *Modern Austrian Literature,* 17 (1984), 93-112; Karl Müller, "Zur (Dis-) Kontinuität österreichischer Literatur seit den 30er Jahren: Karl Heinrich Waggerl (1897-1973). Ein Erfolgsautor der 50er Jahre," in *Literatur in Österreich von 1950 bis 1965*, ed. Wendelin Schmidt-Dengler (Mürzzuschlag: Buchebner, 1984), 52-74; Joseph McVeigh, *Kontinuität und Vergangenheitsbewältigung in der österreichischen Literatur nach 1945* (Vienna: Braumüller, 1988); Karl Müller, *Zäsur ohne Folge: Das lange Leben der literarischen Antimoderne Österreichs seit den 30er Jahren*

(Salzburg: Otto Müller, 1990) and K.M., "Sieben Jahre später in einem Totenhaus," in *Standard* (Vienna: 1998).
[14] Martin Walser, "Heimatbedingungen," in *Wie und wovon handelt Literatur: Aufsätze und Reden*, ed. Martin Walser (Frankfurt: Suhrkamp, 1973), 89-99, and "Heimatkunde," in *Heimatkunde: Aufsätze und Reden*, ed. Martin Walser (Frankfurt: Suhrkamp, 1968), 40-50.
[15] Norbert Mecklenburg, "Poetisches Hinterland," in *Neue Zürcher Zeitung* (Zurich: 4 January 1980), 27.
[16] Jürgen Koppensteiner, "Anti-Heimatliteratur in Österreich: Zur literarischen Heimatwelle der siebziger Jahre," in *Modern Austrian Literature*, 15 (1982), 8.
[17] Cf. Jakob Ebner's comments in a review of the first three parts of Zauner's tetralogy, in *Die Zeit im Buch* 5/95.
[18] Josef Donnenberg, "Heimatliteratur nach 1945—rehabilitiert oder antiquiert?" in *Wesen und Wandel der Heimatliteratur*, ed. Polheim, 45; consult also J.D., "Das Thema Heimat in der Gegenwartsliteratur und Anzengruber als Schlüsselfigur der Tradition der Heimatliteratur," in *Traditionen in der neueren österreichischen Literatur*, ed. Aspetsberger, 67-82.
[19] Cf. Renate Lachinger, *Der österreichische Anti-Heimatroman: Eine Untersuchung am Beispiel von Franz Innerhofer, Gernot Wolfgruber, Michael Scharang und Elfriede Jelinek* (dissertation, Salzburg: 1985), 7-44.
[20] Friedrich Ch. Zauner, *Dort oben im Wald bei diesen Leuten: Roman* (Wien/Hamburg: Paul Zsolnay, 1981); page references from this novel follow citations in the notes in brackets.
[21] *"Von einer Gegend, die man sich einfach nicht vorstellen kann, von der wir irgendwo träumen, die aber dann doch ganz anders ist, viel weniger süßlich, gar nicht so idyllisch"* – 52.
[22] *"Recheuz.... Dieser unbeschreibliche herbe Frieden, den es nur noch dort gibt, wo Land wirklich noch Land ist"* – 59.
[23] *"Das ist nicht das wirkliche Recheuz, ihr habt mir da ein paar Kulissen hingestellt, ein Potemkinsches Dorf, das wahre Recheuz liegt dahinter"* – 116.
[24] *"Wir haben im Grunde ja längst keine Ahnung mehr, was das ist: Land. Wir haben uns selbstmörderisch durch die dicken*

Schichten von Beton und Asphalt von der Erde abgetrennt, wir haben die Welt mit Geraden und Senkrechten verplant und durch den rechten Winkel verdorben. Seither grassiert die Ansicht, Landschaft, das sei ein Stück Natur ohne Städte—was für ein Missverständnis! Die Reiseindustrie macht daraus ein Disneyland in rustikal. Hier riecht der Boden nach Erde, die Häuser riechen nach Erde, die Menschen riechen nach Erde, egal welches Kostüm sie tragen, und da ist nichts von diesem idyllischen Aroma, diesem Fichtelnadelspray, diesem Dirndlblusencharm und Heimatdullióh jener Potemkinschen Urlaubsdörfer" – 173.

[25] *"Ohne Zweifel: Obermann hat viel übrig für Echtes, für Einfachheit, er hat eine große Sehnsucht nach der Natur, nach dem Land, weil er hofft, dort ein Stück von dem wiederzufinden, wovon er sich selbst, seine Person herleitet.... Obermann ist sich klar darüber, daß er mit seinen Gedanken in einen Zwiespalt geraten ist. Was ist wirklich Natur? Oder natürlich? Wir verwenden das Wort ständig und meinen damit natürlich = selbstverständlich. Wenn wir von einem Menschen behaupten, er gebe sich natürlich, meinen wir, daß er umgänglich ist, leger, unkompliziert. Aber ist Natürlichkeit wirklich unkompliziert oder sympathisch? Er sieht den Kater vor sich, der im Sessel döst, faul und breit und selbstbewußt und schön, und dann kommt ihm das Bild in den Sinn, wie er die Maus malträtierte. Warum macht er das? Warum so? Nach welchem Prinzip? Warum verschafft er sich—dieses prächtige, träge Tier!—seine Nahrung auf diese Weise ... unnatürlich, ist man versucht zu sagen! Wenn wir schon von den Tieren ein so verschobenes Bild haben, um wieviel mehr muß unsere Vorstellung von den Pflanzen falsch sein? Und gar von den Menschen! Ist nicht am Ende sogar unsere Abstammung von den Affen eine Projektion von Überheblichkeit, wer weiß, ob Affen mit uns verwandt sein möchten?!"* – 196.

[26] *"Ein paar Stunden noch, ein paar Dutzend Kilometer und er wird den Wald hinter sich gelassen haben, und wahrscheinlich wird es ihm vorkommen, als entstiege er einer Grottenbahn.*

Nur daß ihm diese Fratzen und Gnome, diese Kobolde, diese Feen, diese Moritaten betroffen gemacht haben. Warum? Er, der Städter seit Generationen, der die Wurzeln schon längst im 'Brenngraben' abgeschnitten bekommen hat, kann die Verbindung nicht mehr herstellen. Er fühlt Scham und Schuld, Abscheu, klebrige Betroffenheit, er weiß, daß ihn dieser Roßwald etwas angeht, aber er hat vergessen warum. Im Grunde ist ihm alles fremd und erschreckend. Er weiß doch nicht mehr wirklich, wie ein Baum wächst und stirbt, wie groß die Kraft des Windes ist, wie die Luft schmeckt oder wie man sich gegen den allmächtigen Wald wehrt. Er weiß nicht, wie sich der Kater ernährt, doch, er weiß es, weil es in den Büchern steht, aber er erschrickt, wenn er es erlebt...." – 217-218.

[27] Gauß, "Erkundung der Welt."

[28] Ibid.

[29] Cf. O.P. Zier, "Friedrich Ch. Zauners *Das Ende der Ewigkeit*: Zyklus, Dritter Teil," in *Literatur und Kritik* (Salzburg: April 1995), 89-90; see also Heide Stockinger's review "Eben nicht 'Im Schatten der Maulwurfshügel'!" in *Oberösterreichischer Kulturbericht*, 50 (Linz: November 1996), 11.

[30] This tetralogy is not, strictly speaking, about *Erinnerungsarbeit*, as claimed by Robert Schurz, "Friedrich Zauner: *Das Ende der Ewigkeit*," (Sendung des Hessischen Rundfunks, 14 April 1997, typoscript, 1), for the author deliberately terminates the narrative at the very point in time when his own memory would have set in (Jörg Thunecke's interview with Friedrich Zauner in Rainbach on 11/12 July 1998); compare also the author's comments in an interview with Josef Haslinger, "'Junge entdecken da eine neue Welt!' 3 Fragen an Dr. Friedrich Ch. Zauner," in *Oberösterreichische Rundschau/ Rieder Rundschau* (Linz: 10 November 1995): "Deshalb hört der Zyklus auch zu der Zeit auf, wo meine eigene Erinnerung einsetzt. Da soll keine Spur von Autobiographie sein."

[31] Cf. Haas, "*Im Schatten des Mostkrugs*: Regionale Geschichtsschreibung und akkurate Soziologie in Form einer Bauernchronik"; see also Ilse Tielsch's review "Friedrich Ch. Zauner:

Im Schatten der Maulwurfshügel," in *Literatur aus Österreich* (Vienna: October 1995), 179.

[32] Cf. esp. Theodor Kramer's Gedichtbände *Die Gaunerzinke* (1929) and *Mit der Ziehharmonika* (1936).

[33] Josef Haslinger, "Eine große Geschichte über die Geschichte im Kleinen," in *Oberösterreichische Rundschau/Rieder Rundschau* (Linz: 10 November 1994).

[34] Karl-Markus Gauß, "Der Rand in der Mitte: Die Chronik einer Heimat," in *Die Zeit*, 4 October 1996.

[35] Gauß mentions a *dörfliche Sozialstudie* in his "Kleine Welt, große Literatur," 84; Helmut Salfinger refers to a „*Soziologie des Dorfes,"* in his piece "Prosa," in *Blickpunkte* (Linz: January 1995).

[36] Reinhold Tauber, "Viele Farben im Bild," in *Oberösterreichische Nachrichten* (Linz: 16 November 1994), 16.

[37] Erich Brandl, "Friedrich Ch. Zauner: *Früchte vom Taubenbaum,"* in *Oberösterreichischer Kulturbericht*, 49 (Linz: March 1995), 14.

[38] "*[d]er Kaiser die unumstrittene Leitfigur, der innere Zusammenhalt des Ganzen*" (I, 14).

[39] "*Alles Ungewohnte, jede Veränderung empfindet er [der Bewohner von Thal/Oed/Fegfeuer] als Bedrohung. Heimweh setzt bei ihm bereits ein, sobald die Turmspitze seiner Dorfkirche aus seinem Blickfeld verschwindet. Er weiß, daß er Bürger eines altehrwürdigen Riesenreiches ist, jenen Teil der Welt aber, der ihn selbst betrifft, macht er sich überschaubar"* – I, 14.

[40] "*...so unentrinnbar sie in ihre kleinen Schicksale verstrickt sind, so sehr die großen, internationalen Entwicklungen an ihnen vorbeizulaufen scheinen, [haben sie] sich, nicht weniger als... die Bürger der Städte, als die... österreichische Aristokratie, schon lange vor der Jahrhundertwende einem Umsturz, einer drohenden, gravierenden Änderung im Gefüge der Monarchie entgegengefürchtet"* – III, 106.

[41] The titles of three parts of the tetralogy (vols. 1, 2, and 4) were gleaned from Roswitha Zauner's poetry volume *Meine Liebe— Mein Land* (Steyr: Ennsthaler, 1997), 5, 86, 84 respectively; according to Zier (ibid.), confirmed by the author himself,

Früchte vom Taubenbaum „are yet another symbol of disintegration" (*"ein weiteres Symbol der Auflösung"*), for pine trees carry no fruit (*"Der Taubenbaum trägt nichts"*).

[42] "*...der zur Zeit tobende Weltkrieg berührt Thal nicht mittelbar. Die Fronten befinden sich weit verstreut... verschont freilich... kann sich keiner mehr fühlen. Die Zeitungen strotzen weiterhin von Siegeszuversichte.... Meldungen von glorreichen Siegen kommen aus allen Ecken der Erde, daheim aber wird die Liste der Vermißten an der Tür des Postamtes immer länger. Kaum eine Woche vergeht, da nicht das Totenglöcklein geläutet werden muß, kaum eine Familie, die noch verschont geblieben wäre"* – II, 192.

[43] "*In Thal gehen die Gänge wieder ihren Gang. Vater Schmied hat seinem Sohn die Hand gedrückt zum Abschied, nun kehrt er zurück an seine Esse, der Wegmacher scharrt Roßäpfel an den Fahrbahnrand. Schuster Bartl handelt noch vor dem Feuerwehrdepot eine Stör aus, der Wagner lackiert den eben fertigen Bretterwagen doch wieder grün.... Die Menge vor dem Spritzenhaus zerstreut sich, die Bauern wählen ihre Wege zurück zu den Höfen querackerein und kontrollieren dabei, ob der Knecht seiner Arbeit nachkommt, ob die Mägde, unbeaufsichtigt, nicht etwa faul am Rain hocken.... Mit Genugtuung stellen sie fest, wie schwer die Bäume an Äpfeln und Birnen zu tragen haben.... Gibt Most für zwei Winter.... Die Rüben quellen prall über die Erdkruste hinaus... und auch die Erdäpfel werden bald soweit sein... und man kann mit der Ernte beginnen.... Nur die betroffenen Mütter laufen wie aufgeschreckte Hühner durchs Haus, ihnen ist auch durch gutes Zureden nicht zu helfen"* – II, 54.

[44] Note Graziella Hlawaty, who refers to „the brutal pictorialness" (*"in wuchtig brutalster Bildhaftigkeit"*) of Zauner's description of village life, in her essay "Der ganze Sauhaufen," in *morgen* (Vienna: December 1996); see also the same reviewer's comments on Zauner's syntax, "Ein Roman der anderen Art," in *morgen* (Vienna: May 1995), 87.

[45] "*Es ist eine schwielige Gegend... behäbige, träge, Hügel, die störrisch ansteigen, sich ineinanderschachteln und gegen den*

Horizont zu immer wieder neue Hügel zu gebären scheinen. Wiesen und Felder im Schachbrett. Die Höfe ducken sich in den Boden, verstecken sich hinter Kuppen. Das Land wirkte unbewohnt, tauchte da nicht unvermittelt ein rotes Schindeldach aus einer Mulde, stiegen nicht irgendwo Rauchsäulen aus unsichtbaren Kaminen auf. Die Wiesen sind immer noch grün, dort und da weiden Kühe in gottergebener Gelassenheit, die Felder, braun um diese Jahreszeit und umgebrochen. Und überall Wald. Er kriecht über die Anhöhen, bildet Tobel, wächst in Zungen an Gräben entlang und leuchtet in all den Herbstfarben von Jägergrün, Zinnober, bis hin zum Braun und Hellgelb der abfallenden Birkenblätter. Je weiter entfernt ein Waldstück liegt, umso mehr verdichten sich die Farben, werden düster, fast schwarz.... Daß der Teufel seine Hand mit im Spiel gehabt haben muß, ist allein schon an den Flurnamen abzulesen... und sie sind wohl auch Zeichen dafür, wie höllisch hart, wie teuflisch schwer die Bewohner sich im Fegfeuer ihr Brot verdienen müssen" – I, 141-142.

[46] Cf. Heide Stockinger, "Findelbub, hast kein Stub...," in *Oberösterreichischer Kulturbericht*, 47 (Linz: February 1993), 6.

[47] Cf. Gauß, "Kleine Welt, große Literatur," 83.

[48] Margret Czerni, "Eine Lust, ihn zu lesen," in *Neues Volksblatt* (Linz: 8 September 1993), 24.

[49] See Margret Czerni, "Ausgereifte Erzählkunst," in *Neues Volksblatt* (Linz: 31 March 1993), 3.

[50] *"Hierarchie ist ein tragender Faktor in der Funktion einer jeden Gesellschaft. So dünkt sich der Thaler privilegiert gegenüber den Bewohnern von Oed oder Fegfeuer, die wiederum fühlen sich denen vom Hintern Wald überlegen. Den persönlichen Rang verleiht der Stand. Ein Bauer steht über dem Beamten, der über dem Handwerker, dann folgen Dienstboten und Taglöhner, das absolute Ende der Skala bilden die Lohnarbeiter. Wer sich sein Geld im Steinbruch oder auswärts in der Ziegelei verdient, zählt fast schon zum Gesindel. Die Grenzen zwischen den Ständen sind scharf gezogen. Ein tüchtiger Schreiner hätte keine Chance, um die Hand der Tochter eines Bauern anzuhalten. Selbst wenn er finanziell*

sehr viel besser gestellt wäre als dieser. Andererseits brauchen Kinder von Handwerkern selten in den Dienst zu gehen. Auch innerhalb der Stände ist die Rangordnung genau festgelegt. Bei den Bauern hängt sie ab von der Tradition des Geschlechtes und von der Größe des Hofes.... Unter den Handwerkern rangieren diejenigen am höchsten, die, wie der Schmied oder der Wagner, ausschließlich in der eigenen Werkstatt arbeiten, Schneider, Schuster, Faßbinder und alle anderen, die ihrem Beruf hauptsächlich auf der Stör nachgehen, gelten minder. Streng wird die Rangordnung auch bei den Dienstboten eingehalten. Das reicht vom Roßknecht... bis hinunter zum Kälberbuben, von der Großmagd... bis zum 'Küchenmensch'.... Nur zwischen Arbeitern werden keine Unterschiede mehr gemacht, ihr Ansehen ist zu gering, als daß sich da noch eine Abstufung lohnte.... Trotz des verschlungenen Systems kennt jeder exakt seinen Platz in der Hierarchie, und er wird ständig daran erinnert..." – I, 69-70.

[51] Cf. Ilse Tielsch, "Wie lange noch?" in *morgen* (Vienna: September 1993), 52.

[52] Zier stresses that Zauner utilizes local idioms without ever allowing it to degenerate into *"Dialektdichtung"*; the author himself told me that he had deliberately tried to avoid or eliminate pure dialect terms. In this regard, consult also Reinhard Olt, "Zumpf aus dem Latz: Sprechen Österreicher deutsch?" in *Frankfurter Allgemeine Zeitung* (Frankfurt: 22 July 1995), 7).

[53] Norbert Mecklenburg, "Regionalismus und Literatur: Kritische Fragmente," in *Basis: Jahrbuch für deutsche Gegenwartsliteratur*, 9 (1979), 16.

[54] *"Sie ist im siebten Monat, watschelt tatsächlich daher wie mit einer Kugel vor dem Bauch.... Ausgerechnet zum dritten Kind fühlt sie sich unförmiger als je zuvor. Sie paßt in überhaupt kein Kleid mehr. Die Blusen spannen um die Brust, jeden Moment drohen die Knöpfe wegzuspringen. Den Rock hält sie sich mit Gummibändern am Leib, trotzdem quillt aus den Schlitzen seitlich wie an einer Schlampe das Unterzeug hervor. Wohl sind die Tage der morgendlichen Übelkeit ausgestanden,*

dafür muß sie nun alle fünf Minuten vors Haus, weil ihr der Bauch auf die Blase drückt. Ihre Haut schimmert im fahlen Altweiberton, die Sommersprossen sind zu häßlichen, braunen Flecken auseinandergelaufen, die Nase sticht spitz aus einem hageren Gesicht hervor, ihre Lippen haben sich zu farblosen, schmalen, welken Strichen verengt. Manchmal fühlt sie sich nicht mehr viel jünger als ihre Großmutter, die Altwirtin.... Ihr Haar... ist dünn, kaum zu bändigen, strähnig, stumpf, zottig. Unansehnlich. Sie haßt es, sich in dem Spiegel schauen zu müssen, was ihr da aus wächsernen, blaßblauen Augen entgegenstiert, läßt sie bisweilen Ekel vor sich selbst empfinden" – III, 223.

[55] Elsbeth Wessel, "Kindheit in Österreich: Über die Anti-Heimat-romane Franz Innerhofers," in *Dikt og idé: Festskrift til Ole Koppang*, ed. Sverre Dahl (Oslo: Germanistisches Institut, 1981), 281-293.

[56] "*Zaundürr ist er, hager, ausgehungert ist er, hohlwangig, mit tiefen Furchen um die Nase. Seinen Schädel trägt er... kahl geschoren, dadurch treten die Augen noch stärker hervor, wirken größer in ihren schwarzgeränderten Höhlen und verleihen dem Blick etwas Stechendes. Seine einst vollen Lippen haben sich zu zwei blassen Strichen verengt, das Bärtchen unter der Nase ist abrasiert, stattdessen wuchern Bartstoppeln an Kinn und Kragen.... Er, der stets so heikel auf seine Kleidung gewesen war, hat seit Jahren nichts anderes mehr auf dem Leib gehabt als die alte Landsturmuniform.... Am ersten Tag schon war ihm der Gürtel abgenommen worden, der Mantel bald danach auch. Inzwischen hat das ursprüngliche Feldgrün einen undefinierbaren, schmutzgrauen Farbton angenommen, die Rockärmel sind abgestoßen, die dreizackigen Patten der Taschen ausgefranst.... An Knien und Ellbogen blitzt die nackte Haut durch, das Hemd besteht überhaupt nur mehr aus mühsam zusammengehaltenen Leinenresten, die Füße stecken barfuß in den Stiefeln. Man hatte ihnen im Lager seit über zwei Jahren keine Unterwäsche mehr zuteilen können, so haben sich die Männer in ihrer Not aus Fußlappen Tücher ge-*

schnitten, die sie dann Kinderwindeln ähnlich um den Unterleib gewickelt trugen" – III, 25-26.

[57] *"Im Wirtshaus wird er nicht verkauft, wer immer ein Gewölbe besitzt und ein paar Obstbäume, preßt ihn selbst. Meist aus einem bestimmten Gemenge von Äpfeln und Birnen, und er schmeckt anders von Haus zu Haus, oft sogar von Faß zu Faß. Das hängt vom Mischverhältnis ab, von der Qualität des Obstes, von der Pflege, vom Keller.... Reiner Birnenmost ist rar.... Most aus Birnen ist herb, rauh, er legt sich beim Trinken pelzig an den Gaumen, und da die Frucht mehr Süße mitbringt, entwickelt er einen höheren Alkoholgehalt"* – I, 126.

[58] *"Er kann... alle möglichen Krankheiten lindern, Magendrücken, Kopfweh, Zahnweh. Er wird eingerieben bei Gliederreißen, im Wickel verwendet gegen Fieber, er hilft einem die Kälte loswerden und die Sorgen manchmal auch.... Hauptsächlich gibt es den Obstler, der wird aus einer Maische aller möglichen Kern- und Steinfrüchte hergestellt, je nachdem die Ernte ausfällt. Ein paar wenige Bauern brennen Slibowitz, man erkennt das allgemein an ihren blaugeäderten Nasen. Das Zwetschkenwasser hat den Adel unter den harten Getränken. Reiner Birnengeist ist selten, noch seltener findet man Wacholderbrand. Schnaps ist so ziemlich aus jeder Frucht zu gewinnen... aber Korn wird kaum verarbeitet, das ist nicht der Brauch, die Gerste kommt ins Bier"* – I, 23.

[59] See Jörg Thunecke, "'Die Kritiken sind wie von Verbrechern geschrieben': Zur Rezeption von Günter Grass' Roman *Ein weites Feld* oder: Der Romancier als Fremder im eigenen Land," in *Literatur und Geschichte: Festschrift für Wulf Koepke zum 70. Geburtstag*, ed. Karl Menges (Amsterdam: Rodopi, 1998), 331-343; also Josef Haslinger, "Eine große Geschichte": *"Er will nicht belehren, sondern erzählen."* ('He does not want to educate but to tell a tale.')

[60] Reinhold Reiterer, "Die Entdeckung der Heimat," in *Kleine Zeitung* (Graz: 19 September 1996), 58; see also R.R., "Friedrich Ch. Zauner: Licht und Schatten der Heimat," in *Neue Vorarlberger Tageszeitung* (Bregenz: 12 February 1995), 46.

[61] Karl-Markus Gauß, "Natur, Provinz, Ungleichzeitigkeit: Theodor Kramer und einige Stereotypen der Literaturwissenschaft," in *Theodor Kramer 1897-1958: Dichter im Exil*, ed. Konstantin Kaiser (Vienna: 1983); *Zirkular*, 19.

[62] Norbert Mecklenburg, "Regionalismus und Literatur: Kritische Fragmente," 17; see also Karl Wagner, "Über die literarischen Dörfer: Zur Ästhetik des Einfachen," in *Zeit ohne Manifest? Zur Literatur der siebziger Jahre in Österreich*, eds. Friedrich Aspetsberger and Hubert Lengauer (Vienna: Östereichischer Bundesverlag, 1987), 166-174.

[63] Zauner's father was a cooper ("*Faßbinder/Böttcher*") by trade; since he perished in World War Two, Friedrich Zauner learned details of the craft from his mother, who continued the business at the end of the war.

[64] "*Maurits ist ständig unausgeschlafen, der Grad der Müdigkeit wird beinahe grenzenlos. Phasenweise nimmt er das Leben überhaupt nur mehr wie hinter einer dicken Milchglasscheibe wahr. Halb im Schlaf noch mäht er in der Morgenfinsternis das Gras für die Binderkühe, striegelt und tränkt den Fuchs, wie in Trance stellt er sich die Eichenklötze zurecht, plaziert instinktiv das Ansetzbeil auf die Stelle, wo das Holz sich am besten spalten läßt, wie in Trance hebt und senkt sein Arm sich beim Aushacken der Rohdauben, wie durch ein Wunder ziehen die Finger der Führhand sich jeweils im noch rechten Moment zurück, ehe sie von der Axt durchgetrennt würden. Ohne sich dessen noch bewußt zu sein, feilt er nach Feierabend Scharten aus Spundbohrer und Reifenzieher, schränkt und schärft die Sägen, manche, in Gedanken verloren, gleich doppelt. Nickend im Takt der Hammerschläge, die Augenlieder fast zu, hockt er in der Abenddunkelheit auf der Dengelbank, um frische Schärfe in die Sensenblätter zu klopfen*" – III, 125.

[65] Cf. especially Jakob Ebner's contribution "*Das Ende der Ewigkeit*—linguistisch betrachtet," in a volume of *Die Rampe: Hefte für Literatur* (Linz: 1996, 43-47), dedicated to Friedrich Ch. Zauner in which, among other things, technical terms are listed, which find mention in 'The End of Eternity,' like: *Schaff, Plutzer, Rein, Schiff, Simpel, Zuber, Fürtuch, Leibkittel,*

Kasten, Binder, Stör, Drusch, Überleger, Pfette, Gaupen, Schober, Kleereiter, Grummet, Geißelstecken, Scheiterklieben, Austragbauer, Hube, Dirn, Einleger, Häusler, Gstanzel, Halbe, Nachkirtag, Percht, Salznagel, Brezen, Zeche, Zehrung, Speisgitter, Tafel, Zechpropst, Marterl u. Drud (43-44), as well as—contrary to Zauner's expressed intention—pure dialect terms in areas like milieu and characterization, like, for example: *anlassig, ausdeutschen, Ausschuler, Budel, dasig, entrisch, Fetzentandler, Frischgefangener, Gaudee, Gausterer, gnädig, Göd, Goden, Goder, Haderlump, Hansel, Häuter, Immenhütte, Kalfakter, Kalier, Kittel, klieben, knotzen, Kobel, Krispindel, kudern, Lahmlack, Leich, Leite, mögen, notig, petschiert, Pinkel, Prater, Progroder, Remasuri, Roß, Russen, rußig, sakrisch, Saubarthel, sauber, Scherz, Schluf, Simandl, Speckrenken, Spompanadeln, Springinkerl, stampern, Suderer, Surm, trenzen, Trumm, Tuttel, Tutter, Untam, wuzeln, Zumpfen, zusammenheuen* (44-45).

[66] Cf. Albert Janetschek, "Ein bedeutsamer Dorfroman," in *Podium 90—Literaturzeitschrift* (December 1993), 56: „mitreißende Sprache."

[67] "*Nur der Hölzenreiter, der in allem gern eine Extrawurst brät, hat sich für die Fahrten nach Thal ein Motorrad zugelegt.... Um es der Hölzenreiter Größe anzupassen, war es notwendig gewesen, die Sattelstange auf die maximale Höhe hochzuschrauben. Sitzt der feiste Bauer nun auf, verschwindet der Sattel zur Gänze unter dessen überhängenden Arschbacken. Aussieht das Ganze wie ein Ochs am Spieß, als schiebe sich ein Eisenrohr durch den After des Bauern pfeilgerade in dessen Schmerbauch. Über die Anstiege hinein ins Fegfeuer und unter dem Gewicht dieses massiven Körpers gibt die Maschine von Zeit zu Zeit den Geist auf. So können die Thaler erleben, wie er mit hochrotem Kopf, keuchend, Kreuzschelter ausstoßend, Zündkerzen ausbaut und putzt, den Benzintupfer traktiert, ungeduldig an Verteiler oder Gasgestänge werkt. Helfen läßt er sich von niemandem*" – III, 160.

[68] "*Zur Draufgabe... ein Ausfluß des verschrobenen Humors, wie er Menschen aus dem Hintern Wald eigen ist, haben die*

Bettelhöher Maurer ... einen gemauerten Abort hingestellt, der sich alsbald zur Sensation bei der Oeder Nachbarschaft entwickelt. Kirchgänger, die Kinder auf dem Weg zur oder heim von der Schule, alles, was hausierend, bettelnd oder streunend unterwegs ist, kehrt seither hier zu, um sich zu erleichtern. Man säße buchstäblich, wird gewitzelt, wie der Kaiser auf dem Thron. Als Lichteinlässe dienen an Stelle der Herzen richtige, kleine Fenster, die mittels Holzläden sogar geschlossen werden können, was besonders das Weibervolk als wohltuend empfindet, weil es sich vor ungebetenen Zuschauern sicher fühlen darf. Bisweilen entsteht geradezu ein Andrang vor diesem Luxusscheißhaus, aber die Leute, anstatt, wie gewohnt, in die nahen Büsche auszuweichen, warten lieber mit zusammengezwickten Knien in der Reihe. Sehr zum Ärger der Theres. Ihr schließlich fällt zu, in einem noch unbewohnten Haus das Klosett alle paar Monate zu entleeren, damit der Kegel der dünnen oder festen, hell- oder dunkelbraunen, stinkenden Würste, unterspickt von marmorierten Zeitungsfetzen, mit denen die Ärsche gewischt werden, sich nicht gar bis ans Loch des Sitzbrettes herauftürmt" – III, 193.

[69] See Norbert Mecklenburg, *Erzählte Provinz: Regionalismus und Moderne im Roman* (Königstein: Athenäum, 1982).

[70] Ibid, 49.

[71] Unacceptable is Schurz's claim that 'The End of Eternity' "represents a closed society, a closed life-cycle, during which all things eternally repeated themselves."

[72] Mecklenburg, "Regionalismus und Literatur," 13.

[73] Michael Scharang, "Landschaft und Literatur," in *Kürbiskern*, 3 (Vienna: 1975), 101.

[74] Ibid; see also Ina-Maria Greverus, *Der territoriale Mensch* (Frankfurt: Athenäum, 1972) and I.-M.G., "The Heimat Problem," in *Der Begriff der 'Heimat' in der deutschen Gegenwartliteratur/The Concept of 'Heimat' in Contemporary German Literature*, ed. Helfried W. Seliger (Munich: iudicium, 1987), 9-27.

[75] Scharang, ibid, 101.

60 *Beyond Vienna*

ALOIS BRANDSTETTER
Courtesy of Residenz Verlag
im Niederösterreichischen Pressehaus

"Vienna is far away": Alois Brandstetter's Proclivity to the Provinces

by Paul F. Dvorak

Alois Brandstetter has established himself as one of Austria's most enduring and prolific, if less widely known, authors. Born in 1938 as the youngest child to a miller's family in Pichl, near Wels in Upper Austria, Brandstetter spent his formative years in a close-knit family and community where the conservative values of Catholicism and rural life predominated. Dismissed as a teenager from the seminary in Linz, Brandstetter successfully completed his doctorate in philology and history at the University of Vienna in 1961 at the age of twenty-three. Initially his academic career brought him to the University of the Saarland in Saarbrücken where he worked primarily on linguistic projects, then to Salzburg on a brief visiting appointment, and finally to the University of Klagenfurt where he has been teaching as a professor of medieval language and literature since 1974.

While carrying out his academic duties as teacher and scholar, Brandstetter simultaneously established his credentials as an author and editor. His first literary attempts in the late 1960s resulted in the publication of several works in small printings and reveal the influence of the circle of avant-garde Austrian writers known as the *Wiener Gruppe*, for whom linguistic experimentation stood paramount.[1] However, it was not until the publication of the novel *Zu Lasten der Briefträger* ('The Postmen's Burdens') in 1974 that Brandstetter's defining breakthrough occurred. Over the course of his literary career, Brandstetter has now published eleven novels, most notably *The Abbey*,[2] (*Die Abtei*, 1977), *Die Mühle* ('The Mill,' 1981), *Die Burg* ('The Castle,' 1986), *Hier kocht der Wirt* ('The Innkeeper Does the Cooking,' 1995), and most recently *Der geborene Gärtner* ('The Born Gardener,' 2005). Interspersed among these longer prose works are numerous collections of short prose pieces, essays, edited anthologies of Austrian stories, and collaborative works with photographers, such as *Das Buch der alten Mühlen* ('The Book of Old Mills,' 1984) and *Kärnten im besonderen* ('Carinthia,' 1995). 'The Postmen's Burdens' and *Altenehrung* ('Honoring Ancestry,' 1983) have also been adapted to film. Yet despite his exceptional productivity, only one novel, *The Abbey*, has been translated to date into English, a fact that is closely connected not only to the content of Brandstetter's work but also to the difficulty of capturing the essence of his style and complex use of language.

Residing comfortably in the provinces of Carinthia and Upper Austria, Brandstetter draws inspiration for his writing from the cultural heritage of his provincial homeland and from the wealth of information and experience he gleans from his professional background as professor of medieval language and literature. He remains contentedly immersed in the familiar natural landscapes and settings of his western Austrian roots and the cornucopia of European and Germanic cultural traditions that enrich it. Other than his early appointment in Saarbrücken between 1962 and 1975 and his brief stay in Salzburg, Brandstetter has been firmly entrenched in Carinthia and Upper Austria and infrequently strays far beyond this comfort zone. Ironically, for example, he has never visited the United States, which plays a particularly significant role in his work (along with contemporary Vienna) as the iconic, monolithic embodiment of the shortcomings, artificiality, and ills pervading a modern-day consumer society that threatens the essential uniqueness and individuality of everything over which it casts its shadow.

Having published in both academic and literary circles (his literary publications alone number close to thirty), Brandstetter has established a modest position on the Austrian literary scene for over thirty years and ranks among the most productive and prolific of present-day Austrian authors. His literary work stands in stark relief against the backdrop of a life spanning the period in Austria from the *Anschluss* through the foundation of the Second Republic and Austria's entry into the European Union into our present twenty-first century. Not surprisingly, Brandstetter's novels and prose texts manifest a connectedness to a type of *Heimatliteratur* that is categorically distinguishable from the recent emphasis in contemporary Austrian literature on *Antiheimatliteratur* and on a post-modernist urbanism frequently focused on Vienna and global issues. The term *Heimat* that will occur throughout this chapter (and in such compounds as *Heimatliteratur, Heimatdichter, Heimaterzähler*, etc.) is a difficult concept to translate into English with a succinct word or phrase. *Heimat* implies a deep-rooted connectedness to one's native land and region, to its people, its culture and its relatively simple way of life, and casts them in overtly positive terms. In literature, it denotes a style of writing that draws upon the "topography" of the region, its landscape, and its people. (See note 26 below.) Thus, *Antiheimatliteratur*, a trend cultivated among many Austrian writers in the 1970s, such as Mitterer, Winkler, and Turini, for example, broke with the traditional espousing of local values and positive views of the landscape and countryside in order to expose the negative psychological, spiritual, and physical undercurrents lurking beneath the pristine natural surface.

In contrast to these prevalent current literary trends, Brandstetter writes against the grain by drawing heavily upon the positive personal experiences of his early years growing up in the provincial alpine countryside of Upper Austria. For example, his autobiographical photoessay, *"Meine Römerstraße"* ('My Roman Road')[3] depicts nostalgically in word and picture the formative influences on his development: father and family, home and mill, church, bible and religious devotions, local farmers and neighborliness, postmen (who brought more than the mail), unpaved roads, Greek, Latin, and local dialect, familial Habsburg loyalty, and Roman ruins and remnants. Many facets of these images, artifacts, and figures reveal themselves as recurring motifs in his other literary works, as, for example, the invasion of asphalt surfaces and the *Autobahn* that mar and scar the natural rural landscape in 'The Innkeeper Does the Cooking,' the destruction of historic buildings and relics wrought by modernization in 'Honoring Ancestry,' or the description of his father's religious devoutness in *Über den grünen Klee der Kindheit* ('Enduring Childhood Memories,' 1982).[4] And everywhere along the path of this autobiographical memoir it is the *Schotter*, the broken stone of the gravel roads, that forms these life-sustaining arteries interlocking past to present—the leitmotif of his youth, as Brandstetter calls it.[5] *His* "Roman road" connects his own past to the more distant past and history of Roman ruins and thus to the very foundations of our shared Western cultural heritage.

Brandstetter's deep-rooted familiarity with his native region's local culture and its people as well as his extensive knowledge of its linguistic and literary traditions with their foundations extending back to Latin (and Greek) inspire his creative muse. Through the intricate interplay and interconnectedness of these elements, along with his apparent innate bent for irony, humor, and turn of phrase, Brandstetter has produced a body of literary work that signals an apparent provincialism and staunch conservatism on the one hand and a high level of erudition and insight into human nature on the other. With a critical and observant eye, Brandstetter crafts his colorful, highly intertextual prose against the backdrop of rural Austrian life and culture. Modern readers not fully familiar with his native Upper Austria and his adopted Carinthia or those disinclined to identify with the ironical, scholarly, erudite characteristics many of his occasionally overbearing narrators embody may find his work prosaic, impenetrable, and even pedantic. Yet it is Brandstetter's exacting and literal use of language, his skillful connotative playfulness, and a rich vocabulary firmly rooted to its etymological underpinnings that supports a style that ranges from the serious to the self-parodying. The combination of these factors with his own somewhat reclusive temperament has contributed to casting him in the mold of a regional author, and consequently has also resulted in the fact that there has been relatively little interest in translating his work into other languages.

Yet through his predominantly first-person narrators, Brandstetter critiques the cultural foundations of his native homeland and himself as an integral part of it. The pervasive irony and humor in much of Brandstetter's writing enriches the depiction of characteristics that are both essentially Austrian and genuinely human.

In addition to exhibiting an intimate familiarity with the Austrian mindset, especially that of the provinces, Brandstetter's work is founded upon an encyclopedic familiarity with the Western literary tradition and especially with its Classical Roman and Germanic linguistic heritage. The author's predilection for linguistic analysis and preoccupation with the power of exactness and literalness in the use of language as well as of its connotative and associative suggestiveness characterize a body of work that is both imaginative and challenging. The resulting product contrasts the common themes of *Heimatliteratur* with the scholarly, linguistic interests the author simultaneously advances. Like Handke, Bernhard, Jelinek, and other contemporaries, Brandstetter walks in the long shadows of the established Austrian tradition of linguistic analysis and the relationship of language, meaning, and reality that can be traced back to the likes of Hugo von Hofmannsthal and the *fin-de-siècle* obsession with appearance and reality (*Schein und Sein*). This quintessential Austrian preoccupation with the interrelationship between language and meaning constitutes a critical component of Alois Brandstetter's writing.

The fact that Brandstetter prefers relative obscurity to basking openly in the limelight has also contributed to his modest public profile as author and citizen. His unassuming, conservative lifestyle, coupled with the predominantly nonconfrontational nature of his works, has not provoked scandal or created controversy and has kept him at arm's length from the major literary and political debates of the day. Unlike his activist, contentious contemporaries Handke, Bernhard, and Jelinek, who have consistently served as lightning rods for the Austrian *status quo*, Brandstetter as both person and author remains a relatively unknown, unalluring, and unprovocative figure for the Austrian public at large. Nevertheless, Brandstetter's works, which offer his readers highly reflective, autobiographical glimpses into a worldview that conveys his value system, personality, and humanity in an array of prose genres, have quite clearly achieved considerable popularity and a relatively high level of success among a limited but loyal readership within the German-speaking world, if not beyond. His consistent pattern of publication has helped preserve this modest ranking amongst the field of contemporary Austrian writers. For many of his avid readers he is, in contrast to the often-vilified Bernhard, an author that one loves to read rather than an author one loves to hate.[6]

Literary critics have described Brandstetter as a "conservative annihilator of stories" and a "destroyer of literature who preserves language."[7] Both of these descriptors invite comparisons to Brandstetter's fellow Upper Austrian countryman, Thomas Bernhard. But whereas the designation "conservative anarchist"[8] might aptly describe Bernhard, Brandstetter might best be labeled a medieval Catholic anomaly.[9] Yet despite this label, Brandstetter reveals himself as an enlightened intellectual fully capable of questioning even his own traditional cultural and religious values. A recent example is his novel 'The Born Gardener,'[10] in which the fictional narrator, Abbot Konrad von Burghausen, serves as the mouthpiece questioning Wernher the Gardener's apparent abandonment of his horticultural duties in order to pursue his literary avocation. In the abbot's mind Wernher runs the risk of allowing writing to become an all-consuming process, one that the abbot rejects categorically because it diverts his young subordinate from the fulfillment of his essential vocation as a monk in a highly structured hierarchical order. Brandstetter leaves it for the reader to decide whether the pursuit of diverse interests and the ability to serve both God faithfully as monk and writer are, in fact, incompatible. It is the intersection of this baroque dichotomy, pitting the heavenly against the worldly, around which the novel revolves. However, in the end the gardener's open-mindedness appears to have gained the upper hand over the abbot's inflexible adherence to established rules and regulations based on his "Catholic" interpretation and understanding of history and tradition. And so, too, it would seem that Brandstetter's own sympathies as *Heimatdichter* lie with the title figure's literary aspirations rather than its narrator's limiting prescriptions. Once again, Brandstetter's sophisticated sense of irony reveals itself in the interplay of these polar opposites.

Brandstetter's reliance on irony can be traced back to his earliest work. In *Start*, a collection of prose texts written several years before its publication in 1976, Brandstetter opens with a letter addressed to his cherished readers in which he expresses his thanks for their purchase of his modest book and his hope that their support will continue as he embarks on his journey along his literary writing path. Furthermore, he expresses his intention of offering his readers relaxation and enjoyment, even though he surmises that "progressives and pop artists" will laugh at his work in pity. The goal he sets for himself is measured: he characterizes himself not as someone who writes so that his readers will fall off their chairs with laughter while reading, but rather as someone who will occasionally cause his readers to grin and smirk along the way. Moreover, he describes himself as a writer who draws upon personal experiences but who also creates his own texts. As one reads the letter, the inherent self-effacing irony it contains is difficult to overlook. The essential elements of a literary style that will characterize him throughout his long career—irony, humor, self-deprecation, turn of phrase—are all clearly evident in this early effort.[11]

With regard to the type of prose Brandstetter crafts, Bernhard's quip about avoiding plot and action—"If I see a plot rising up from beyond the hill, I shoot it down immediately"[12]—

is equally suited to describe his lesser-known countrymen's tendency toward a narrative style that both shuns plot development and action and refrains from the treatment of themes involving crime and sexuality. Both authors share a tendency toward verbosity and an often rambling, repetitive style as they weave their narratives in long passages with minimal reliance on paragraph, heading, or chapter subdivisions. Although both authors rely heavily on humor and irony, Brandstetter's variety is by far the less confrontational and politically charged. True to his professional background as philologist, Brandstetter "etymologizes"[13] and engages in linguistic associations and experimentation in a concerted effort to bridge the gulf between historical past and traditions and the contemporary world, as in the aforementioned 'My Roman Road,' which conjoins personal experience with historical and cultural artifact.

In 'The Postmen's Burdens,'[14] Brandstetter's narrator bemoans the influx of urbanites into the rural regions. What these encroachers from the city label the country houses or *Landhäuser* they build are in fact merely city houses, *Stadthäuser*. Their country homes are designed with all the amenities and conveniences of contemporary city dwellings. As such these trespassers and the houses they construct symbolize a distortion of the authenticity of country life that the narrative voice seeks to defend and preserve. The entire text is developed around the basic polarity between the land, earth, and simple rural life on the one hand and the city, urbanization, and consumer lifestyle and society on the other.

Brandstetter's perceptive insight into the etymological denotation of words, phrases, and idioms uncovers similar incongruities in 'The Innkeeper Does the Cooking.' Contrasting the *haute culture* of Vienna's Carinthian Street or *Kärntnerstraße* and what the simplicity, naturalness, and earthiness that the provincial culture of Carinthia represents for him, the narrator, innkeeper Peter Glandschnig, staunchly upholds his firmly held sense of regional identity and proclaims that "Vienna is far away" (*"Wien ist weit"*). Yet he is forced to acknowledge the inroads that the demands and norms of the national authorities have made on regional custom and individual inclination. Defiantly, Glandschnig continues to act independently on his own authority insofar as he is able. He operates his inn not according to the prescriptions of law as to when and how an establishment may be open, but according to local circumstances and his own sense of appropriateness; he acts in accord with the old saying: "The innkeeper doesn't open up for just *one* customer."[15]

Moreover, it is the innkeeper who does the cooking, as the title indicates; he is in charge, he determines who will be served what and when. As Brandstetter's narrator, he is also in charge of the course of the text and the barrage of information with which he assaults his Viennese visitor. This Viennese art aficionado has traveled to the province to see first-hand the famous frescoes of Thomas of Gerlamoos in the village church to which Glandschnig also controls the keys and must acquiesce to his manner of doing business. Like the famous flood and mudslide of 1993 for which the area is best known by contemporary society, Glandschnig overpowers his Viennese visitor with a deluge of information about the region and specifically about the frescoes of the famous artist that he considers to be the area's real claim to fame. While inundating his visitor with his self-acquired knowledge about Thomas' art and various other issues, Glandschnig affirms through the text he quotes that language is the memory of mankind and explains that many proverbs and sayings still current have their original meanings deciphered only in dictionaries. The circumstances and conditions that originally inspired them may have long since died out in reality, but the linguistic phrases and idioms that they spawned may still exist.[16] As the keeper of the keys, Peter (*"nomen est omen"*) feels fully justified in delaying the Viennese visitor's entry into the church as long as he sees fit.

The novel 'The Castle' is also rich in regional overtones connecting present to past.[17] In its denotative and connotative incarnations, the castle is the central image of the novel that bears its name and conjures images of Carinthia's landmark

Hochosterwitz, which was first mentioned in documents dating to 960 and has existed in its present form since the sixteenth century. Brandstetter's autobiographical narrator, Arthur, a serious-minded university professor of medieval literature who bemoans the loss of understanding of and appreciation for the past, takes the reader on a journey through his professional career, his family life as the married father of two young sons, and his forced adaptation to the advances of contemporary society. Arthur's whole life and being is framed within the context of the medieval world.

His older boy's favorite toy is a Playmobil model of a medieval castle whose multiple parts and figures find themselves strewn about the family's cramped living space and impinge upon Arthur's attempts to engage in his academic research as a medievalist because his writing desk has been invaded and occupied by the boy's toy. True to his personality and scholarly interests, Arthur recounts: "I could describe my situation very well in the language and with the vocabulary of a siege, of an assault, and of the final conquest of a medieval fortress."[18]

One of the more illuminating scenes of the novel is the family outing to the unnamed castle. At least for Arthur, the outing is spoiled by the nearby din of a motocross race that detracts from the reverence he deems appropriate to this superb example of medieval fortresses and mars and scars its environment audibly and visually. The natural setting, the earth, the ground, and the soil as components of an entire eco-system are juxtaposed with the non-biodegradable plastic bottles and containers littering the natural environment around the medieval castle as visitors and tourists besiege the surrounding area for the race. The juxtaposition of the genuine *Burg* to the model toy and to contemporary society's overrunning of the serene castle surroundings allows Brandstetter through Arthur to explore his central themes. In his profession as an underappreciated member of a progressive-thinking university faculty, in his family life and the struggle to balance his role as husband, father, and breadwinner, in his misaligned relationship with the consumerism and shortsightedness of contemporary society, Arthur engages in skirmishes his author shares at least in part. Arthur's practical, level-headed wife, Ginover, serves as a counterweight to her pedantic, serious, moody, misfit husband as she repeatedly and calmly draws him back to a world view that can coexist with these contradictions.

Brandstetter's *The Abbey* typifies the essential characteristics of his narrative techniques.[19] Although ostensibly a detective novel, *The Abbey* will disappoint the avid reader of whodunits looking for suspense, twists of plot, and an investigator driven by the sole task of finding his man. Brandstetter's main character, police investigator Dr. Einberger, is an astute but unconventional law-and-order type. Considered an unsophisticated member of the rural law-enforcement establishment by his superiors in Vienna, Einberger employs a questionable investigative methodology that raises the eyebrows and elicits the derision of those in Vienna until the case is actually solved. Noteworthy is also the fact that the novel fails to exploit lurid details of sex or of crime. In fact the typical detective-story murder is not part of the crime: the central deed is the theft of the Arnulf Chalice from the fictional Upper Austrian monastery of Freimünster.

The entire novel is narrated from the first-person perspective of Dr. Einberger. Any insight into the minds of other characters, most notably that of the Abbot, who bears the brunt of Einberger's continuous harangue, is filtered through the unique logic and logos of the main character. The narrative contains no chapter subdivisions or subheadings other than those of the paragraph. With its associative powers, Brandstetter's creative mind is the sole driving force behind the narrative as the inspector, like his counterparts in 'The Innkeeper Does the Cooking' and 'The Castle,' for example, launches into dissertations on various and sundry topics, such as the environment, pollution, theology, biology, education, sport, food and drink, among others.

It is evident in virtually everything Brandstetter writes, both literary and academic, that he exploits and exhausts the power of language and of the written word, both as a means of "teaching" as well as of preserving his own sense of self-identity that is so inseparable from his cultural and provincial landscape. Language and the written word shape the very essence of his being. The didacticism is expressed, often ironically, in the range of erudite characters Brandstetter presents. From Einberger in *The Abbey* to Arthur in 'The Castle,' to Peter Glandschnig in 'The Innkeeper Does the Cooking,' to Feuerbach in *So wahr ich Feuerbach heiße* ('Yes, My Name is Feuerbach'),[20] to the fictional Abbot Konrad von Burghausen in 'The Born Gardener,' Brandstetter presents a series of narrators with an *idée fixe*. The focus of their intent—often unapparent and impenetrable in the eyes of the recipient (reader)—leads to expositions and dissertations on innumerable topics apparently with little connection to the apparent expectation of the reader or to plot. While preserving the centrality of language, Brandstetter destroys literature in its conventional form. It is in following the contorted, associative path of the narrative without the aid of the usual narrational props of plot, chronology, and even logic that eventually leads to the conclusion and to the ultimate enjoyment of the reading process as the reader has to let himself go with the flow of the text and enjoy it as a type of impressionist painting where the overall image changes and reshapes itself at every moment. It is in this creation of art through the skillful use of language that Brandstetter expresses his mastery and that ultimately leads to the enjoyment of his work as author and reader engage in a head-to-head battle of wits.

Brandstetter's literary work can thus be categorized as a compendium of highly stylized first-person prose texts from very short one-page commentary to his "novels" of several hundred pages. As seen earlier, his first-person narrators frequently bear highly autobiographical markings. Even the several works that bear the description "novel" (*Roman*) are ones that are difficult to place within the framework of normal literary terminology. The relationship between objective and subjective truth raises interesting questions regarding the relationship between fact and fiction, autobiography and novel.[21]

Brandstetter unfolds narratives in which the narration itself, often in the minutest detail, takes precedence over the development of plot.

Two other works, 'The Mill' and *Das Buch der alten Mühlen* ('The Book of Old Mills'),[22] blend literary elements with scholarly ones and ease the transition from Brandstetter's creative writing to his more scholarly work. These two particular works go hand in hand in recreating the symbiotic relationship between mill and water and the etymological basis of the "miller" as *"Curator aquarum."* Nostalgically, the uncle in 'The Mill' relates to his nephew that in Roman times both language and water were transparent, clearer and pure.[23] These two works affirm Brandstetter's affinity for language and etymology that he succinctly expressed several years later in *Kleine Menschenkunde* ('A Small Anthropological Study'): "I love the so-called 'etymological figures,' figures of speech and of writing, in which words from one stem emerge as members of a 'family.' And how very different, how strangely dissimilar even brothers can be!"[24]

An examination of some of Brandstetter's editorial and scholarly contributions reveals a similar value system and world-view to that presented in his own literary contributions. An early example, *Daheim ist daheim* ('Home Sweet Home'), is according to the editor's foreword a collection of recent *Heimat* stories (*"neue Heimatgeschichten"*) by sixteen writers of local color from the German-speaking world.[25] Brandstetter goes on to state that the common denominator among the stories is what he describes as a precision and exactness in the narration that makes itself evident to the non-indigenous reader of the texts. As conceptualized by Brandstetter, it is this ability of an author to create a supra-regional plausibility in the representation of country and its inhabitants that defines what he calls good *Heimatliteratur*.[26] Authors' individual methods may vary widely, but their ability to capture the essence of their topic with precision is what makes their work genuine. The title for the volume 'Home Sweet Home' (taken from the common German folk saying *Daheim ist daheim*) reflects what Brandstetter further describes as a personal recollection of innate familiarity.

In 1984 Brandstetter published his second anthology of Austrian prose, *Österreichische Erzählungen des 20. Jahrhunderts* ('20th-Century Austrian Stories'), which includes an afterword important to understanding both his conception of *Heimatliteratur* and also of narration (*"Erzählen"*) in general. With regard to its association with *Heimatliteratur per se*, Brandstetter's afterword *"Vom Ärgernis des Erzählens"* ('Narration as a Nuisance') cites the familiar sounds of the *Heimat*[27] as one of several primary characteristics that can serve to identify and characterize Austrian literature. He specifically references the contributions of writers like Stifter to the tradition of Austrian *Heimatliteratur* and goes on to reveal much about his own proclivities as a writer (*Heimatdichter*). The stories in this anthology—and by extension, his own—embody what he describes as a reasoned reflection on the humane. Storytelling signifies for him a conscious, calm, reliable, and cultivated undertaking, a task that is considerate of humanity. In the best sense of the word he considers narration (*Erzählen*) to be slightly middleclass and cognizant of traditions and heritage. Finally, he concludes that storytelling requires time and demands patience from the recipient.[28] Again, whether it is reading through a succession of his short early prose in collections such as *Von den Halbschuhen der Flachländer oder die Größe der Alpen* ('Of the Half Shoes of the Lowlanders or the Majesty of the Alps'),[29] the lengthy novel 'The Mill,' or the more modest 'Yes, My Name is Feuerbach,' Brandstetter's reader needs to allow himself to be moved along on an even keel with the flow of his text and not become impatient when great twists of plot fail to emerge. For Brandstetter it is the give-and-take between reader and writer that is of central importance.

As alluded to above, Brandstetter holds Adalbert Stifter in high regard and considers him the greatest of Austrian narrators. The retreat from the misery and discomforts of the world into a world of appearance and dreams that can be described as "*biedermeierlich*"[30] is a common denominator between the two of them. Brandstetter goes on to say that narrating and writing stories has always involved a kind of defiance, an ignoring of the times and its ongoing crises, and not at all only in Austria.[31] Much of Brandstetter's work can be described as embodying the principles Stifter outlines in his preface to *Colored Stones* (*Bunte Steine)*, in which he writes about the general laws of nature where the exceptional is an isolated expression of these laws and where a sense of ethics pervades the soul and interaction among human beings and describes the marvels of the moment as the expression of these general laws of nature.[32] The movement of the air, the rustling of the waters, the growing of the grain pervade Brandstetter's works, too, from short autobiographical texts such as the aforementioned 'My Roman Road' to the lengthy novel 'The Mill,' to the ironic, humorous meanderings of the eccentric innkeeper, Peter Glandschnig, in 'The Innkeeper Does the Cooking.'[33]

The "noble simplicity and quiet grandeur"[34] of Winckelmann's classical ideal is expressed in both Stifter and Brandstetter. Not the noble characters of classical antiquity or of German classicism, but the Christian exponents of Rousseauian natural man seem more aligned with Brandstetter's image of man. Of course not all of Brandstetter's subjects achieve or measure up to the "classical" ideal, but it is this ideal against which the foibles of those who do not are measured. The relationship between culture and nature as well as between nature and man are examined continually in his writings.

When one strips away the artificiality of art, the lesson or the exemplary in the story is revealed.[35] Brandstetter's own texts are associative, contemplative, and impressionistic as opposed to the linearity of the typical novella and short story. As it was for Franz Nabl and Karl Heinrich Waggerl, Brandstetter's style reveals his inclination toward "native sounds of quiet happiness, of cheerful indigence, the blessings of the earth, of patience and resigned suffering.[36] In 'The Mill,' Brandstetter writes through the figure of the uncle that a person who can't take pleasure in the simple things of life is and might just as well be dead.[37] Brandstetter thus sees himself standing firmly in the Austrian tradition of *Heimatdichtung* while simultaneously incorporating a strong dose of linguistic experimentation. Given the recurring juxtaposition of these two components of his writing, he has been labeled—and personally does not dispute being called—a mixture of Peter Rosegger and Karl Kraus.[38]

In the anthology *Advent, Advent: Geschichten zur Vorweihnachtszeit* ('Advent, Advent: Stories for Pre-Christmastime,' 1988), Brandstetter integrates his deep sense of religiosity and Christian tradition into the broader scope of his cultural material. The collected contributions by roughly fifty German-speaking authors, including Brandstetter's own piece titled "*Advent*," and the introduction "*Adventus. Zum Geleit*" make the connection between the Christian season of Advent and the values of the *Heimat* clear. In tracing the continuum of word and thought throughout the ages, Brandstetter highlights the comparison between the idyllic poetry of the pre-Christian Vergil and the rustic tales of Peter Rosegger.[39]

Another anthology, *Heiteres aus Österreich: Von Artmann bis Zeemann* ('Cheerful Stories from Austria: From Artmann to Zeemann'), responds to the rhetorical question the editor raises in the preface as to whether such a thing as Austrian humor exists. Similar to his published anthologies of nineteenth and twentieth century Austrian authors, this collection serves to interrelate a varied group of authors from the same time frame. The use of exaggeration and parody characterizes many of them and serves to associate them with the stereotypical Austrian quality of lightheartedness and lack of seriousness. Many clearly fall into Brandstetter's conception of *Heimatdichter*, both old and new.[40]

But it is Brandstetter's collaborations with two photographers that deserve a closer look. Both works stand on the periphery of conventional "literary" publications. The first, 'The Book of Old Mills,' a joint effort with photographer Gerhard Trumler, integrates a lengthy essay by Brandstetter among the photographs of mills and their surroundings collected from throughout the Austrian countryside. Brandstetter's essay is part historical, part scholarly, part personal. Himself the son of a miller,

Brandstetter dedicates the book to his father, who has earlier been described as a dominant influence in his son's life as the embodiment of the cultural values and traditions of the *Heimat*. The essay begins with one of Brandstetter's typical etymological explications. He traces the roots of the word "mill" through its relationship with the Austrian courtly poet or *Minnesänger*, Der von Kürenberg, who used the millstone as his symbol. He reveals the relationship between the stem "*kürn*" and the modern derivative "mill" or "*Mühle*," which is in turn derived from the Latin "*molina*."[41] Brandstetter the linguist and scholar cannot refrain from indulging his predilection toward etymological analysis, and it is in exploring such linguistic intricacies that the aforementioned quote about his love for etymology proves its validity.[42]

As a conservator of the written word, Brandstetter also incorporates several historical texts dealing with mills and milling into this eclectic, intertextual volume. The first, 'Regulations for the miller in the upper forest region, issued under Emperor Karl VI, 1724,' (*Handwerksordnung der Müller für das obere Waldviertel, erlassen unter Kaiser Karl VI. 1724)* was a text discovered in the Rosenmayer mill in Klein Gundholz (*Waldviertel*); the second, 'Milling regulations, issued under Emperor Franz 1, 1814' (*Mahlordnung, erlassen unter Kaiser Franz I. 1814*) dates from a century later. The volume embodies the elements Brandstetter considers essential to both his life and that of the native regions with which he identifies: the preservation of rural, rustic life through the specific exploration of the significance and function of the mill; the sense of historical, cultural, linguistic continuity that ties past to present; his personal kinship with this past; and the linguistic, philological conservation of the written word through the inclusion of historical documents.

A second photographic collaboration with Michael Leischner, the pictorial essay of Carinthia entitled *Kärnten im besonderen*,[43] is perhaps even more revealing of Brandstetter's deep personal attachment to his Austrian rootedness. Imparting much more than the typical coffee-table edition of nostalgic landscape pictures of a country or region, this volume represents a genuine blending of image and word. The flow of photographs of Carinthia's landscape, people, and architecture captures visually the patterns and themes of the Carinthian heritage that Brandstetter skillfully expresses in his insightful introduction. Both textually and visually, what attracts Brandstetter's attention and where the soul and spirit of the author reside is clearly evident. Ancient Carinthia, whose roots precede those of the thousand-year documentation of *"Ostarrichi,"* is portrayed in a series of pictures that elicit the ethos of the land and its people in moods that evoke an atmosphere of timeless beauty, tradition, and serenity. Vistas of majestic natural mountain landscapes and relics of man-made ecclesiastical marvels intermingle with scenes of simple provincial life with mills, streams, fields, and farmhouses that conjure up the calm, harmonious bliss of an eternal goodness. Thus it is easy to correlate the author's close personal attachment to this landscape and the values he then examines in the bulk of his other creative writing. It is also not much of a leap to understand why so much of Brandstetter's creativity derives from highly personal and autobiographical elements.

Yet a tinge of melancholy—a frequent byproduct of Austrian lightheartedness and frivolity—invades the words and images of the text as well. Brandstetter quotes actor-comedian Karl Valentin, whose remark that only jovial people have the capacity to be truly sad [44] helps capture the mood and mitigate the chasm between idyllic nature and harsh reality. The baroque contradiction manifest in the Austrian spirit reveals itself here as it did in the work, life, and eventual death of nineteenth-century compatriot Adalbert Stifter. Another descriptive passage in Brandstetter's introduction that clearly evokes a sense of melancholy and loss is the one noting the fact that one of the twelve extant copies of the Gutenberg Bible, once owned by the Benedictine Abbey of St. Paul in the Lavanttal, had to be sold to the United States in 1930. For Brandstetter the removal of the five-hundred-year-old edition from its historical and geographical roots represents "a particular wound"[45] that is difficult to heal. It may very well be that few Carinthians or Austrians are even aware of the sale of the Bible or that in fact few would even particularly care that it had been sold. But for Brandstetter the personal wound resulting from the sale bears implications proportional to those of Kafka's Gregor Samsa and thus touches upon the central nerve of Brandstetter's work. So much cultural and linguistic heritage is lost and sacrificed to the questionable values of a modern world overrun by industrialization, technology, and consumerism. Brandstetter's creative and edited work draws the reader's attention repeatedly to this fact. He is the conservator of history, culture, religion, and language, and by extension, of the environment and natural landscapes that are being compromised as modern civilization encroaches more and more upon the idealized tranquility of the past.

Perhaps a quote from the innkeeper about his persistence and tireless provocation offers a fitting conclusion. As he explores the casual unconcern expressed in the phrase *"es ist mir wurst"* ('It's all the same to me') and the gastronomical manifestations of *Wurst* ('sausage') he as cook might prepare, the innkeeper Peter Glandschnig states: "Sometimes I think to myself that I've been a real fool, because I've gotten angry and upset about so many things. Earlier on I ought to have taken on the attitude of indifference, then I would have spared myself a lot of grief."[46] The play on the word *Wurst* and its compound in the quote is regrettably lost in English translation. It is in the essence of these wordplays that so much of Brandstetter the writer is contained. Through his narrators Brandstetter frames his own personal struggle to keep the past alive, a struggle he never abandons, but he mitigates the seriousness of his concerns about modern civilization through the use of irony and humor.

Notes

[1] The Wiener Gruppe included the influential figures Friedrich Achleitner, H. C. Artmann, Konrad Bayer, Gerhard Rühm, and Oswald Wiener.

[2] *The Abbey*, translated by Peter and Evelyn Firchow (Riverside, CA: Ariadne Press, 1998).

[3] "Meine Römerstraße" in *Vom Manne aus Pichl: Über Alois Brandstetter*, Egyd Gstättner, ed. (Salzburg: Residenz Verlag, 1998), 7-27.

[4] *Über den grünen Klee der Kindheit* (Salzburg und Wien: Residenz Verlag, 1982).

[5] "*als Leitmotiv meiner Jugend*," 9.

[6] In this regard, see Gstättner, 5-6.

[7] "*ein konservativer Geschichtenzerstörer*" and "*ein sprachbewahrender Literaturzerstörer*" – Gstättner, 5.

[8] "*konservativ[er] Anarchist*"– Gstättner, 5.

[9] Gstättner overstates the case by labeling him a "*katholischen Misanthropen.*" While both Brandstetter and his narrators may be relative outsiders who frequently mock and brood over the foibles of modern-day man and society and who are grounded in an essential Christian (Catholic) belief system, he and his narrators are by no means cynical hatemongers or religious zealots.

[10] *Der geborene Gärtner* (München: Deutscher Taschenbuch Verlag, 2005).

[11] *Start* (Wien: Europäischer Verlag, 1976), 5.

[12] "*Sehe ich hinter dem Hügel eine Handlung auftauchen, schieße ich sie sofort ab*"– Gstättner, 5-6.

[13] Gstättner, 6.

[14] *Zu Lasten der Briefträger* (München: Deutscher Taschenbuch Verlag, 1976), 27.

[15] "*Wegen einem hängt der Wirt den Reif nicht auf.*" From *Hier kocht der Wirt* (Salzburg: Residenz Verlag, 1995), 7.

[16] "*Die Sprache, sagt man, ist das Gedächtnis der Menschen. Und so bewahren unsere Wörterbücher bereits manches auf, was es in der Wirklichkeit gar nicht mehr gibt, die Wörter sterben offensichtlich langsamer als die Sachen. Die Arten sterben schneller als die Redensarten: Immer binden wir noch Bären auf, obwohl sie hier ausgerottet sind*" – 29.

[17] *Die Burg* (Salzburg: Residenz Verlag, 1986).

[18] *"Ich könnte meine Lage ganz gut in der Sprache und mit dem Wortschatz der Belagerung, des Berennens und der endgültigen Einnahme einer mittelalterlichen Burg beschreiben"* – 6.
[19] *Die Abtei* (Salzburg und Wien: Residenz Verlag, 1977).
[20] *So wahr ich Feuerbach heiße* (Salzburg und Wien: Residenz Verlag, 1988).
[21] See, for example, *The Fiction of the I: Contemporary Austrian Writers and Autobiography*, Nicholas J. Meyerhofer, ed. (Riverside: Ariadne Press, 1999).
[22] *Die Mühle* (Salzburg und Wien: Residenz Verlag, 1981); *Das Buch der alten Mühlen* (Wien: Edition Christian Brandstätter, 1984).
[23] *"Die Sprache und das Wasser seien damals durchsichtig, lauter und rein gewesen."* – *Die Mühle*, 58.
[24] *"Ich liebe die sogenannten 'etymologischen Figuren,' Rede- und Schreibfiguren, in denen Wörter aus einer Wurzel und somit Mitglieder einer 'Familie' auftreten. Und wie verschieden, wie merkwürdig ungleich können selbst Brüder sein!"* From *Kleine Menschenkunde* (Salzburg: Residenz Verlag, 1987), 85.
[25] In the foreword Brandstetter refers to these writers as *"Topographen." Daheim ist daheim*, ed. Alois Brandstetter (Salzburg: Residenz Verlag, 1973).
[26] *"Eine derartige regional-überregionale Plausibilität in der Darstellung von Land und Landsleuten kennzeichnet meines Erachtens die gute Heimatliteratur"* – Foreword.
[27] *"heimatliche Töne"* – 430.
[28] *"In keiner der Geschichten fehlt meines Erachtens eine Besinnung auf das Humane... 'Erzählen' ist ein bedächtiges, oft geradezu geruhsames, immer verläßliches und kultiviertes Geschäft, eine menschenfreundliche Angelegenheit, Erzählen ist im besten Sinn des Wortes auch immer ein wenig 'bürgerlich,' das Herkommen und die Traditionen achtend. Das Erzählen braucht seine Zeit und es verlangt vom Zuhörer Geduld"* – 425.

[29] *Von den Halbschuhen der Flachländer oder die Größe der Alpen* (Salzburg und Wien: Residenz Verlag, 1980).
[30] *"eine biedermeierliche Schein- und Traumwelt"* – 425. The term Biedermeier implies the solid yet philistine qualities of the bourgeois middle classes and emphasizes sobriety, domesticity and often sentimentality.
[31] *"Erzählen und Geschichtenschreiben hat immer schon eine Art Trotz bedeutet, ein Ignorieren der Zeit und ihrer dauernden Krisen, gar nicht nur in Österreich"* – 425.
[32] *"So wie in der Natur die allgemeinen Gesetze still und unaufhörlich wirken und das Auffällige nur eine einzelne Äußerung dieser Gesetze ist, so wirkt das Sittengesetz still und seelenbelebend durch den unendlichen Verkehr der Menschen, und die Wunder des Augenblickes ... sind nur kleine Merkmale dieser allgemeinen Kraft."* 'Vorwort' zu Bunte Steine, 1853.
[33] *Das sanfte Gesetz: "Das Wehen der Luft, das Rieseln des Wassers, das Wachsen der Getreide, das Wogen des Meeres, das Grünen der Erde, das Glänzen des Himmels, das Schimmern der Gestirne halte ich für groß. Ein ganzes Leben voll Gerechtigkeit, Einfachheit, Bezwingung seiner selbst, Verstandesmäßigkeit, Wirksamkeit in seinem Kreis, Bewunderung des Schönen... halte ich für groß. Wir wollen das sanfte Gesetz zu erblicken suchen, wodurch das menschliche Geschlecht geleitet wird. Es liegt in der Liebe der Ehegatten zu einander, in der Liebe der Eltern zu den Kindern, der Kinder zu den Eltern, in der Liebe der Geschwister, der Freunde zueinander, in der süßen Neigung beider Geschlechter... So wie in der Natur die allgemeinen Gesetze still und unaufhörlich wirken und das Auffällige nur eine einzelne Äußerung dieser Gesetze ist, so wirkt das Sittengesetz still und seelenbelebend durch den unendlichen Verkehr der Menschen, und die Wunder des Augenblickes... sind nur kleine Merkmale dieser allgemeinen Kraft. So ist dieses Gesetz, so wie das der Natur das welterhaltende, das menschen-erhaltende."* 'Vorwort' zu Bunte Steine, 1853.
[34] *"edle Einfalt und stille Größe"*

[35] *"Manchmal ist das...die Künstlichkeit der Kunst, bloß Einkleidung, und es steckt in den Geschichten, wenn man sie entkleidet, eine starke Lektion..."* – 426.
[36] *"heimatliche Töne vom stillen Glück, der fröhlichen Armut, dem Segen der Erde, vom Dulden und ergebenen Leiden"* – 430.
[37] *"Wer sich über das Einfache nicht freuen könne, sei soviel wie tot und gestorben."* – 57.
[38] *"eine Mischung von Peter Rosegger und Karl Kraus"* – 430.
[39] *"Adventus: Zum Geleit"* in *Advent, Advent*. Alois Brandstetter, ed. (Salzburg und Wien: Residenz Verlag, 1988), 5-9.
[40] *Heiteres aus Österreich: Von Artmann bis Zeemann* (Salzburg und Wien: Residenz Verlag, 1994).
[41] *Das Buch der alten Mühlen*, 8.
[42] See note 23 above.
[43] Michael Leischner and Alois Brandstetter, *Kärnten im besonderen* (Klagenfurt: Verlag Carinthia, 1995).
[44] *"Wirklich schön traurig sein können nur lustige Leute"* – 10.
[45] *"eine besondere Wunde"* – 10.
[46] *"Manchmal denke ich mir, daß ich ein rechter Narr gewesen bin, weil ich mich über so vieles geärgert und aufgeregt habe. Ich hätte schon früher den Wurstigkeitsstandpunkt einnehmen sollen, dann hätte ich mir viel Ärger erspart"* – from *Hier kocht der Wirt*, 241.

ANNA MITGUTSCH
Courtesy of Verlagsgruppe Random House

Landscapes of Suffering: The Depiction of Rural Austria in Anna Mitgutsch's Novel, *Punishment*[1]

by Kathleen Condray

'I believe that writing is always a grating against reality, against society, and I believe that a narrowness reigns in Austria, especially in provincial Austria —and almost all of Austria is, of course, provincial—that provides much more of this area of contact where, when writing, you get inflamed or upset, much more so than in a more open and more diffused federal republic.'

Anna Mitgutsch[2]

Anna Mitgutsch[3] is not the only modern Austrian author to recognize the particular literary attraction of the Austrian countryside over the bright lights of the capital, Vienna. Indeed, one scholar notes that a whole generation of Austrian authors who came of age from the 1960s to the 1980s did so in rural provinces and that their experiences are reflected in their work.[4] The debut novel of Anna Mitgutsch is also not the only Austrian work that depicts rural Austria as a background for harsh brutality. As early as 1974, Franz Innerhofer described life in the countryside as a rustic concentration camp or "*Bauern-KZ*," and works by Egyd Gestättner, Marianne Gruber, Manfred Rumpl, and O.P. Zier in the 1990s echoed Mitgutsch's unflinching portrayal of the violent side of rural life.[5] In *Punishment* (*Die Züchtigung,* 1985), however, the Austrian countryside is much more than a backdrop for the events of the novel; it plays a central role in the narrative itself, as the main protagonist is both drawn to ownership of the land for the power it represents and repelled by the violence inherent in the agrarian society. In Mitgutsch's novel, the countryside becomes synonymous with violence in an exceptionally clear way that allows Mitgutsch to criticize not simply the "*Land*" (countryside), but also her homeland, Austria.

While definitively not a documentary novel, realistic aspects of the violence described by Mitgutsch have led many critics to read this work as a type of semi-autobiographical portrayal of both the author and her regional home. Leonore Schwartz's first reaction to the novel was that it is a "risk, a personal one, because only the most radical search for the truth can be mobilized against such an inescapable psychological strain;"[6] Maria Frisé commented "that it seems doubtful that the figures in this novel are imaginary."[7] Sigrid Löffler also made a direct connection to the author in reviewing her first novel: "Every person has a novel in him—his own."[8] Further, in considering the extent to which the book has been read as an accurate account of rural Austria, it is interesting that critic Anne Linsel felt compelled to add this note to conclude her review of the novel in 1985:

> 'P.S. No one should think of situating this torture-mother caught in the orbit of violence as a lower middle-class horror story occurring only in the past and in an Austrian borderland. Corporal punishment is still considered a legal educational method. Most parents beat their children because they themselves were beaten, at all levels of

society. 30,000 cases of child abuse are reported annually. 100 children died from beatings in 1984."[9]

Following the critics' lead, the residents of her hometown also read Mitgutsch's first novel as a realistic portrayal and regarded her as an ungrateful traitor ("*Nestbeschmutzer*") after the publication of *Punishment*.[10]

Other critics protest this equating of fiction with real life. Kristin Teuchtmann remonstrates reviews that tend to reflect "the curiousity concerning the private life of the author" more than the work itself.[11] Kecht notes how "many journalist-critics, with almost fanatical thoroughness, place special importance on the autobiographical content."[12] Mitgutsch herself has also expressed irritation with the ubiquitous charge of critics and the reading public that female authors must to some extent be drawing on personal experiences, while male authors, who also utilize topics from their own lives, are not subject to this criticism.[13]

Mitgutsch laments that readers assume the material in *Punishment* is a journalistic accounting of real life. Moreover, in the interview with Kecht in her hometown of Linz, the author also comments on the tendency of readers to interact with the narrative on a personal level: "People read this very personally. Everyone thinks: 'Yes, my mother was just like that, too.'" For her part, Mitgutsch insists: "But, as far as I am concerned, it was a political book."[14] She has also described it and her later work *Ausgrenzung* ('Ostracism') as books about society, or "*Gesellschaftsbücher*," in contradistinction to her novels *Das andere Gesicht* ('The Other Face') and *In fremden Städten* ('In Foreign Cities'), which she regards as 'relationship books' or "*Beziehungsbücher*".[15]

Whether or not the central story is drawn from the author's life, the rural setting of *Punishment* is one that Mitgutsch knows from experience. The shocking violence of the child abuse is what initially drew the greatest attention of critics, but it cannot be ignored that the abuse is a localized phenomenon associated solely with the countryside and rural ways in the novel. (Although the maltreatment of the narrator occurs largely in the city, the ostensibly learned behavior is attributed to her mother's childhood in the country, which will be discussed below). The present essay will examine both this landscape of suffering, in which violence and ownership of the land determine societal structure, and the extent to which it is contrasted with the city and mountains as a separate realm.

Punishment is the story of Marie Kovacs who came of age during World War II, told in retrospect by her daughter, Vera. The recounting is occasioned by Vera's daughter, who asks what her grandmother was like, leading Vera to reflect on the details of her mother Marie's life. After a brutal childhood in the country, filled with beatings at the hand of her father (sometimes instigated by her mother, who also abuses her verbally), torture by her brothers, and the hard physical labor of the farm, Marie moves to the city with her husband, Friedl Kovacs. Marie regards her husband as unworthy, due both to Friedl's standing in the rural community as the son of a logger and his occupation as a streetcar conductor, which places them firmly in the shameful status of the working class, at least as it is viewed by Marie.

Over the years, Marie endures a loveless marriage and the drudgery of her work as a housewife, while attempting to mold her daughter into something better, regrettably through constant abuse, both physical (in early childhood through the young teen years) and emotional (for the rest of Vera's life). Although Marie dies when Vera is still a young woman beginning her college studies, the shadow of her mother follows Vera through her own marriage and divorce, and through the raising of her daughter. While Vera does not beat her daughter as she was beaten, she fears that she has not been able to break the cycle of abuse when she realizes that her daughter's apparently unhappily bohemian childhood is a direct result of her avoidance of the nuclear family, which she associates with abuse.

Immediately after a brief introduction, the reader is confronted with a depiction of the farm of Marie's childhood as a desolate landscape full of brutality and neglect. The descriptions of country life are related in plain language,[16] which serves to draw attention to the violence that is not hidden behind an idyllic reminiscence of the beauty of the natural setting. In the first scene at the farm, the laming of Marie's legs is attributed to the neglect of farm servants who leave her outside in the cold while they are supposed to be watching her during her mother's recovery from a breast cancer operation. Then, the narrator travels farther back to show that Marie was also unwanted before she was even conceived, and that she exists because her father viciously raped her mother immediately after she gave birth to their first child because he could not control his sexual urges: 'The baby had been large, the slashes had to heal by themselves, and in his euphoria of fatherhood he poured his semen into her torn vagina, night after night.'[17] This graphic portrayal of domestic violence directly follows the first scenes in the book in which the narrator, Marie's daughter Vera, recounts the brutality of the child abuse she suffered at her mother's hands, a narrative choice which seems to offer a justification of the violence. Later in the text, in a discussion with a boyfriend, Vera does indeed plead her mother's case as a victim of violence who is passing on learned behavior.

One should note that the narrative style of the text also leaves some doubt as to the veracity of these initial depictions. It is not plausible that Marie could remember the events of her first months in such detail, nor obviously could know the circumstances of her conception, unless inferred from her father's later behavior, which includes the drunken rape of Marie's sister Fanni. When Marie deduces that Fanni became pregnant through incest, she is again beaten terribly by her father, although she has become an adult in the meantime. The narrator herself refers to these events as an account of her mother's childhood meant to induce sympathy in her daughter,[18] which would seemingly indicate a bias perceived by Vera, but this qualifying statement is given only after they have been presented to the reader as fact.

This doubt about the truth of her mother's account has its basis in her aunts' later disputation of the extent to which the family farm was a setting for violence. This denial takes place after Marie's death and after Vera has believed Marie's accounts for years.[19] Teuchtmann also notes that the aunts' refusal to acknowledge the abuse that took place during their childhoods on the farms directly mirrors their inability to recognize the violence of the Third Reich: '"That was a lovely time, between '39 and '45,' Aunt Rosi said."[20] Another explanation is that the beatings directed toward Marie did not stand out to the women who were accustomed to the daily violence present in the rural milieu: 'Beaten? It's possible that Father beat her once in a while—he beat us all up from time to time.'[21]

Ultimately, however, these portrayals do fit into a larger pattern of violence in the account, violence which the narrator Vera witnesses first-hand in later returns to the country, when she sees her mother, aunts, and cousins beaten in a similar fashion. Evidence of the pattern also can be found in the broken dolls in the attic of Vera's childhood house, which she "disciplined" by beating just as she was beaten, and her father also admits to the abuse administered by his wife, while hypothesizing that the brain tumor found after Marie's death perhaps made her insane.

In addition to the beatings, Marie endures hard physical labor, which is an element of the rural lifestyle depicted throughout the book (as opposed to the mountainous way of life discussed later in this essay). As early as her childhood, Marie is recognized for her ability to work hard, an ability that is regarded as her duty, since she is never paid for her labor. As a six-year-old, she is expected to care for her infant brother, while her barely older sister Fanni is rewarded with money when she performs tasks such as carrying wood. This is a pattern repeated throughout her life, a life filled with hard labor but without the expected accompanying compensation, which drives Marie's obsession to procure her own piece of land as an adult. In later childhood, Fanni is kept in the kitchen to perform the physically less demanding tasks, while a nine-year-old Marie is sent outside to milk cows, feed pigs, and mow hay, which are regarded as women's work (*"Weiberarbeit"*). Marie proves to be less than competent at the womanly task of milking (a scene which later mirrors the difficulty she has as a new nursing mother), and her father proclaims: 'You lazy cow, you'll never become a farmer's wife.'[22]

While Marie is perhaps not intended to be a farmer's wife, she proves more than capable of completing the manly tasks on the farm. When she is fourteen years old, her father sends the farmhand away since she was as strong as a man.[23] Her work on the farm replaces the formal schooling at which she excelled, and effectively ends her dream of becoming a convent teacher. Marie comes to associate the farm with an endless cycle of work, punctuated only by breaks for meals needed to keep her strength up:

> 'Milking, cutting grass, creamy potato soup with little chunks of bread for breakfast, forking over the hay, cleaning out the stables, fertilizing the fields, pork belly with flour dumplings and beets for lunch, feed cattle, carry wood, pile hay on the wagon and unload it in the stuffy-hot barn, milk, strain the milk and cart the milk cans to the village stall, bacon, curd cheese and bread with sour creamy potato soup for dinner, and that would be her life now, day by day, until some man came and took her away, to some other farm where it would begin all over again under the thumb of her mother-in-law.'[24]

Although Marie believes she has found a way out of this rustic cycle by marrying Friedl and moving to the city, she freely returns to the country often over the course of her life, drawn to the setting where her ability to work is recognized, if not properly compensated. At first, the return is necessary to earn food in the shortages immediately ensuing after the war, but time and again Marie returns to work on the farm, justifying it to her mother-in-law as necessary for her daughter, referred to always by the less-than-affectionate term 'the child' (*"das Kind"*): "'I'm only doing it for the child's sake, the damp apartment, the bad food—out here she's got fresh air and good farm meals."'[25]

Marie is welcomed back by the country residents only grudgingly, but she is received back because of her physical strength at harvest time. Marie even returns yearly to help her sister Angela, who suffers under the very fate that she has avoided: 'Year after year she was pregnant, six births in eight years, and her husband beat her, pregnant or not, whether he had a reason or not, all the while her mother-in-law was crouching behind the staircase, listening, and grinning.'[26] While Marie dutifully does the farm work, it is her brother-in-law's intimation that she no longer belongs in this setting; during an argument he refers to her as 'city trash' (*"Stadtgesindel"*), that sends her straight home to the city.

While she henceforth avoids this farm where her connection to the country is disavowed, Marie continues to return to her own family's farm. The tolerance of Marie's presence in the country comes to an end only some eighteen years later, when it is clear that Marie has exceeded her physical usefulness: 'She stayed for two days, helped harvest potatoes, cut the grass, but by now it was all too strenuous, after all she wasn't young anymore and had to lie down a while after work.'[27] This time, after a fight concerning Marie's lack of inheritance, the connection to the country is permanently severed, and the narrator portrays this very night as the beginning of the illness that ultimately causes her death; the physical cause is the fact that Marie has to wait outside in the sudden cold for over an hour for the bus to take her back to the city, while the emotional reason is the rejection: 'That's what happens when you go off somewhere, that's what happens when you think there's someplace where people are glad to see you.'[28] Noticeably, the end of the tolerance for Marie's returns to the country directly coincides with a diminution of her physical ability and her usefulness on the farm, and this rejection is final.

Throughout her life, Marie exhibits a double relationship to the agrarian society of her upbringing. She wants to belong to the community, however violent and flawed, because she understands the societal rules there. Foremost among the rules is that those who have land belong to the privileged class, of which she was a member before her marriage to a man of lesser standing in the rural society. In order to re-establish herself, she attempts to buy land of her own, which would represent the compensation for hard work that is denied her by others. At the same time, she is contemptuous of the backward rural ways and continuously attempts to depict herself as a city dweller ("*Städter*") when she returns home.

This assumed identity in the country begins before she has even left the community, and she is frustrated in her playacting by Friedl, who arrives in the village, much to her chagrin, to pick her up "in the midst of the church-goers, in the midst of the stage on which she is playing the role of 'the wealthy farmer's daughter who marries and moves to the big city.'"[29] When she returns later, she has indeed become 'the important lady from the city'[30] in the eyes of the rural community, and her efforts to maintain this illusion grow ever more elaborate: 'The preparations for her entrance before the church could last two hours.'[31] Marie's self-worth is directly tied to the contrast between herself and the women of the farming community: 'Which farmer's wife had such smooth skin, which farmer's wife could afford such lovely clothes?'[32] During visits to the country church, she especially feels superior to her sister Fanni, who has become the abused farmer's wife.

This portrayal is, however, overwhelmingly an external one, marked by outward bearing and good clothing, costumes that must be carefully put away after each performance. As the narrator notes: 'By this time, Marie had been away from home for eight years, and still felt as if she were in exile in the city.'[33] At her core, Marie remains a farmer's daughter (*"Bauerntochter"*), which is why she is not accepted in the city, no matter how well she is able to fool the residents of the country with the trappings of urban society. Ultimately, Marie is forced to give up this charade of belonging to the city at the end of her life. At the hospital, Marie does not cling to the only vestige of the urban lady (*"Stadtdame"*), her proper High German, but rather 'cursed in the broad, guttural rural dialect of her youth.'[34] This linguistic change represents an end to Marie's dreams of belonging to either society: 'The retreat to the language of her youth represents her resignation, Marie no longer needs to disguise herself, the exertion was in vain.'[35]

For her daughter Vera, who of course knows the discrepancy between her mother's public portrayals and private lifestyle, the association with the country is not dependent on sartorial or linguistic evidence. Rather, she views her mother's hands as 'farmer's hands' (*"Bauernhände"*) when connoting them with the violence of the eponymous castigation. In this case, violence is additionally paired with the other major association with rural living in the novel, namely work: 'Sometimes she collapsed lengthwise on the floor, and I became afraid, hoped she hadn't fainted from the hard work of the punishment.'[36] Even the instrument of the abuse, the rug beater, is not merely an instrument of torture, but a household tool simply put to another use.

It should be noted that the negative portrayal of the countryside in *Punishment* is a societal critique of rural Austrian society and not a depiction of nature or the farm in and of themselves, which are seen in a more positive light. In Vera's earliest memories, she is bundled up and taken for a sleigh ride with her father through the snow-covered countryside: 'I've never felt more snug and secure.'[37] This description is immediately followed by the memory of arriving in the country with her mother after a terrifying train ride: 'The parlor in the evening, warm as a cow's belly...'[38] Home from the front and visiting Marie, Friedl regards the farmhouse as a welcoming place before he recognizes the danger there inherent in his lower status: 'Friedl was so happy. He was sitting in a warm parlor, in a *farmhouse* parlor.'[39]

Even the work itself can be pleasant when removed from the coercion of the farm setting. When Vera is three, the family moves to a house near the Danube River. While both she and her father are happy spending time in the nearby woodland, it is the chance to cultivate earth again that excites her mother: 'My mother was happy, she could work her own land, and under her hands everything thrived.'[40] Later, in this same house when Vera is studying as a teenager, she is irritated by her mother's singing while performing typical country chores, such as caring for the chickens, not because of the sound, but because of her happiness in performing this kind of labor: '...it reminded her of home, where she was in her element, and she sang softly all the while... but her singing made me furious, it followed me throughout the house and left me no breathing space for my own dreams.'[41]

While Marie is depicted on the family farm as either a mechanized or masculinized work force, the work in her own garden emphasizes her womanliness and sexual attractiveness: 'She worked so absentmindedly... in her blue jumper with her shoulders naked... She didn't see the men, ogling her full figure over the fence, or the jealous glances of their wives.'[42] The obvious difference between the country and suburban settings is that Marie is working for herself in the garden. Only once is Marie's work on the family farm associated with eroticism: she flirts with the worker Lois, and in her nightshirt, the contrast of the skin that has been browned by the sun with the normally covered white flesh of her breasts has erotic appeal.

In spite of the violence inherent in country life, Marie's marriage and resettlement are no panacea. First, Marie only marginally moves to the city. Her husband Friedl, who does not understand the relationship between land ownership and social power that dominates in the country, mistakenly believes a similar environment will make the transition easier for his new wife and rents rooms from a farmer on the outskirts of the city. No longer in the privileged position of daughter of the resident farmer, Marie is scorned by the other women and even subjected to public humiliation when she is dragged through the courtyard by her braid, after she refuses to turn over the leaves she has picked for her pet goat. As is the case with the farm back home, Marie is not allowed to retain what she has worked for, but the humiliation is increased because her efforts do not go to the good of the family.

Friedl tries to encourage her to go into the city as she becomes increasingly more isolated on the farm where they rent rooms, yet she refuses, because she has no money to spend there. As a result of this segregation from city dwellers, she still has the country attributes with which she left her parents' farm even a year later when she is giving birth to her daughter: "'I thought right away that you had to be from the country,' the woman in the next bed said later on, 'when they brought you in, your long, red braids.'"[43] Although Marie later rids herself of the country hairstyle and the accent, the shame over her heritage continues years later when Marie and Friedl contemplate letting Vera learn to play the zither, which they can acquire from the family, rather than the expensive piano: "Nevertheless they bought a piano, because Marlene's mother [the woman from the hospital] laughed contemptuously and said, 'Zither, that's about right, of course, country music.'"[44]

Vera's earliest memory of her mother's life in the city is based on the societal rejection that she encountered there. In the metropolitan setting, one's occupation, rather than property ownership, is the paramount factor in social status. Upon moving to the city, Marie's contempt for this lack of respect for land ownership is clear: her husband is a mere train conductor which makes acceptance into society impossible as Marie attempts 'to eke out a place in society for her and her child among the engineers, doctors, architects, and professors.'[45] Unlike in the country, where land ownership assures societal status, no attainable mechanism for social advancement is available to Marie in the city.

In every new school from the elementary level to the *Gymnasium* that Vera attends in the city, it is not the academic performance of the child that is inquired after, but rather the profession of the father. In spite of Marie's endeavors to portray the family as middle-class rather than working-class, she cannot hide her husband's identity and is ultimately rejected by metropolitan society. Although Marie manages to mimic the urban inhabitants in outward appearance through attire and food and in the plans for her daughter's future, Friedl lacks the ambition and ability necessary to secure a higher position, which is the only measure that is acknowledged in the city. Thus she falls back on the social status that is familiar to her from her rural upbringing: she must acquire her own piece of property.

This constant preoccupation with owning property that pervades Marie's life is directly linked to her grandfather's premonition, recounted by the narrator early in the book that they would all become beggars.[46] Indeed beggars (*"Bettelleut"*) in the form of refugees seem to be ubiquitous in the story, even if their presence is not emphasized: Marie's father (the *"Bauer"*) turns away refugees from the city with the dismissive term, Vera is named after a refugee who came to the farm and made the first friendly overtures that Marie experiences in her life, and the house to which Vera returns is initially bought from a refugee family from Hungary (the land on which the home stands is leased). Occasionally, city dwellers also use the term 'beggar woman' (*"Bettelweib"*) to refer to Marie, and Marie berates her daughter as a gypsy or *"Zigeunerin."*

The danger that was prophesied by the grandfather, however,

is not an overt one; the origin of the fear is that the family will be reduced to begging because they have no connections to the land and thus will not be able to produce their own food. The narrator indicates that this lack of control over one's own destiny has come to pass (and seemingly has little to do with land ownership in spite of the rural mindset):

> 'What had become of the beautiful, proud farmer's daughters? Nothing had become of them. Grandfather had been right, you'll all be beggars, someday all you will be beggars. Two oppressed, regularly beaten farmers' wives, one divorcée, and two who have tried to get away from their rental apartments, to get a place of their own, to scrimp on food so that their children could have something.'[47]

In point of fact, however, it is the daughters who move away from the country and the family farm, namely Rosi, Marie, and Heidi, who ultimately have the best chance of improving their situation. Rosi, a successful seamstress, enjoys her own apartment in the city, where Marie and Vera feel welcome. When an early marriage turns out poorly (her drunken and womanizing husband beats her), she is rejected by her rural family because she simply refuses to put up with the abuse, as the women in the country do, and divorces the man. It is Marie who gives her refuge, albeit unsympathetically, until she can reestablish herself in the city; her fate is happily resolved with a husband younger than herself and a child of her own late in life.

The other sisters who escape their parents' farm village are Marie and Heidi. Donald Daviau comments that "Marie is portrayed as being different from her sisters...."[48] However, it is clear that Mitgutsch creates the character of Heidi as a doppelgänger for Marie. Both Marie and Heidi have an opportunity to succeed because they are trying to obtain property for themselves, something that would never have been possible for them as *Bäuerinnen* had they remained in the country. While each is equally burdened by the disgrace of having married a logger's son, Heidi is the sister who is able to be successful in her quest to own her own land because she is not afraid to leave the established role of housewife and earn extra income, as Marie refuses to do, since Marie aspires to be in the middle class (in which wives do not have to work) rather than working class.

Although Marie attempts to circumvent the societal role of "*Arbeiter*" assigned to her family by the city dwellers through the purchase of land, working outside the home would make this designation as a worker fact rather than opinion. She is not willing to do so even in order to earn money to buy land, the only measure of status that is important to her: 'I'd rather starve than clean up after the big shots.'[49]

While her pride and concern over social standing will not allow Marie to work outside the home, she manages the household budget like a dictator, immediately demanding that her husband hand over his paycheck upon arriving home. She carefully decides what is important enough to spend money on, which curiously enough does not include improvements to the house on the rented property.

Even at the end of her life, Marie clings to the possibility of belonging either to the country or the city society. She suddenly begins to demand that those who have remained in the country give her a portion of her inheritance, either in land or money, to make the dream a reality. When the inheritance of her rural upbringing is denied to her, she still has hope for eventual acceptance in the city via the one thing she does possess, her child: 'The child was her only possession that she jealously, anxiously guarded and felt was continuously threatened.'[50] Marie realizes that society is changing and sees the possibility of approval at long last: 'Vera no longer needed to go around with the children of doctors and architects in order to be socially accepted; she had shown them that a high school degree opened all doors.'[51] However, in order to fulfill this goal, Marie must part with her only possession, which she predicts will kill her, and she does indeed die during Vera's first year of college.

In addition to the portrayals of the violence of rural life and the social rejection of city life, Mitgutsch also introduces a third landscape to her novel: the woodland. The forest is largely associated with her husband Friedl's family, as his mother had a small house there, and is thus also regarded as enemy territory by Marie. Although she was initially welcomed to the forest house as an honored guest, her first visit after the wedding reveals the *Waldhäusl* as a setting for more work; after being angered when she sees that Marie is likely eating all the rations allotted the married couple, her mother-in-law orders her to cook, to also engage in work here, since she is now a housewife. The association of Marie with the country and Friedl's mother with the forest is intensified when Vera as a child visits her grandmother and is accompanied by each woman only until the domain of the other (be it forest or country) is in sight. Even after her mother-in-law has died, Marie cannot enjoy a vacation in the old house in the woods (in contrast to Friedl and Vera who revere the forest setting) because of what her husband refers to as her farmer's pride or "*Bauernstolz.*"

While both are natural settings, the main distinction between the country and the forest is the manner of work done in each. The woodland is a realm in which nature offers gifts given freely to be collected. As a child, Vera brings back berries and flowers from a forest near their house in order to appease her mother so she will not be beaten (though to no avail). The forest hills around the city offer healing at no cost from a respiratory ailment when Vera is a child; since the family cannot afford an actual trip to the mountains, Marie carries her there when the doctor prescribes mountain air ("*Höhenluft*") as a remedy.

As a child, Vera remembers her grandmother's *Waldhäusl* as a place of freedom to play, with bountiful and better food to eat. While the farm is also a place of plenty, the earth only yields its fruits here with hard work. Further, the inhabitants of the forest are happy to share the gifts of nature. After the war, Friedl's mother scolds Marie because her family will not share their food as Friedl's family does, although they have more than enough; even after Friedl shares his take-home portion with Marie against the instructions of his mother, Marie still hates him for the fact that his family is more generous than her own, a fact emphasized by the narrator. Interestingly, Friedl first glimpses Marie and presumably falls in love with her when she is picking raspberries, engaged in the work of gathering associated with the forest rather than cultivating associated with the farm.

Throughout this novel, which Teuchtmann refers to as the "only truly-Austrian novel" of Mitgutsch's oeuvre,[52] rural Austria is depicted as a landscape of extreme suffering and brutality, yet the central protagonist nevertheless feels compelled to continue to try to live according to the rules of the agrarian society that prizes land ownership as a status symbol and sign of hard work. The question remains as to what end Mitgutsch portrays this abuse. In an interview regarding her writing, Mitgutsch notes that it is the repeated exposure to brutality that makes the great majority of the citizens of Austria numb:

> 'For me that is a pivotal point for an education of horrendous cruelty, an education that allows the growing youth, the child, no room to become an individual. This complete subjugation and crushing of a person in the name of order, punctuality, cleanliness, and all these values that one can identify as fascist.'[53]

In the work itself, the author makes numerous direct references to the Nazi past. While later in life her father shows no interest in the mother's obsession with owning property, Vera confronts Friedl with his own longings for a piece of land no matter the cost: 'And you nevertheless wanted to settle a piece of land in the Ukraine with your wife after the final victory?'[54] And while Marie never goes more than 100 kilometers from her birthplace and ostensibly wishes to avoid traveling in order to stay close to the land of her home, Mitgutsch also hints at another need for the generation of the second World War to remain in Austria: '...the partisans in the Balkans were more feared than anything on the entire Eastern Front, Greece was a mess, and you all got seasick on the isthmus, and who knows whether somebody in France might recognize you again.'[55] Although the book primarily deals with the violence of the countryside, Mitgutsch does not allow those in the cities to pretend that they did not participate in the Third Reich. Uli Reisinger, Vera's rival from the upper classes throughout her childhood, is the daughter of a father who has been de-nazified ("*entnazifiziert*"), and the family obviously did not suffer in any way from their association with the Nazis, continuing to belong to the upper echelons of society and experiencing no change in their status even after the war was lost. Marie even accuses the father of continued loyalty to the Nazi cause in spite of his rehabilitation.

This mirrors the situation in the countryside, where the Third Reich is seen as a continuation of the quotidian order. When the Nazis first come to power, only the local pastor and a professor recognize and fight the danger, though they are soon taken away: 'He [the priest] and the professor were the only ones in the community who had any idea of what was going on; the others experienced the takeover as if it were an exciting movie.'[56] Marie actually welcomes the Third Reich as an era when she is not the only one being beaten: '... if you were unpretentious and didn't stand out in a crowd, for a change the others got beaten first.'[57] So, Marie goes about her rural life, finding her first dances in traditional dress (*Dirndl*) of more interest than the Nazi movement.

Mitgutsch includes extraordinarily little material about life during World War II in this self-described political book, and this obvious lacuna bothers the narrator, Vera. More than just an attempt to cover up the past, the lack of information is an indication that this period of extraordinary violence simply was not remarkable compared to the brutishness of life under normal circumstances in the country. One critic, in an essay on Austria's coming to terms with its Nazi past, its *"Vergangenheitsbewältigung,"* notes that the attempt to portray Austria as Nazi victim was successful to the extent that even those within the country believed it.[58] However, the lack of willingness to acknowledge the past is similar to the hidden violence that originates in the countryside but nevertheless comes to the surface in Mitgutsch's novel; although the narrator Vera seems to overcome the heritage of violence, she is still lamed by it; it predetermines her future and that of her child.

Punishment is a complex work that draws on many themes. Other critics have investigated its portrayal of the mother-daughter relationship, patriarchal values, and narrative technique. Mitgutsch herself has noted that it is the story of a mother and daughter, but that it is also something more. The something more is an elegant allegory of Austria as beaten child; one victim (Marie) is a woman who knows the violence that awaits her in the countryside, yet finds it difficult to resist returning; while another, Vera, suffers both the physical and emotional scars of this violent legacy and is unable to overcome the brutality of her rural heritage as she raises her own daughter.[59] The novel ends tellingly with Marie figuratively refusing to stay buried, rising from her grave, from the earth of the countryside, to torment her daughter.

In the landscape of suffering that is the Austrian countryside as portrayed here, violence begets violence, passed along through generations. The fear of becoming *"Bettelleut,"* of losing one's connection to the land and its way of life, sustains even those traditions which are unhealthy. Similarly, Austria must face its past before being able to function as a modern nation. With the negative ending of the book, that is, Vera's knowledge that she has been unable to prevent herself from acting in the shadow of her mother's abuse, Mitgutsch shows her belief that this is perhaps an impossible task, an opinion later reflected in the interview with Kecht: "I hate the word 'coming to terms with the past—'*Vergangenheitsbewältigung.*' That is something you can never overcome."[60]

Notes

[1] All references to the primary source in this essay are from the following edition: Anna Mitgutsch, *Die Züchtigung* (München: dtv, 2002), and will indicate the relevant page(s). As translated by Lisel Mueller, the work was originally published in English with the title *Punishment* (London: Virago, 1987, 1988), and also appeared as *Three Daughters* (New York: Harcourt Brace Janovanovich, 1987), 216 pp. All English translations in this text are those of the editor.

[2] "*Ich glaube, daß Schreiben immer ein Sich-Reiben an der Wirklichkeit ist, an der Gesellschaft, und ich glaube, daß in Österreich eine Enge herrscht, besonders im provinziellen Österreich—und es ist ja fast ganz Österreich provinziell—, die viel mehr diese Reibungsfläche bietet, an der man sich schreibend entflammt oder entzündet, sehr viel mehr als in einer offeneren und diffuseren Bundesrepublik.*" Quoted in Maria-Regina Kecht, "Gespräch mit Waltraud Anna Mitgutsch," in *Women in German Yearbook*, 8 (1992), 128.

[3] *Die Züchtigung* and subsequent novels originally appeared under the name "Waltraud Anna Mitgutsch," but the author ceased using her first name after the publication of *Abschied von Jerusalem* in 1995, according to Peter König's "Konsensualisierung von Wirklichkeit als Intervention gegen Fremdheit zu den Romanen von Anna Mitgutsch," in *Fremde und Fremdes in der Literatur*, Joanna Jablkowska and Erwin Leibfriend, eds. (Frankfurt am Main: Peter Lang, 1996), 223.

[4] See Klaus Zeyringer, *Österreichische Literatur 1945-1998: Überblicke, Einschnitte, Wegmarken* (Innsbruck: Haymon-Verlag, 1999), 106.

[5] Zeyringer, 107, 440, 445.
[6] *"...Wagnis—ein persönliches, weil gegen den unausweichlichen Leidensdruck nur die radikalste Wahrheitssuche aufgeboten werden kann...."* From Leonore Schwartz, "'War deine Mutter so wie du?' Waltraud Anna Mitgutsch: Der erste Roman," in *Deutsches Allgemeines Sonntagsblatt* (2 June 1985), 25.
[7] *"Daß die Gestalten dieses Romans frei erfunden sind, scheint zweifelhaft."* Maria Frisé, "War deine Mutter so wie du? Die Züchtigung–Das Romandebüt von Waltraud Anna Mitgutsch," in *Frankfurter Allgemeine Zeitung* (3 April 1985), 26.
[8] *"Jeder Mensch hat einen Roman in sich—seinen."* Sigrid Löffler, "Körperfeindschaft," in *Profil* (13 May 1985), 65.
[9] *"P.S. Es komme ja keiner auf die Idee, diese Folter-Mutter im Kreislauf der Gewalt als kleinbäuerliche Horrorgeschichte nur in Vergangenheit und im österreichischen Grenzland anzusiedeln. Die Prügelstrafe gilt noch immer als legales Erziehungsmittel. Die meisten Eltern schlagen, weil sie selbst geschlagen wurden, in allen gesellschaftlichen Schichten. Jährlich werden 30000 Kindesmißhandlungen registriert. 1984 wurden 100 Kinder zu Tode verprügelt."* Anne Linsel, "Im Teufelskreis: Waltraud Mitgutschs Roman *Die Züchtigung*," in *Die Zeit* (19 July 1985), 39.
[10] Donald Daviau, "The Problems of Identity, Reality, and Estrangement in the Works of Waltraud Anna Mitgutsch," in *Literaturkritik und erzählerische Praxis*, Herbert Herzmann, ed. (Tübingen: Stauffenburg, 1995), 109.
[11] *"der neugierige Blick auf das private Leben der Autorin"*, in Teuchtmann, 12.
[12] *"von vielen journalistischen Kritikern mit fast fanatischer Akribie besonderen Wert auf den autobiographischen Gehalt gelegt [wird],"* in Kecht, 132.

[13] See Kecht, 132.
[14] *"Das ist sehr persönlich gelesen worden. Jeder meinte: 'Ja, ich habe auch so eine Mutter gehabt.' Für mich aber war es ein politisches Buch."* Kecht, 129.
[15] Teuchtmann, 16.
[16] One should note here that while Mitgutsch uses some Austrian vocabulary such as *"Engerl"* (instead of the High German *"Engel,"* 'angel') and *"Erdäpfel"* (instead of High German *"Kartoffeln,"* 'potatoes') the scenes that take place in the countryside are not depicted with an attendant dialect, as is the case with the poetry of authors such as Christine Nöstlinger, Annemarie Regensburger, and Anna Nöst (Cf. Zeyringer, 311).
[17] *"Das Kind war groß gewesen, die Risse mußten von selbst verheilen, und er stieß ihr in der Euphorie der Vaterschaft seinen Samen in den zerrissenen Schoß, Nacht für Nacht"* – 13.
[18] *"Leidensgeschichte ihrer Jugend"* –16.
[19] Zeyringer notes that Vera so identifies with her mother's perspective and terminology that she often refers to herself as *"das Kind"* during the narrative (185-86).
[20] *"Eine schöne Zeit war das, zwischen 39 und 45, sagte Tante Rosi"* – 51. See Teuchtmann for an extended discussion of the problems of the concept of memory in this novel, especially on p. 55.
[21] *"Geschlagen? Kann schon sein, daß der Vater sie manchmal geschlagen hat, er hat uns alle manchmal hergenommen"* – 33.
[22] *"... du faules Luder, aus dir wird nie eine Bäuerin"* – 22.
[23] *"sie hatte Kraft wie ein Mann"* – 26.
[24] *"Melken, Grasmähen, Rahmsuppe mit Brotbröcklen zum Frühstück, Heu umkehren, Ausmisten, Mistführen, Bauchfleisch mit Mehlknödeln und Rüben zu Mittag, Vieh füttern, Holz tragen, Heu auf Leiterwagen schupfen und in der stickig heißen Scheune abladen, Melken, Milch abtreiben und Milchpitschen*

zum Dorfstand schleppen, Speck, Topfen und Brot mit Rahmsuppe zum Abendessen, das würde jetzt ihr Leben sein, Tag für Tag, bis ein Mann sie wegholte und auf einem anderen Hof unter der Fuchtel der Schwiegermutter dasselbe von vorne beginnen würde" – 27.

[25] *"Ich tu's ja nur wegen dem Kind, die feuchte Wohnung, das schlechte Essen, hier hat sie die frische Luft und gute Bauernkost"* – 88.

[26] *"Jahr für Jahr war sie schwanger, sechs Geburten in acht Jahren, und der Mann schlug sie, schwanger oder nicht, mit und ohne Grund, während die Schwiegermutter hinter der Hausstiege horchte und sich eins grinste"* – 192.

[27] *"Sie blieb zwei Tage, half Erdäpfel sammeln, ging Gras mähen, aber alles war schon so anstrengend, sie war halt auch nimmer jung, mußte sich nach der Arbeit ein wenig niederlegen"* – 229.

[28] *"Das kommt davon, wenn man wohin fährt, das kommt davon, wenn man glaubt, irgendwo sei man doch willkommen"* – 230.

[29] *"…mitten unter die Kirchgänger, mitten auf die Bühne, auf der sie gerade 'Reiche Bauerstochter heiratet in die Stadt' spielte"* – 60.

[30] *"die große Dame aus der Stadt"* – 139.

[31] *"Die Vorbereitungen zu den Auftritten vor der Kirche konnten zwei Stunden dauern"* – 140.

[32] *"Welche Bäuerin hatte eine so glatte Haut, welche Bäuerin leistete sich so gute Kleiderstoffe?"* – 140.

[33] *"Marie war seit acht Jahren von zu Hause weg und fühlte sich in der Stadt noch immer wie im Exil"* – 117.

[34] *"fluchte im breiten, gutturalen Bauerndialekt ihrer Jugend"* – 241.

35 "*Der Rückzug in die Sprache der Jugend stellt eine Resignation dar, Marie braucht sich nicht mehr verstellen, die Anstrengung war umsonst*"– in Teuchtmann, 42.
36 "*Manchmal ließ sie sich der Länge nach auf den Boden fallen, und ich bekam Angst um sie, hoffte, sie sei nicht ohnmächtig geworden von der schweren Arbeit der Züchtigung*" – 8.
37 "*Nie habe ich mich geborgener gefühlt*" – 81.
38 "*Die abendliche Stube, warm wie ein Kuhbauch...*" – 82.
39 "*Friedl war selig. Er saß in einer warmen Stube, in einer 'Bauernstube'*" – 42, [emphasis mine]. Friedl gradually learns to avoid the farmhouse when he has returned from the war. Although he lives nearby in the city and is courting Marie, he does not go to the country on his free days, recognizing that the locals would regard him as a "*Tagesdieb*" or "lazy bones" (56) for not working when everyone else is, so pervasive is the compulsion to work on the farm. Similarly, Vera also learns fear at the farmhouse as she grows older—of being left in the field, of the animals, and most of all of being compared to her cousin raised on the farm, who is more outgoing and attractive (84-86). In both cases, the initial appreciation of the farm turns negative after each person comes to recognize the underlying social structure of the setting, one in which they cannot hope to belong.
40 "*Meine Mutter war glücklich, sie konnte mit ihren Händen ihr eigenes Land bearbeiten, und alles wuchs unter ihren Händen*" – 92.
41 "*...das erinnerte sie an zu Hause, da war sie in ihrem Element, da sang sie leise dazu, ... aber mich machte ihr Singen wütend, es verfolgte mich durchs Haus und ließ mir keinen Freiraum für meine Träume*" – 181.
42 "*Sie arbeitete so selbst vergessen... in ihrem blauen Trägerkleid mit nackten Schultern... Sie sah nicht die Blicke der*

Männer über den Zaun, die an ihrer fülligen Gestalt hängenblieben, und nicht die eifersüchtigen Blicke ihrer Frauen" – 92-93.

[43] "Ich hab mir ja gleich gedacht, daß Sie vom Land sein müssen, sagte ihre Bettnachbarin später, als man Sie hereingebracht hat, die langen, roten Zöpfe" – 77.

[44] "Sie kauften trotzdem ein Klavier, weil Marlenes Mutter verächtlich lachte und sagte, Zither, das paßt, natürlich, Bauernmusik" – 126.

[45] "... sich und dem Kind einen Platz zu erkämpfen unter den Ingenieuren, Ärzten, Architekten und Professoren der Gemeinde" – 94. Reviewer Leonore Schwartz fails to recognize the ignominy of Friedl's position and sees his work positively, as an opportunity to earn money, rather than negatively due to the insurmountable social rift it creates. It should also be noted that Friedl is rejected by the rural society as well, but there because of his status as a cottage renter who owns no property.

[46] "Bettelleut, alle werdet's einmal Bettelleut" – 22.

[47] "Was war aus den schönen, stolzen Bauerstöchtern geworden? Nichts war aus ihnen geworden. Der Großvater hatte recht gehabt, Bettelleut werdet's, alle werdet's einmal Bettelleut. Zwei geschundene, regelmäßig geprügelte Bäuerinnen, eine Geschiedene, und zwei, die versuchten, aus den Miet-wohnungen herauszukommen, sich was Eigenes zu schaffen, vom Mund abzusparen für die Kinder" – 193.

[48] Daviau, 110.

[49] "Bei den Großkopferten putzen gehen, fragte sie empört, lieber verhungere ich" – 117.

[50] "Das Kind war ihr einziger Besitz, den sie eifersüchtig, ängstlich bewachte und ständig bedroht glaubte" – 89.

[51] "Sie [Vera] brauchte nicht mehr den Umgang der Arzt- und Architektenkinder, um gesellschaftsfähig zu sein, sie hatte es

ihnen gezeigt, mit Matura standen einem alle Türen offen" – 215.

[52] "*einzig wirklich 'österreichischen' Roman,*" in Teuchtmann, 19. Space, such a central part of *Die Züchtigung*, has, however, continued to be an important general theme in Mitgutsch's life and works. Mitgutsch herself left Austria to pursue opportunities in the United States, South Korea, and Israel, although she has now returned. And three of her later novels all carry allusions to physical locations: *In fremden Städten*, *Abschied von Jerusalem*, and *Haus der Kindheit* (Teuchtmann, 277). Indeed, Teuchtmann notes that relatively few of Mitgutsch's literary characters remain in Austria (292).

[53] "*Für mich ist das schon ein Angelpunkt für eine Erziehung von ungeheurer Härte, von einer Erziehung, die dem heranwachsenden Menschen, dem Kind keinen Raum läßt, um Individuum zu werden. Dieses totale Unterwerfen und Brechen eines Menschen im Namen der Ordnung, Pünktlichkeit, Sauberkeit und all dieser Werte, die man faschistoid bezeichnen kann.*" In Kecht, 130.

[54] "*Und wolltest trotzdem ein Stück Land in der Ukraine besiedeln mit deiner Frau nach dem Endsieg?*" – 53.

[55] "*… auf dem Balkan waren die Partisanen gefürchteter als die ganze Ostfront, Griechenland war schmutzig, und auf dem Isthmus seid ihr alle seekrank geworden, und wer weiß, ob euch in Frankreich nicht einer wiedererkennen würde*" – 55.

[56] "*Er [der Pfarrer] und der Professor waren die einzigen in der Gemeinde, die ein Bewußtsein von dem hatten, was vorging, die anderen erlebten die Machtergreifung wie einen spannenden Film*" – 34-35.

[57] "*… wenn man sich klein machte und nicht auffiel, kamen die anderen zur Abwechslung einmal zuerst dran*" – 35.

[58] Karl-Markus Gauss, "Verklärer und Verächter: Über die Schwierigkeit, Österreich zu entdecken," in *Was wird das*

Ausland dazu sagen? Literatur und Republik nach 1945, Gerald Leitner, ed. (Wien: Picus, 1995), 20.

[59] Kecht, 130.

[60] "*Ich hasse das Wort 'Vergangenheitsbewältigung.' Das kann man nie bewältigen.*" In Kecht, 130.

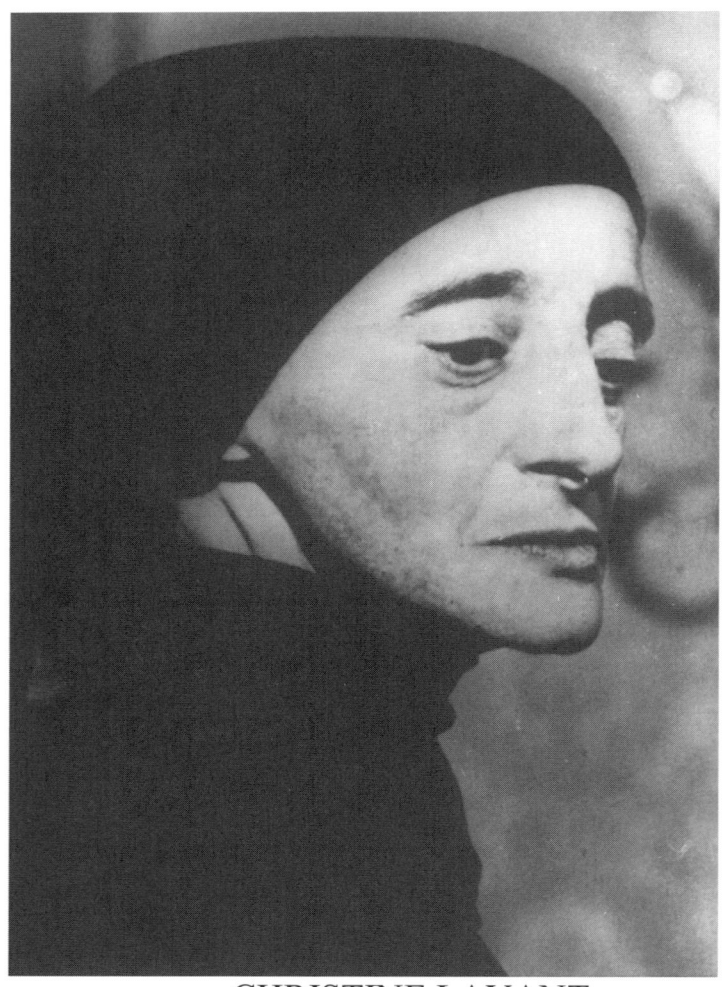
CHRISTINE LAVANT
Courtesy of Otto Müller Verlag

Christine Lavant 113

Madness in the Landscape: Christine Lavant's Provincial Modernism

by Geoffrey C. Howes

Christine Lavant (1915-1973), born Christine Thonhauser in the tiny village of Gross-Edling in the southern Austrian province of Carinthia, in many ways epitomizes the provincial writer. Except for two years in the Carinthian capital Klagenfurt, she lived all her life in the village of St. Stefan. Both St. Stefan and Gross-Edling are now incorporated into Wolfsberg, a mining town in the valley of the Lavant, the river from which the author took her pen name. Although she was recognized by the literary establishment, winning among other honors the Trakl Prize twice (1954 and 1964), the Wildgans Prize (1964), and the Grand Austrian State Prize for Literature (1970),[1] she maintained, and apparently cultivated, the persona of a country woman, with her headscarf and traditional garb.[2]

Lavant's poetry teems with images drawn mainly from four spheres: the rural Carinthian landscape, the Catholic Church, the skies, and the human body. Herbs, flowers and wild plants, domesticated and wild animals and birds, stones, gravel and dust, fields and streams, village greens ("*Anger*"), and plain foods like bread, onions, and grains fill her texts. She derives more abstract vocabulary mostly from the Bible and the Catholic liturgy. The persons of the Trinity, especially Christ, and the promise of salvation, but also the burdens of guilt and sin and hopelessness, furnish the conceptual mortar to bind the bricks of the landscape images. Somewhere between the earthly milieu and ethereal Catholicism are the heavenly bodies: the sun, the stars, and especially the moon. The body of the poems' speaker, especially its heart, brain, and hands, is also frequently present. The modern world, with its cities, technology, mass production, secularism, high culture, and concentrations of population, is strikingly absent. Indeed, even the rural population is largely missing, and persons, when they do appear, are not individuals, but fill the archetypal roles of family and village life: mother, daughter, sister, beggar, or priest.

One of the central questions in research and criticism on Christine Lavant has thus been how an apparent naïf who suffered chronic and serious childhood illnesses, which left her partly blind and deaf, could blossom in spite of geographical, social, physical, and gender-related limitations into a recognized poetic talent who contributed some of the finest German-language lyric poetry of the twentieth century. A corollary to this question is her relationship to modernism: how is it that a writer of such limited experience, whose repertoire of images and themes seems circumscribed by the boundaries of a village, could produce work with so many earmarks of literary modernism, which was produced in large part by urbanization, industrialization, and individualism? Modernist features, like illogicality, reliance on images rather than rational structures, and the demand placed on readers to participate in the construction of meaning, typify Lavant's texts and lend them a poetic sophistication that seems alien to the piety and privation of their subject matter. Why is this provincial literature so unprovincial, and how does imagery that is almost exclusively pre-modern add up to modernistic poetry?[3]

Many of Lavant's modernistic literary qualities are traceable to her encounter with the texts of Rainer Maria Rilke and Georg Trakl in her late twenties,[4] as well as to her overcoming the derivative work that her admiration for these poets initially produced.[5] Part of her modernism, however, also derives from a central conflict in her oeuvre that mimics on an individual scale (and with some historical delay) one of the broad upheavals of European modernity: the failure of religion to provide comfort or make sense of the world and its suffering. Many urbane Europeans of the late nineteenth and early twentieth centuries, of course, resorted to art for spiritual nourishment when the assurances of Christianity were laid bare and broken down by the natural sciences, historiography, and Enlightenment and post-Enlightenment philosophy. Christine Lavant, in her Carinthian isolation, faced a similar crisis on a personal level when her ancestral belief in Catholicism, which seemed to guarantee hope and charity, provided no answers to why she had to suffer poverty, illness, and loneliness. She turned to her art as a form of compensation, even though she regarded it as a second- or third-rate substitute for a pain-free, hopeful life. "Art like mine is nothing but mutilated life," she wrote to a friend.[6]

This essay will explore Lavant's apparent "provincial modernism" through a close reading of her poetry with occasional supportive reference to her prose texts, and by concentrating on one important aspect of her texts: the theme and motif of madness. According to Louis A. Sass in *Madness and Modernism*, there are fundamental parallels between schizophrenia and modern art: "Modernist art has been said to manifest certain off-putting characteristics that are reminiscent of schizophrenia: a quality of being hard to understand or feel one's way into."[7] Sass, however, uses this correlation not to reduce modern art to madness, but to remove madness from its traditional image as a diminution of awareness and the alienation from reason. What, he asks, "if madness, in at least some of its forms, were to derive from a heightening rather than a dimming of conscious awareness, and an alienation not from reason but from the emotions, instincts, and the body?"[8] The aspects of modern art that parallel madness are "antithetical to notions of primitivity and of deficit or defect, for these art forms are characterized not so much by unreflectiveness and spontaneity as by acute self-consciousness and self-reference, and by alienation from action and experience—qualities we might refer to as 'hyper-reflexivity.'"[9]

"Hyper-reflexivity" applies well to nearly all of Lavant's oeuvre, as does "acute self-consciousness" and "self-reference." Her poetry expresses the ordeal of a self, thrown back on its own meager resources by the silence of God. The poems' self-reflexivity parallels Sass's description of the "schizoid personality type," a typically modern form of consciousness that is also a feature of much modern art. "The most prominent characteristics of schizoid persons are an apparent asociality and indifference, often combined with introversion. Seldom do such people feel in harmony with their bodies or with the environment.... Often they will seem detached, 'as if something unnatural and strange divided them from the world.'"[10] Lavant's poetic persona corresponds further to the "hypersensitive" subtype of the schizoid personality, which Sass adapts from Ernst Kretschmer's "hyperaesthetic" type: "'timid, shy, with fine feelings, sensitive, nervous, excitable... abnormally tender, constantly wounded.'"[11] Sass identifies Franz Kafka as a prototypical "hypersensitive" or "hyperaesthetic" sensibility, noting his isolation, his feelings of vulnerability and inferiority, his "extreme self-consciousness," and endless "self-scrutiny."[12]

Lavant's lyrical persona shares this sense of vulnerability and inferiority, and this endless self-scrutiny, which allows us to compare it with the hypersensitive type of the schizoid personality. Living in a remote Carinthian village, partly debilitated by illness, Lavant was certainly alienated from her "action and experience."[13] Since, however, her lyrical persona is not a personality, but a component of her art, I will not argue on the basis of Lavant's biography or psychology. Nor will I maintain that her texts are somehow an expression of a schizoid personality or of madness itself. Rather, staying within the literary system created by Lavant's texts, I will argue that madness has a poetic function related to the hypersensitivity of the poems' voices.[14]

What is this function? These poems neither express madness nor portray madness. From within their intense self-reflexivity, they rather convey the *desire for madness*. In order to understand why the lyrical self would desire such a harrowing condition, one must grasp that madness in Lavant's poetry holds out the prospect of compensation for the impossibility of religious salvation. In Lavant, this is not a general impossibility; it is a specific one that for unknown reasons affects the speaker of the poems who believes in Christian salvation but, in her schizoid sense of inferiority, does not believe that it applies to her. Lacking spiritual hope, and feeling thus relegated to the material realm, the "I" in many of Lavant's poems finds in madness an intimation of transcendence, a whiff of secular ecstasy.

It is important at this point to distinguish between the schizoid and the schizophrenic, between neurosis and psychosis. In discussing the schizoid personality, Sass investigates the "chronic" as opposed to the "acute" dimension of the type, "the so-called pre-morbid personality that often precedes the psychotic break."[15] In Lavant's poems, the chronic schizoid dimension is fully present, since they typically portray the desperate, alienated self's attempts to gain hope. Yet in the absence of hope, they often press in the direction of the acute condition, of full-blown madness itself, of psychosis as a presumed release from the constant disappointment of fruitless belief.

Tracing the images and language of madness in several of Lavant's poems will reveal a conceptual gradation, more subtle than the binary oppositions of saved-versus-lost, or spiritual-versus-material, or God-versus-devil. In this earthly limbo, a graduated system of meaning between apotheosis and damnation, the three realms of content outlined at the outset—everyday objects, religious ideas, and heavenly bodies—take on new roles. The poet wrests them from their practical functionality into a poetical functionality that depends on their place in the system of meaning created by the lyrical voice of the poems. This system shifts and oscillates, so that its components often change their respective functions while maintaining their valences, as it were. Nonetheless, the system exhibits an overall stability in which material values and objects are substituted for religious values and objects. This shift away from conventional expectations imposes a constant vigilance over things, whose function is now unpredictable. Furthermore, religious salvation is no longer assured, since the promises of the Church do not seem to apply to the speaker of the poems. The poetic "I" must plead for salvation, maneuver for it, and at times even demand it, and still it does not come. This pleading, maneuvering, and demanding, often in the form of prayer or supplication, is a tactic repeated in many, if not most of Lavant's poems.

If values have lost their efficacy, and material objects stand in for these absent religious values, then the realm of religion is reduced or downgraded to the material realm, at least for the speaker of the poems. Hence the transcendent promises of religion—reuniting with the godhead, an end to earthly suffering—are removed from the range of hope, and a worldly substitute for them must be found. One possible secular substitute for religious transport is madness, with its seeming release from cogitation and hence from the torments of the schizoid brooder.[16] Ultimately, however, madness itself is beyond the hopes of the lyrical self. Lavant's lyrical alter ego yearns to go mad, for this would mean a loss of painful individuation and isolation, yet even this hoped-for surrogate for rapture betrays the believer.

In order to explore Lavant's "provincial modernism" by way of the function of madness in her poems, I will discuss examples of what are arguably her most representative texts: three volumes of poetry published in her lifetime, 'The Beggar's Bowl' (*Die Bettlerschale*, 1956), 'Spindle in the Moon' (*Spindel im Mond*,

1959), and 'The Peacock's Cry' (*Der Pfauenschrei*, 1962).[17] Considering these three collections chronologically will show a progression in Lavant's use of the images of schizoid sensibility and madness: from diffident hope, to defiance, to despair.

Typically, the poems in 'The Beggar's Bowl' express a schizoidal self-scrutiny, isolation, vulnerability, and inferiority, along with a desire or prayer-like request for relief. I have selected the poem 'My temples fill with *Foehn*' ("*Die Schläfen füllen sich mit Föhn*"), both because it is an important instance of the role of madness in Lavant's work, and because Johann Strutz interpreted this poem at length in the first comprehensive study of Lavant's poetry, published in 1979. Contrasting my threefold interpretation of Lavant's universe with Strutz's twofold conception will permit us to see precisely what is gained by inserting the middle ground between abjection and exultation. Here is the poem with my translation, which is intended less as a poetic rendering than as an attempt to reproduce the poem's semantic structures.

> My temples fill with *Foehn* -
> Lord, do you want to drink my memory?
> No drop must fall upon the earth,
> it is so glassy and so fine
> full of immaculate signs.
> Drink my skull blamelessly empty,
> for you there is no drink too heavy,
> nothing can soften your brain.
> I have sped up here so high,
> the hair of the woods below undulates
> like manes about the lamb
> of the white town, a cock's comb
> blooms burning red at the roadside,
> where earlier my mind stood
> before your son's dead body.
> Who knows how far I'll stray?
> Already I don't recognize the pain anymore

that drove me in the *Foehn* to the savior-;
Lord, feel your way along the thorn,
graciously drink my skull empty.[18]

The wish for deliverance is a request to the Lord to drink the memory of the poem's speaker:[19] 'My temples fill with *Foehn* - / Lord, do you want to drink my memory? / No drop must fall upon the earth, / it is so glassy and so fine / full of immaculate signs.' Seeking relief from the *Föhn*—the warm, dry wind that comes over the Alps from the south and is believed to cause headaches, circulation problems, irritability, nausea, and fatigue, and even to increase crime, suicide and accident rates—the speaker of the poem asks the Lord to take away her memory. As Johann Strutz notes, this is a reversal of the situation of communion, in which the communicant drinks of the Lord in memory of him. The Foehn's attributes summarize the schizoid sensibility, which fills the head of the speaker. This mental content, this memory, is seen as sullied, as unworthy: not a drop must fall to the earth, which is 'immaculate.' Strutz sees this as a duality: the content of the head is holy, and the earth, which is of glass, is artificial; hence the holy contents of the speaker's head should not be mixed with the profane earth.[20] But this reading does not account for the 'immaculate signs' of the earth. If we see the poem operating with three conceptual realms instead of two, the interpretive paradox noted by Strutz—having to develop the opposite of an extrapolated concept and use this as a hypothesis—is eliminated. Instead of a holy realm with which the speaker is identified through her ecstatic, *Foehn*-induced state, contrasted with a deceitful earthly realm, we now have an intermediate earthly realm that has received the Lord's blessing, a holy realm represented by the Lord Himself, and a lower realm, occupied by the speaker of the poem, which is rejected by both of the others. The later association of the city with a symbol of Christ (the lamb) and a pure color (white) further underscores the association of the earth with blessedness.

The Lord can imbibe the *Foehn*-contaminated memory without ill effect, for He need fear no mental suffering. His brain will not be softened like the supplicant's: 'Drink my skull harmlessly dry / for you there is no drink too heavy, / nothing can soften your brain.' If we adopt the triple division of the poem's world suggested above, we can see several remarkable things happening in these first lines. First, the abjectness of the speaker's condition is made clear not only by her distance from God, but also by her distance from the earth, which is 'immaculate,' and which she fears fouling with the contents of her head. She is at home neither with the Lord nor in the terrestrial realm. Second, she tries to relate to God not by comparing herself to Him, but by comparing Him to her. The metaphor is not that she has a mind or soul like God's infinite one, but that God has a brain as she does. (This takes the perversion of the communion scene further in the direction of impiety.) But God's brain is far more powerful than her own—'nothing can soften' it. She implies that the *Foehn* has softened her brain, made it liquid and potable—that she has become "soft in the head" (in German "*weich im Gehirn*"). The rough—one might say, surgical—physicality of the images of brain and skull contrasts with the emptiness that the speaker seeks: she wants to lose her mind. The schizoid humility of her request is expressed in her reminder to God that He has nothing to lose by relieving her. The tone, though, is both humble and impatient. Helping her would cause God no trouble, so why doesn't He do it?

The next lines establish a narrative that has led to the present condition: the speaker has quickly climbed above the town and the trees. She has been insolent ('I have shot up so high'—"*Ich habe mich sehr hoch geschnellt*" [21]), and she has increased her distance from the town, which is identified with Christ and purity ('the lamb of the white city'), [22] and from a majestically depicted nature ('the hair of the woods... like lions' manes'), and now she is standing before a plain cockscomb, one of the medicinal herbs that pervade Lavant's poetry.[23] The 'burning red' of this wild plant is contrasted not only with the pure white of the civilized town, it has also replaced the image of Christ in the speaker's consciousness: 'a cockscomb / blooms burning red at the roadside, / where earlier my memory stood / before your son's dead body.' Strutz interprets the cockscomb as replacing the speaker's memory, but since her memory is still present (how else could she ask God to drink it?), it makes more sense to view it as having replaced Christ; both Christ and the cock's comb stand by the side of the road; the speaker has moved on from one to the other. The speaker seems thus to challenge God for the inefficacy of His conventional solutions, indicating that she will go as far as she needs to in order to find succor: 'Who knows how far I'll go [away]?' (*"Wer weiss, wie weit ich weiche?"*). This line stands out not only because of its heavy "w" alliteration; it is also the only line, in a poem full of enjambments, dashes, and commas that is syntactically independent. It is a turning point. An impish challenge to God is a common motif in Lavant's poems, as if the speaker, having no hope for salvation anyway, is testing how far she can go. She has already moved past the traditional scene of piety, a crucifix, a *"Bildstock,"* one of the roadside shrines common in rural Austria, where she was driven by the *Foehn*, and now she stands before an earthly, pagan curative. Her question is both rhetorical and a challenge to God. *"Wer weiß, wie weit ich weiche"* can mean 'who knows how much I'll give in,' or 'give way,' but also 'who knows how far I'll go away' and even 'who knows how much I'll soften' (echoing the verb *"er-weichen"* earlier in the poem). God may be powerful enough not to weaken, but the speaker wonders how much she will give in, how weak she can become, how much she'll stray before she finds relief.

The two final lines renew the request to the Lord to drink dry her skull: 'Lord, feel your way along the thorn, / graciously drink dry my skull.' The first image is a bold one inviting the Lord to revisit His suffering, to approach someone whose suffering has not ended. The second image repeats the equally bold image of

Christine Lavant   123

the skull as God's chalice (again reversing the roles of holy communion), ending this time on the word 'empty' (*"leer"*).

In the poem I have selected from the second published volume, 'Spindel in the Moon' (*Spindel im Mond*, 1959), the lyrical "I" addresses madness more directly. It is also one of the poems that Johann Strutz interprets in detail, and so I will again contrast my tripartite construction with his dualistic conception. 'I wish to break bread with the madmen' draws a three-fold landscape of the soul: the bottom of the water, associated with the inorganic and melancholy; the waters themselves, associated with the organic, but also with madness, anger, and misery; and the 'wilderness' above the waters, associated with the human (in the form of bells) and the divine (in the form of the symbol of the Holy Spirit, the dove).

> I wish to break bread with the madmen,
> daily one piece of the great horror,
> and also the bell in my heart,
> there where the dove is nesting
> and has her minuscule refuge
> in the wilderness over the waters.
> Long I have dwelt as a stone
> at the bottom of things.
> But I have heard the bell
> speaking softly of your secret
> in the flying fish.
> I will learn to fly and swim
> and leave what's of stone among the stones,
> and bed the melancholy in mother-of-pearl,
> but uplift the rage and the misery.
> My wings are older than your patience,
> My wings flew ahead of the courage
> That took error upon itself.
> I wish to share the bread with the mad
> there in the terrible wilderness of the dove,

where the bell thirds the great horror
to the threefold sound of your name.[24]

The poem opens with the speaker's wish to share bread—the physical manifestation of Christ—with the madmen or "*Irren.*" But this communion takes on a perverse cast when the bread is identified with 'the great horror': 'I wish to break the bread with the madmen, / daily one piece of the great horror.' The impishness encountered in 'My temples fill with *Foehn*' has become more defiant. Christ's earthly appearance through the bread, usually a positive sign of His risen presence, is linked again to the sufferings of His life. At this physical level of pain—as opposed to the abstract theological level of resurrection—the speaker can identify with the Deity.

Yet the more ethereal realm does manage to communicate as well, through the sound of the bell—the summons to worship—and the symbol of the dove. The heart is the organ that these messages reach, as opposed to the mouth and digestion addressed by the bread. The speaker also wishes to share the merciful message of the bell with the 'madmen': 'and also the bell in my heart / there where the dove is nesting / and has her minuscule refuge / in the wilderness over the waters.' The symbol of the Holy Spirit is not at home in the organic world, and therefore It has only a 'minuscule' or 'tiny' ("*winzig*") refuge in the organ of compassion. The image of the 'wilderness' combines both the scene of Jesus' baptism by John ('one crying in the wilderness') and the image of the spirit of God over the waters in Genesis, when the world was still Chaos. The world inhabited by the speaker still has a large element of chaos, and this accounts for why the spirit of God—the dove—must seek refuge in the heart. (This is probably also an allusion to the dove sent forth by Noah over the waters of the deluge, returning to the ark for refuge, but with a sign of hope.[25]) The generosity of the speaker, her wish to share the bread and the bell, is a modest one, on a 'tiny' scale, and it extends only to those most distant from God, and with whom she can identify: the mad.

In the next lines we discover that the speaker is not even among the mad, that her position is even lower, and so the wish of the first lines is a wish to rise out of a depressed condition, represented by the inorganic image of the stone, to a more animated, yet by no means peaceful state, represented by the fish 'flying' in waters that lie overhead relative to the bottom:

> Long I have dwelt as a stone
> at the bottom of things.
> But I have heard the bell
> speaking softly of your secret
> in the flying fish.
> I will learn to fly and swim
> and leave what's of stone among the stones,
> and bed the melancholy in mother-of-pearl,
> but uplift the rage and the misery.

The 'flying fish'—in the organic, living realm—have access to the spiritual, however tenuous this contact might be: the bell is 'speaking softly' of a 'secret.' The muted message is enough to arouse in the speaker the wish to 'leave what's of stone among the stones,' to escape the state of melancholy and 'learn to fly and swim.' Strutz interprets the 'stone at the bottom of things' as the image of a divine origin in God[26]—the 'ground' ("*Grund*") to which the speaker yearns to return, so that he sees the poem's movement as circular, from stone (a 'grounding' in God), to the earth (the water and air), and then back to God. The 'but' in 'But I have heard the bell,' however, contrasts the call to God with the stony, melancholic existence, as does the wish expressed in the next sentence to 'leave what's of stone among the stones.' The startling thing about the images of movement away from these stones, of flying and swimming, is that they are correlated not as might be conventionally expected with joy, but with 'rage and misery.' In other words, the speaker of the poem wishes to rise above the immobilized condition of melancholy, of depression. Even if this is an elevation to madness, anger, and suffering, it is still preferable to schizoid melancholy. The German word for melancholy, "*Schwermut*," literally 'heavy spirit' or 'heavy mind,' relates directly to the stone image, connecting the mental and physical. To put the melancholy behind her, she will imitate the action of a mussel or oyster that coats the inorganic irritation with a mineral shield of mother-of-pearl.

Instead of this lifeless state, the lyrical "I" aspires to a condition of animation. The psychosis, rage, and distress it promises to entail are preferable to anhedonic, impassive dejection. Strutz urges us not to read the image of 'the mad' as literally mentally ill persons, but rather as all mankind ('humans themselves') in their fallen state.[27] But the concept of madness is exclusionary, not inclusive, and the mad are those others who, like the speaker, are abandoned by God's promise, and therefore a point of identification for her. They are not 'normal' Christians, who seem to believe in salvation, but those rejected by society, and by God. This is also shown by the intensity of the speaker's wish to transcend her state and commune with the mad. In fact, her strong emotion surpasses even the normal Christian virtue of patience, which seems to have sentenced the speaker to lifelessness and passivity. The 'you' addressed by the poem, Jesus as Lord, is able to wait longer than the speaker of the poem is willing to wait for relief from her condition: 'My wings are older than your patience / my wings flew ahead of the courage / that took error upon itself.' This courage can be interpreted as the courage of Jesus himself, Who in becoming human also assumed human limitations. 'Error'—in German "*das Irren*"—is related both to mad ("*irr*") and to the archaic sense, present in both English 'err' and German "*irren*," of straying or wandering. Jesus subjected Himself to the organic realm of straying and madness, and is thus supposed to understand human suffering and help alleviate it. But for the speaker, this imperfect Jesus shows too much patience, and now she extends the impudence noted in the previous poem to the point of blasphemy, saying that her wings—the ones she will use to swim and fly—are older than Jesus' patience and outstrip His courage.[28] She has lost her patience with Jesus' all-too protracted patience. To the extent that this patience has kept her in the state of wretchedness, it is associated with 'the great horror,' which at the end of the poem is divided into three parts, corresponding to the Trinity: 'where the bell thirds the great horror / to the threefold sound of your name.' Now the 'great horror,' connected at the poem's outset with Jesus under the sign of the bread, is extended to invoke all three members of the Trinity. This is the message the speaker wishes to share with the mad.

If, in 'My temples fill with *Foehn*,' straying (*"weichen"*) is a desperate attempt to gain relief from the schizoid or depressive state associated with the *Foehn*, here straying (*"irren"*) goes even further. The speaker wants at least to share the human status that Jesus assumed, but she actually aspires even further, to flying, swimming, and breaking bread with the mad. This means she is content to stay in the fallen, organic world, even if she thus abandons hope of the (endlessly delayed) salvation intimated by the dove and the church bells. An unredeemed mortal state is preferable to the lifelessness of melancholy, which combines hopelessness and impassivity by relinquishing agency to another entity. And, blasphemously, one's own agency is preferable to waiting eternally for God's intervention.[29]

The blasphemy of Lavant's poems, however, is not flagrant. It is encoded within complex imagery, which reflects the poems' precise attempt to represent complicated relationships between authority and servitude, mercy and cruelty, good and evil, humility and arrogance, and immobility and liveliness. The poetic ciphering of sacrilege also reveals the poet's caution, her wish to explore territory that is beyond the pale of the Catholic traditions she has internalized, but without giving up any and all chance for communion with the Deity. This is one reason why so many of her poems, including the three examined here, are in the form of prayer. These are the genuine supplications of a believer. But these prayers are mixed with a desperation and defiance that would be considered sinful in the speaker's religious frame of reference. She cannot, however, do otherwise. She has lost patience with the virtue of patience, and this loss is a form of doubt, a deficit in the cardinal virtues of faith and hope. Indeed, the poems' speaker is in a double-bind: she wants to escape the sin of sloth, represented by the images of melancholy, and the sin of envy, shown in the images of the things she cannot have. But in order to escape these, she must commit the sins of pride and wrath (*"Zorn"*). Yet even in the midst of pride and anger, she remains humble, faithful, and hopeful. She does not aspire to more than what God's most abject human creations—the mad—possess. Even madness, with its rage and misery, is preferable to dwelling 'as a stone at the bottom of things.'

The third poem for consideration, from 'The Peacock's Cry' (*Der Pfauenschrei* of 1962), chosen like the others for its directly expressed theme of madness, has a greater dose of anger and impatience than the two we have looked at so far. It is addressed not to Christ or another member of the Trinity, but to a patron saint (*"Schutzpatron"*)—the unnamed patron saint of madmen.[30]

You patron saint of madmen,
I do not know your name,
nor what scream glorifies you
and whether you can even bear
the clangor of my cracking heart.
Master Succorer, are you already
pondering in secret your escape
and sneaking away untested
from the wringing of my hands?
Do you know how angels sing
when you use your temple bone
as a hammer or a stone,
to try breaking out

of solitary confinement?
Do you know the image-power
at your head's crown, and the speech
at the rib-knot spot?
How far are you already gone
from my finger-cradle,
you alien patron saint?
The moon, that son of a bitch,
is mocking me as I lie,
twisted and nerve-racked,
chilled to the bone and scorched.[31]

The lyrical "I" has lowered its sights from Jesus to an intercessor. Once again, the speaker seeks admission, not to salvation, not to the kingdom of heaven, but at least to the same consideration that madmen receive. The desperation found in 'My temples...' and the anger in 'I wish to break bread...' have turned here, however, into outright derision and skepticism: 'You patron saint of madmen, / I do not know your name, / nor what scream glorifies you / and whether you can even bear / the clangor of my cracking heart.' The prayer has turned to a cry or scream (*"Schrei"*), and even that is not certain to reach and flatter the saint. The speaker doubts that the saint can even bear her pain, to say nothing of helping her. She already senses that the entreated mediator is slipping away: 'Master Succorer, are you already / pondering in secret your escape / and skulking away untested / from the wringing of my hands?' The German verb for 'skulk' (*"sich schleichen"*) is of low diction and expresses contempt—it could also be translated as 'sneak,' 'slink,' 'tiptoe,' or even 'weasel out.'

The next rhetorical question directed at the saint is a stark instance of the attempt to escape melancholy: 'Do you know how angels sing / when you use your temple bone / as a hammer or a stone, / to try breaking out / of solitary confinement?' That battering one's head against the wall produces the voices of angels is an irony similar to identifying the Trinity with 'the great horror,' as in the previous poem. The irony, however, is stepped up here, for the self-abuse is portrayed as a form of prayer or religious observance. 'Solitary confinement' can be seen as parallel to being a 'stone at the bottom of things,' but in this poem there is even less hope of escape.

The ironic representation of self-imposed pain as worship or devotion is then taken further when the body itself is seen as communicating images and words. The points of the body where the nerves and the blood vessels come together, the crown of the head (*"Scheitel"*) and the heart, marked by the 'rib-knot spot' where the ribs join the breastbone, produce grotesque versions of icons (*"Bilder"*) and the word (*"das Sprechen"*). Headache and heartache are the channels of spiritual transmission. The speaker doubts if this 'alien' saint can even know what she is talking about, and she imagines him already far away from the 'finger-cradle' (*"Fingerwiege"*) of her praying hands.

The last four lines move to a new image, that of the moon, an impersonal denizen of the heavens, possibly even an object of pagan worship, and traditionally associated with madness (lunacy).[32] But even this second-rate deity, this idol, does not heed her cries: 'The moon, that son of a bitch / is mocking me as I lie, / twisted and nerve-racked, /chilled to the bone and scorched.' Once again, the speaker is denied even the release of madness and is instead reduced to a low, schizoid state: ('I lie') like that of the stone on the bottom, with a body contorted in pain, and tortured by both heat and cold. The paradoxical images of being simultaneously 'chilled to the bone' (*"durchfroren"*) and 'scorched' (*"verbrannt"*) have in common not only extreme pain, but also the reduction of life to its elements, the degeneration to an inorganic state that likewise resonates with the image of the stone.

In these three poems, then, we find a repeated pattern of the speaker's wish to escape what I have called a schizoid or depressive state. Using these terms interchangeably may seem inexact, but this is not a clinical diagnosis, it is a rhetorical analysis, and so it is useful to connect the schizoid with what Lavant calls "*Schwermut*." The condition portrayed by Lavant fits Louis Sass' description of the schizoidal type as noted above: "constantly wounded," with feelings of vulnerability and inferiority, "extreme self-consciousness," and endless "self-scrutiny."[33] There is also isolation and detachment, a sense of division from the world.[34] The descriptions also correspond to melancholy—sullenness, sadness, annoyance, introspection, and vexation—and depression—misery, anguish, and guilt, accompanied by headache or insomnia. The *Foehn*, the 'stone at the bottom of things,' and 'solitary confinement,' are all images of this, and the actions of escaping the town, 'uplifting' anger and misery, and battering one's head against the wall are all attempts to gain release. As we move from book to book, both the symptoms and the attempts at relief become more acute.[35] But all three express the sense that losing one's mind, communing with the mad, or becoming lunatic might provide respite. None of the poems attains resolution, however, for not only do the holy figures who are entreated—God the Father, Christ, the Holy Spirit, and the 'patron saint of madmen'—remain unresponsive, but the desired substitutes for religious salvation—having one's brain drunk dry, learning to swim and fly with the fish and commune with the mad, and becoming moonstruck—also remain vain hopes.

What does this have to do with what I have called Christine Lavant's "provincial modernism"? What seems particularly "modern" about Lavant's poetry is the portrayal of the individual, the subject. In his study of Robert Musil and the "history of subjectivity," Stefan Jonsson describes the modern or postmodern subject as one no longer subject to the "expressive paradigm." In other words, in much of modern literature, there is no subject that expresses its inner identity, but there are subjects who have lost this identity because it no longer corresponds to any outward characteristics or identities such as nationality, citizenship, gender, or profession.[36] Lavant's poems likewise do not so much *express* the inner emotions of the lyrical "I" as they search for identity among the structures provided by the provincial environment. The most significant of these are familial (daughter, mother, sister, wife), economic (farmer, miner, shopkeeper), and ecclesiastical (communicant, priest). It is also characteristic of premodern, rural societies that these roles are not neatly distinguishable: family roles are also economic, as everyone contributes to farm work and related functions; and there is an intimate connection through the sacraments between familial and churchly identities. Although the speakers of Lavant's poems occasionally appear in family roles, they almost always lack any of these identities. That is to say, the subject position in these poems is empty, and most crucially empty of a Christian identity. As Crystal Mazur Ockenfuss writes, "lack" is Lavant's business: "She is not in the poems. They are empty and revolve around an absence."[37] The poems try again and again to establish identity, but in the last analysis they fail, and the only identity there is the missing subject demarcated by the poems. According to Evelyn Schlag, it is not only the subject position that is empty, the addressee of the poems—God—is also absent.[38] But since these poems are written only for these two absentees, and not for a larger audience, their critique of the power of God, hence their blasphemy, is all the more convincing. Schlag writes that in a more frequent model of the poet—the "bard" who speaks for an audience—the bard cannot attack power, for he himself depends on it for his authority. Not so with Lavant's poetry, whose radicality, for Schlag, resides in its powerlessness. "There is no more radical critique of power than that from the mouth of powerlessness."[39]

That Christine Lavant herself had a theoretical understanding of the powerless "subject without an identity" that speaks in her poems is attested to by a statement made in an interview, reproduced in the commentary to her *Memoirs from a Madhouse*: "The self is a glorious secret behind a thousand and one miseries and never describable... The truly experienced realm or rather the fragmentary mirror images of it can be found more or less magically transformed—poeticized in my books."[40] The phrase "magically transformed—poeticized" ("*verzaubert-verdichtet*"), might also be rendered 'enchanted-condensed,' in which 'enchanted' does not modify 'condensed,' but is combined with it to render what the poetic act does: it both enchants—makes magical—and condenses—concentrates and solidifies—experience. The difference is significant: not the process, but the product of writing poetry is magical. And while *"verdichtet"* could be interpreted as 'poeticized' (an intensive form of *"dichten"*), it could also be simply 'to solidify, concentrate, condense.' The juxtaposition of fairy tale and almost scientific vocabulary is characteristic of Lavant's sense of irony.

These texts are positioned precisely between a premodern or *Gemeinschaft*-conception of the individual as part of a community, defined by birth and ascribed roles, and a modern or *Gesellschaft*-conception of the individual as defined by functions within a community.[41] Lavant's poems signify a space between these two, in which the speaker no longer has access to the identity-providing roles of mother, worker, or Church congregant, and yet has assumed no compensatory function that might be supplied by an urban environment. This intervalic space is similar to the role of the mad, who are too idiosyncratic to take on a specific role (other than "mental patient," "fool" or "village idiot") and unsuited to the sort of negotiations required to function in society, in the *Gesellschaft*. Christine Lavant at one point hoped she might find a sense of belonging in the madhouse. In *Memoirs from a Madhouse* she wrote: "It is good to be crazy among the crazed, and it was a sin, and intellectual arrogance, to act as if I weren't. Why shouldn't I too for once be wholly and completely at home?... They, the ones here, are willing to accept me...."[42] Yet she is pronounced cured and released, unlike most of the patients portrayed in the *Memoirs*, whose psychoses are clearly different from Lavant's depression. Even her attempt to be mad among the mad does not provide her with an identity.

Christine Lavant's modernism, her radical refusal of traditional explanations of her place in the cosmos, distinguishes her from her provincial surroundings, while the exclusively provincial content of her images distinguishes her from modernism proper. This can be traced in part to her personal circumstances, and in part to the relatively late modernization of provincial Austria. Although mining connected the Lavant Valley with the industrialized world, it involved exporting resources, not importing ways of life. After the Second World War, the modernization proceeded more rapidly with new and more widely available means of communication, improved infrastructure, and a fundamental change in attitude from the fatalistic, cyclical, and nature-bound rural outlook to an acceptance, or at least an awareness, of change, progress, and the prospect that an individual could change herself and improve her position. Without these changes, the outside world of the cultural scene would probably not have come to Christine Lavant's attention, and her own poetry would not have found an outlet and come to the attention of the Austrian and German literary establishments. Yet there is a strong sense in which the poems belong neither to the countryside nor to the city. They enjoy neither the stability (not to say immobility) of the rural world nor the individual freedom (for better or worse) of the urban world. They reject the *status quo*, the tormenting patience demanded by rural Catholic existence, but do not attain the alternative, self-determination or self-creation. They are depressive, schizoid, but not mad enough to find the release that their writer imagined might come with psychosis. The intense self-reflection, the uncanny isolation, and the seemingly incurable melancholy of Christine Lavant's texts remain unrelieved in poem after poem, and the precision and honesty with which this limbo is described are excruciating.

Notes

[1] A time line of Christine Lavant's life, including prizes and publications, is presented in Inge Glaser, *Christine Lavant: Eine Spurensuche* (Wien: Edition Praesens, 2005), 27-31.

2   On Lavant's public image, see for example Wolfgang Nehring, "Zur Wandlung des lyrischen Bildes bei Christine Lavant," *Über Christine Lavant: Leseerfahrungen, Interpretationen, Selbstdeutungen*, Grete Lübbe-Grothues, ed. (Salzburg: Otto Müller Verlag, 1984), 18-38. Nehring notes that in her public appearances, the poet left an impression of an herbalist from the countryside, 'a naïve, innocent person unaware of herself and her art' (18, my translation). Wieland Schmied said that this image was a "mask behind which a natural, unspoiled human being... a woman of great charm" was hidden (Schmied, in Christine Lavant, *Wirf ab den Lehm* (Graz and Wien: Stiasny, 1961), 7; quoted in Nehring 18-19. Nehring (19) still insists that much of the image of the simple Carinthian farmwoman was true. It is useful to be able to accept apparent contradictions when approaching Lavant.

3   Franz Josef Czernin defines the problem of Lavant's modernism thus: her subject matter (especially the religious element) is unusual and even alien to contemporary literature, yet her poems are aesthetically convincing ("Zum Verhältnis von Religion und Poesie in der Dichtung Christine Lavants," in *Profile einer Dichterin: Beiträge des II. Internationalen Christine-Lavant-Symposions Wolfsberg 1998*. Arno Russegger and Johann Strutz, eds. (Salzburg: Otto Müller Verlag, 1999), 46. After his comparative analysis of irrationality and paradox in religion and poetry, Czernin asks whether the question is not so much whether religion can be taken seriously in modernism, but whether poetry, which is still given lip service, has not also been made obsolete the modern tendency to unmask fiction and illusion (70-71).

4   On Lavant's reception of Rilke, see especially Johann Strutz, *Poetik und Existenzproblematik: Zur Lyrik Christine Lavants* (Salzburg: Otto Müller Verlag, 1979), 23-43.

5   On Lavant's overcoming of Rilke's influence, see Strutz, 43-47.

[6] This statement provides the title of a collection of posthumous and scattered texts by Lavant: *Kunst wie meine ist nur verstümmeltes Leben: Nachgelassene und verstreut veröffentlichte Gedichte—Prosa—Briefe,* selected and edited by Armin Wigotschnig and Johann Strutz (Salzburg: Otto Müller, 1978).

[7] Louis A. Sass, *Madness and Modernism: Insanity in the Light of Modern Art, Literature, and Thought* (New York: Basic Books, 1992), 8.

[8] Sass, 4.

[9] Sass, 8.

[10] Sass, 77.

[11] Sass, 81.

[12] Sass, 82-83.

[13] Sass, 8.

[14] Otto Scrinzi, in "Dichtung und Krankheit am Beispiel Christine Lavants," in *Profile einer Dichterin: Beiträge des II. Internationalen Christine-Lavant-Symposions Wolfsberg 1998,* Arno Russegger and Johann Strutz, eds. (Salzburg: Otto Müller Verlag, 1999) notes that Lavant was a great poet not because of her illness, but in spite of it (190). His approach to the question of mental illness, especially depression, in Lavant's work is enlightening, but it mainly connects the poet's biography with ideas in psychology and psychiatry rather than analyzing the poems.

[15] Sass, 76.

[16] One other secular substitute for religion is romantic love that shares with madness the sense of transport and loss of individuation. Indeed, love is probably more pervasive and important than madness in Lavant's poems, as Evelyn Schlag emphasizes in her essay "'Vierfach nach unten geht des Himmels Richtung.' Über Christine Lavants Radikalität," in *Alte Meister, Schufte, Außenseiter: Reflexionen über österreichische Literatur nach 1945,* Manfred Müller, ed. (Wien: Sonderzahl, 2005), 135-51. It is not always easy (or necessary) to distin-

guish between the addressees of Lavant's poems, whether God, a person of the Trinity, a saint, or the unattainable lover. This lover is unnamed in the poems, but Werner Berg was his name in real life. He is the artist whom we have to thank for the striking woodcut portraits of Christine Lavant that adorn the dust jackets of her books and can be seen in the book *Für Christine Lavant* (Wien: Verlag Guberner & Hierhammer, 1965), with an introduction by Ludwig von Ficker and an afterword by Wieland Schmied.

[17] Johann Strutz, in his *Poetik und Existenzproblematik: Zur Lyrik Christine Lavants* (Salzburg: Otto Müller Verlag, 1979), regards these three books as her 'Main Poetical Works' (66). Inge Glaser includes Lavant's first volume of poetry, *Die unvollendete Liebe* ('The Incomplete Love'), in her detailed discussion of representative poems, but because she is most interested in the connection between biography and work, they interest her more as part of a broad portrait of the poet herself than for their aesthetic qualities and originality (50). Glaser herself notes, however, that there is a crucial shift between the first book and the three that followed: the lyrical voice becomes an accusatory one, and it also displays a split persona (190). In other words, Lavant's distinctive voice and style are established only after the first book. A fourth volume, *Hälfte des Herzens* ('Half of the Heart') collects individually published poems that were not selected by the author herself.

[18] *"Die Schläfen füllen sich mit Föhn –*
Herr, willst du mein Gedächtnis trinken?
Kein Tropfen darf zur Erde sinken,
sie ist so gläsern und so schön
voll makelloser Zeichen.
Trink meinen Schädel schadlos leer,
für dich ist kein Getränk zu schwer,
dein Hirn kann nichts erweichen.
Ich habe mich sehr hoch geschnellt,

> *das Haar der Wälder unten wellt*
> *wie Löwenmähnen um das Lamm*
> *der weißen Stadt, ein Hahnenkamm*
> *blüht brennendrot am Straßenrand,*
> *wo früher mein Gedächtnis stand*
> *vor deines Sohnes Leiche.*
> *Wer weiß, wie weit ich weiche?*
> *Schon kenne ich die Qual nicht mehr,*
> *die mich im Föhn zum Heiland zwang –;*
> *Herr, taste dich den Dorn entlang,*
> *trink gnädig meinen Schädel leer.*
> From: *Die Bettlerschale* (Salzburg: Otto Müller, 1956), 25.

[19] Johann Strutz interprets the *Foehn* positively here, on the basis of its positive connotations in other occurrences (97), but within this poem it is associated with 'torment' (line 17), which drove the speaker to the Savior, presumably to seek relief.

[20] Strutz, 97-98.

[21] Strutz interprets the rapid rising as ecstasy, the self leaving the body, and a neo-Platonic mystical union with God (99). But if the union has already taken place, there is no reason for the pleas for an inverted communion that open and close the poem.

[22] Although Strutz acknowledges the association of the city with Christ, his original interpretation of the earth as artificial and deceptive leads him to reverse this meaning into an ironic one (98). If we see the speaker as equally ostracized from both the earth and heaven, then we do not need to speculate so much.

[23] Strutz interprets the cockscomb literally as a metonym for the rooster itself, which he interprets as a 'guard and Biblical warner' (98). The frequency of wild herbs in Lavant's poetry, and the fact that it is depicted as blossoming by the roadside, speaks for viewing this cockscomb as a plant.

[24] *"Ich will das Brot mit den Irren teilen,*
täglich ein Stück von dem großen Entsetzen
auch die Glocke im Herzen,

dort, wo die Taube nistet
und ihre winzige Zuflucht hat
in der Wildnis über den Wassern.
Lange hab ich als Stein gehaust
am Grunde der Dinge.
Aber ich habe die Glocke gehört
leise von deinem Geheimnis reden
in den fliegenden Fischen.
Ich werde fliegen und schwimmen lernen
und das Steinerne unter den Steinen lassen,
die Schwermut betten in Perlmutter,
doch den Zorn und das Elend erheben.
Meine Flügel sind älter als deine Geduld,
meine Flügel flogen dem Mut voraus,
der das Irren auf sich nahm.
Ich will das Brot mit den Irren teilen
dort in der furchtbaren Wildnis der Taube,
wo die Glocke das große Entsetzen drittelt
zum dreifachen Laut deines Namens.

From: *Spindel im Mond* (Salzburg: Otto Müller, 1959), 79.

[25] See Beda Allemann, "'Die Stadt ist oben auferbaut,'" in *Doppelinterpretationen: Das zeitgenössische deutsche Gedicht zwischen Autor und Leser*, Hilde Domin, ed., 2nd ed. (Frankfurt am Main: Fischer Taschenbuch Verlag, 1971), 111 (quoted in Strutz, 137).

[26] Strutz, 139.

[27] Strutz, 139.

[28] Strutz does see this as a 'Promethean' level of suffering that even exceeds God's suffering (140), but he nonetheless remains within his dualistic framework, saying that the tragic conflict between human love and divine love is the problem of this poem, and that the interpreter must unite these two poles. I would take the Promethean aspect of the speaker's impatience as a sign that she is in a third category, neither human nor di-

vine, but consigned to either melancholy (the passive version of her distinction) or psychosis (the active version). That these two sides correspond to the poles of bipolar illness does not give us leave to "diagnose" the speaker as bipolar, but it does provide a metaphorical model of two opposite ways of suffering that are expressions of the same basic isolation from "normal" humanity.

29 Wolfgang Nehring (1984), interpreting a poem from *Spindel im Mond*, 'He who now brings me the steely bread' (*"Der jetzt das stählerne Brot mir bringt,"* 12) says that the entire poem is a 'flaming protest against an ungodly God, the expression of a refusal to accept such a god—only not out of an outrageous overestimation of herself, but rather from an especially high conception of God' (33, my translation). While I would agree that what I have called "blasphemy" is not rooted in haughtyness, still, adhering to a holier-than-God conception of the deity seems to fall into the category of blasphemy or irreverence. What makes Lavant's rejection of the traditional conception of God and His servants so radical is her knowledge that according to the systems she knows, she is condemning herself.

30 The saint most commonly associated with the mad is St. Dymphna. See Hiltgart L. Keller, *Reclams Lexikon der Heiligen und biblischen Gestalten* (Stuttgart: Reclam, 2001), 187. There seems to be no connection with her here, however, since Lavant does not invoke any of her attributes or call her by name, and the German term for "patron saint" is used in the masculine. The saint seems to function as a sort of bureaucrat of the heavenly host who frustrates the poem's speaker and becomes the target of her wrath. Identifying him or her with an actual saint, by making it seem a specific personal attack rather than an attack in principle, would distract from this more general purpose.

31 *"Du Schutzpatron der Irren,*
ich weiß nicht, wie du heißt,

nicht welcher Schrei dich preist
und ob du auch das Klirren
des Herzsprungs noch erträgst.
Herr Helfer, du erwägst
wohl heimlich schon die Flucht
und schleichst dich unversucht
aus meinem Händeringen?
Weißt du, wie Engel singen,
wenn man das Schläfenbein
als Hammer oder Stein
benutzt, um auszubrechen
aus seiner Einzelhaft?
Kennst du die Bilderkraft
am Scheitel und das Sprechen
am Rippenknoten-Ort?
Wie weit bist du schon fort
aus meiner Fingerwiege,
du fremder Schutzpatron?
Der Mond, der Hundesohn,
verhöhnt mich, wie ich liege,
verkrümmt und angespannt,
durchfroren und verbrannt."
From: *Der Pfauenschrei* (Salzburg: Otto Müller, 1962), 10.

[32] While the pervasive image of the moon has a great variety of meanings and functions in Lavant's poetry, occasionally (as here) it seems to be associated with lunacy. Following Johann Strutz, Inge Glaser associates Lavant's moon metaphors with an endangering of the integrity of the mind or soul as the emotional and irrational element dominates them—in other words, madness (*Christine Lavant: Eine Spurensuche*, 123).

[33] Sass, 81-83.

[34] Sass, 77.

[35] Wolfgang Nehring states that there is no fundamental difference between the poems in the three collections (30).

There is more variation within the books than between them. One difference that does obtain, however, is the density of the images, which increases in the later books. Nehring cites Lavant herself to argue that this is a movement from articulated thought to suggestive image as the basis of the poems' expressiveness (30). This is more than a stylistic difference; it also reflects an increase in urgency, in desperation, which I have tried to exemplify in these three poems. Still, my remarks address more a progression in the function of the trope of madness and madmen than a fundamental progression from book to book.

[36] See Stefan Jonsson, *Subject without Nation: Robert Musil and the History of Modern Identity* (Durham, NC: Duke University Press, 2000), esp. Chapter 1, "Topographies of Inwardness: The Expressivist Paradigm of Subjectivity," 21-59.

[37] Crystal Mazur Ockenfuss, "*Mutter Wurzel Name*," *Profile einer Dichterin: Beiträge des II. Internationalen Christine-Lavant-Symposions Wolfsberg 1998*, Arno Russegger and Johann Strutz, eds. (Salzburg: Otto Müller Verlag, 1999), 108. [my translation].

[38] Schlag, "Vierfach nach unten," 137.

[39] Schlag, 137 [my translation].

[40] Christine Lavant, *Memoirs From A Madhouse*, translated by Renate Latimer, preface and afterword by Ursula Schneider and Annette Steinsiek (Riverside, CA: Ariadne Press, 2004), xx.

[41] "*Gesellschaft*" and "*Gemeinschaft*" are complementary sociological terms that have been borrowed into English, coined by the German sociologist Ferdinand Tönnies (1855-1936) in his 1887 book *Gemeinschaft und Gesellschaft*. The *Oxford English Dictionary* defines Gesellschaft as a "social relationship between individuals based on duty to society or to an organization" and Gemeinschaft as a "social relationship between individuals based on affection, kinship, or membership of a community, as within a family or group of friends." In *The Austrian*

Mind, William M. Johnston nicely summarizes the "pattern variables" within Tönnies's terms identified by the US-American sociologist Talcott Parsons (1902-1979): "According to Parsons, Gemeinschaft society is particularistic and ascriptive. Paricularistic means that local rather than universal standards prevail, while ascriptive means that a person is evaluated in terms of who he is, not what he can do. Gesellschaft society is universalistic—uniform standards govern everyone—and achievement-oriented. Not birth but performance determines status" (20).

[42] Lavant, *Memoirs From A Madhouse*, 53.

FELIX MITTERER
Courtesy of Haymon Verlag

Felix Mitterer, Attorney Of The Weak And Suffering

by Gerlinde Ulm Sanford

Felix Mitterer is one of the most important and prolific contemporary Austrian writers. He has achieved special renown with his many stage plays and also films. In all of his works he takes up issues that deserve attention, individual or social evils that should be remedied; in particular, he takes up the cause of the weak and suffering.

He was born on February 6, 1948 in Achenkirch in Tyrol as the tenth child of a peasant farmer's widow and a Rumanian fugitive and was then adopted by the Mitterers, a married couple who were farm workers. Until 1962 he lived in Kitzbühel and Kirchberg. Then, having completed primary school at the age of fourteen, he began teacher's training at the college for teachers in Innsbruck. He did not finish his degree, terminating his studies after only three years. From 1966 to 1977 he worked at the customs office in Innsbruck and began writing; his first literary production was a radio play, *"No Place for Idiots" ("Kein Platz für Idioten,"* 1970),[1] which was broadcast by the Austrian radio station ORF and later also appeared on stage. He continued with stage plays,[2] television scripts and radio plays,[3] screenplays, short stories, stories in dialect, and children's stories. Since 1977 Mitterer has been a free-lance writer and actor, and in 1995 he and his family moved to Castelions in Ireland.

His native Tyrol, its people, and their manifold fates play a dominant role in many of Mitterer's works. While many could be classified as *"Heimatdichtung"* insofar as they are set in a regional and often rural setting, Mitterer is not a *"Heimatdichter"* in any pejorative sense of the term. Tyroleans in general are very attached to their homeland, so it follows that Mitterer would explore in his writings the significance that the concept of "home" or "homeland" might have for the individual and/or society. "Homeland," *"Heimat,"* can refer to a territorial unit for which individuals, tribes, peoples, or nations subjectively and collectively feel special closeness and attachment. The idea of a "homeland" develops as a result of experiences in early childhood and youth, though adults sometimes adopt a homeland later on.[4]

Even at a cursory glance, the titles of Mitterer's works point to the importance the term "homeland" holds for him. Titles such as 'Lost Homeland' (*"Verlorene Heimat"*) and 'Sold Homeland' (*"Verkaufte Heimat"*) are proof of that. Other titles, such as *"No Place for Idiots,"* 'Blessing of the Earth' (*"Erdsegen"*), *"Home" ("Heim")*, and *"There's Not a Finer Country" ("Kein schöner Land"*) arouse associations belonging to the concept of homeland. Yet more than that, one could maintain that most of Mitterer's works are, in one way or another, variations on the topic of "homeland."[5] At the same time, however, in plays and also in his video broadcasts he avoids portraying folkloric clichés that might have an inherited defect because of their function during the Nazi-times.[6] In the play 'Lost Homeland,' Mitterer illustrates how Protestant farmers from the Ziller valley had to leave their homeland because the Catholic power structure made it impossible for them to confess their creed. The begging and vagabonding children in the play *"Children of The Devil" ("Die Kinder des Teufels"*) are a nuisance to the Church authorities as their homelessness renders them difficult or impossible to control. The same is true for the old man in the monologue play *"Siberia":* The young family considers him a nuisance, and he is therefore transferred into a "home" which, however, is not at all a home in the true sense of the word.

The play *"The Wild Woman"* (*"Die Wilde Frau"*), for example, touches on the "homeland" theme. The conflict among the lumberjacks is based at least partially upon the different degrees of their attachment to a "home." Jock has a house and a family; Mutt likewise considers himself a farmer who always enjoys the time when he can go home (*"hoam"*). Lex on the other hand says: "At home! To hell with that! The only kind of luck I've had at home was bad luck![7] He is only a smallholder, a "*Kloanhäusler*," who had to spend time in prison because he had been caught poaching. Elias and Wendl, too, can be considered homeless in one sense: Elias, since he is old and has remained a farm hand all his life, because he has not been able to acquire a family or a true home; Wendl, since he has no real parental home and—like Elias—will most likely always remain a poor farm hand at his master's beck and call. The Wild Woman herself is an outsider, not only because of her mystical traits, but also in several realistic aspects:[8] she cannot or will not speak the language of the lumberjacks. Mutt suspects that she is "*welsch*," a term that implies in this context that she comes from Italy.[9] She does not come from a specific place, she comes out of the darkness and in the end disappears again into the darkness. Furthermore, being one woman among five men, she is an outsider in that respect. Homeless in different degrees and ways, no reconciliation is achieved between the lumberjacks: Elias dies from old age. Jock and Mutt lose their lives in a gruesome brawl with Lex who also is mortally wounded. Lex' last desperate words are: "You win! You've killed us all! Damned whore! Damned whore!"[10] In the end, Wendl remains behind, more homeless than ever; the Wild Woman disappears into the snowy night.

In the play *"There's Not a Finer Country*,"[11] the village tries to force the livestock dealer Stefan Adler—up to then highly esteemed—to leave his Tyrolean home village because his proof of ancestry shows that he is a Jew. After initial resistance, Adler accepts his newly discovered racial identity, although he had even become a member of the Nazi Party prior to the discovery. He is, however, not willing to leave his homeland and finally perishes under the pressure of the Nazis. In order to rescue their son and daughter from this conflict, Adler's wife claims that the children have Arian fathers. Adler himself is finally imprisoned in a concentration camp where he is shot by his own son, an SS-officer, who then shoots himself. The conflict between attachment to home and family on the one hand, and political machinery on the other, has brought both father and son to ruin. Adler's wife and daughter survive the Nazi-times and remain in their homeland, albeit with broken hearts. The mayor in this play, however, is portrayed as a low-minded bastard; he holds on to the office of mayor in his home village by changing direction like a weather vane: initially he is against the Nazis, then for the Nazis, and in the end advocates forgetting the past and building up the future Austria.

The theme of homelessness is also apparent in the play entitled "*Munde*," the name of a mountain. Four roofers and a secretary make a tour to the top of Munde mountain. In the course of their journey, latent conflicts come to the surface. Two of the characters can be considered as having been displaced from their home. The Turkish worker Memet had to give up his original homeland, because poverty has made the existence of his family impossible there. He has tried in vain to find a new home together with his family in Tyrol. In order to prevent his wife from being sexually abused by his boss, he has to send his family back to Turkey; he does not want them to be destroyed as well. He has tried so very hard to adjust to the new land that he almost has become a stranger to himself. Yet all of these attempts to find a new home in this new country have been in vain. After his master Willi, whom he adored, has hurled himself off the mountain face in the dark, his grief breaks out in broken Tyrolean dialect:

'I have had it with Europe, I tell you! You ruin us! I denied my religion, so that I might please you! So that I am not so strange to you! I drank beer and told my wife that she should put on a short skirt and do away with the scarf! All for nothing! All for nothing! When she said that she wanted to take on a job, I knew, Memet, now you have to be careful! She wanted to take on a cleaning job at the boss's house! The boss would have taken her! Yes, the boss would have liked her! No way! No way! I'm already ruined enough, you mustn't be ruined also, I said! I am already a stranger to myself, do you understand that? I do not recognize myself anymore! Then she said that she could not stand it anymore in the apartment, that she is always alone and has to think of our old homeland all the time! That she would prefer to go home! OK, I said, then you go home! You and the children go home! And I work, and I work, and I save what I can, and then I go home again also, home where the sun shines, where everyone opens his heart and his house, and where one can enter everywhere and where one is welcome everywhere!'[12]

Just like Memet, the master Willi is pushed into an outsider position too. His work on the roof and the shaping of sheet metals are his life and his home. When his new boss's greed for profit and power makes it impossible for Willi to be proud of his work, Willi begins to drink. During a mountain tour, the young and ambitious Gerhard surprises Willi with the news that Willi will be dismissed from his post as master. This brings Willi's world to collapse. He hardly speaks anymore; instead he drinks again and again from his brandy, listens with sad empathy to Memet's vain attempts to acquire a new home, and finally walks off into the dark in the direction of the mountain face. Loss of his beloved profession, which had—in a sense—been his home, drives him to commit suicide. Memet, having been devoted to Willi as to a father, is shaken. He knows, however, that Willi has now finally found a secure home. The play ends with Memet exclaiming: 'So long, master! You are safely kept in Abraham's lap.'[13]

In *"Abraham,"* a young man loses his homeland because of his homosexuality and the resulting consequences. In this play, the love for family and homeland conflicts with the protagonist's sexual preference, which is unacceptable for the family and also for the rural area. It is the love of a homosexual partner that is unacceptable. In the play *"There's Not a Finer Country,"* Anna's love of the mayor's son Erich would likewise be unacceptable if Anna's mother had not lied by maintaining that her children were fathered by Arian men, rather than by her Jewish husband; Anna as daughter of a Jew would not have been acceptable as daughter-in-law of the mayor.

In *"Home"* (*"Heim,"* 1987),[14] Mike has decided to leave his hometown, because his youthful acts of rebellion are strictly repressed by his family. He is regarded as inconsiderate because he acquires a hairdo with colors, because he spends nights in the city when he is only sixteen, etc. He does not adjust to the world of grownups because this world is hardly suitable to further youthful ideals. Mike has found out that behind the outward order and decency of this grown-up world, immorality and deceitfulness are often lurking. Therefore he has become a runaway. Still, he does not feel at home in the world of drug addicts either. He is a runaway, yet one who would like to go back home, as Mitterer puts it in his index of characters. Mike is in search of a home or a homeland where he can feel at home outwardly and also inwardly.

Mitterer shows that home or the homeland can pressure an individual too much toward adjustment. Such pressure leads either to the loss of individual character and moral principles or to leaving the home. Mike ran away, yet he tries to return home in order to arrive, perhaps, at a compromise between individual freedom and pressure from traditional home conventions. The attempt fails, because everything that Mike did not like before turns out to have gotten even worse. The most drastic example is Nina's rape by Ossi, who, toward the outside world, is the highly respected branch manager of the local supermarket.

Mike says to his father: 'I really wanted to come back home. Someday.—But now everything is worse than before.'[15] Then he leaves his home for a second and most likely final time. His father remains behind with a broken heart, and recognizes: 'I've made a mess of everything! Everything!'[16]

As previously indicated, Mitterer's plays demonstrate time and again that the individual often either has to suppress his/her "otherness" within the familiar homeland or has to suppress his/her "remaining the same" within a changing homeland, or else becomes an outsider who must leave the homeland or perish under the pressure of society in the homeland. Richard B. Reich concludes that Mitterer is a *"Heimsucher."*[17] The German expression *"Heimsucher"* implies on the one hand someone who indeed "seeks a home" – in that sense, Mitterer repeatedly portrays characters who seek a home, a homeland, a place of security. Yet at the same time *"Heimsucher"* may also mean someone who "inflicts some kind of plague." Mitterer himself can be considered a *"Heimsucher"* in the latter sense. He frequently criticizes a concept of homeland that is too much associated with "blood and soil" (*"Blut und Boden"*) and that leads to prejudice against anything or anyone foreign and thus "different."

Martin Walser has demanded that a grown-up society shape its state such that it can be a home for everyone.[18] Mitterer shows again and again that we are still far away from turning this ideal into reality, that our society is intolerant towards outsiders of various kinds. There are signs of improvement, but overall, we are still not near the goal. In almost all of Mitterer's plays there are examples of human beings whose concept of home or homeland is not based on "blood and soil" principles, but whose true home is humanity as such. In most cases, however, these individuals cannot survive in the long run.

The right to seek, to have, and to defend a homeland is one of the basic human rights. If the human being becomes expelled from his homeland, it can happen that he or she perishes. In Mitterer's works the loss of the homeland is mostly caused by a combination of failure on the side of the one who is being expelled, and of coldness or lack of understanding on the side of the environment that tries to get rid of an individual because he or she does not fit any more, for various reasons, the homeland image of his environment. A striking example is the death of the old man in *"Siberia."* The old man "fails" because he can no longer adjust. His environment, his home(land) changes every day, for the better, but also for the worse. He becomes more and more an outsider who cannot adjust anymore because of various weaknesses related to old age, but also because, for philosophical reasons, he does not want to adjust. Within the world of the young family, he is perceived as tiresome and out of place. The young ones do not react with lenience, but rather with harshness or at any rate with lack of understanding. Thus the old man is shoved off into an old-age home, a home that is exactly not a home, but instead only a place where he can barely exist, a place where more and more he loses everything that used to be familiar, a place where his living space becomes more and more restricted. Finally he dies, with nothing left except memories of his former life.

One might observe two trends in recent years in respect to the concept of home and homeland: on the one hand there has been an increased interest in the study of local history, geography, tradition, provenance, etc.; on the other hand, however, criticism of political, economic, and social conditions within the homeland that often lead to losing the home(land). Mitterer's works mirror these trends. He writes primarily serious plays dealing with problems of the present day or else with problems of past times that still remain relevant for us. (Nonetheless, there are numerous comic elements in his plays, as Mitterer is well aware of the important role comic relief holds for stage-effectiveness.) He takes up explosive topics and treats them in his stage-effective plays unsparingly and with an open mind; for example, he demonstrates that nonconformists or outsiders of various types have a hard road in a society that prides itself on its tolerance, yet on closer inspection turns out to be anything but tolerant. Mitterer criticizes bigotry, conformism, and fanatic patriotism, as shown in such works as *"Stigma," "Children of the Devil,"* and *"There's Not a Finer Country,"* while defending the handicapped in *"No Place For Idiots,"* the elderly in *"Siberia,"* guest-workers (*"Gastarbeiter"*) in *"Munde,"* and juvenile runaways in *"Home,"* to name just a few of the most prominent examples.

Many, perhaps most of Mitterer's plays came into existence because someone who had heard of him approached him and suggested that he might be interested in taking up this or that pressing issue, this or that tragedy that had occurred. Friends as well as complete strangers have sent him newspaper articles or other documentation in order to convince him of a worthy topic. For example, in 1987 the director of the Munich 'Theater for Youth' (*"Theater der Jugend"*) made Mitterer aware of a topic for a possible play: he told Mitterer of a witch trial against children and youngsters that had taken place in Salzburg in the years from 1675 to 1681. It was an extended and extremely bloody trial. In the center of it was a young man called Jakob Koller, nicknamed 'Jackie the Sorcerer' (*"Zauberer-Jackl"*), who was accused of seducing youngsters to satanic practices. Koller was hunted all over Central Europe, yet despite a significant reward he was never apprehended. Instead, many hundreds of children and teenagers who roamed the countryside as beggars were incarcerated; under torture, they produced the most horrible confessions, and 133 of them were condemned to be burned at the stake. These murdered youngsters were soon forgotten, yet

Koller is still a well-known character in the Salzburg area and figures in many legends.

Mitterer's interest was immediately aroused. He, too, had been neglected as a boy and would probably have also been apprehended and burned at the stake had he lived in those dark times. He then set out to write a play around the topic of those mistreated children. His play, *"Children of the Devil*,"[19] however, is not a play adjusted to the sensibilities of a 'Theater for Youth'—instead, Mitterer attempted to write the story the way it happened, with all its attendant horror and suffering. Mitterer ends his introduction to the book edition by assuring his readers that all confessions of the accused are authentic and can be verified at archives in Munich and Salzburg; he also points to the relevance of this topic by remarking that nowadays begging children are still disposed of in cruel ways in several major Latin American cities.

Mitterer's play consists of a series of interrogations and tortures of children and teenagers and of arguments between the Commissioner, the Scribe, and an Executioner who, together with his two Henchmen, performs the tortures. The first scene of the play does not consist of any action or actors; instead, to achieve an alienation effect, a sign indicates an ominous event: "Barbara Koller is burned at the stake."[20] The 21st and final scene is a repeat of the first, except for the name change in the title: "Magdalena Pichler burns at the stake."[21] Perhaps the spectator was less touched by the burning of Barbara Koller at the outset, not knowing who Barbara Koller was. However, after having seen and heard Magdalena Pichler's cruel interrogation and torture and knowing that she, like many other hapless youth, is helpless and completely innocent, the spectator cannot help but be extremely moved by Magdalena's merciless end at the stake.

In the course of the play, children, ages six to fourteen, and a young man of eighteen are interrogated, as well as the abovementioned Magdalena Pichler, who is seventeen years old; all are questioned about their connections to 'Jackie the Sorcerer.' Under current law of the day, children over the age of ten could be subjected to torture. However, under torture or immediately after their ordeal, children will say just about anything, including the most terrible and disgusting things, as long as they believe that such statements might favorably affect their fate. Their answers are contradictory and contain strange details caused by various circumstances. Some children are overcome by fear, others enjoy being the center of attention and relish fabricating fantastic stories, while each hopes to derive some advantage from his or her narrative.

One of these children is a fourteen-year-old cripple named Veit. He demonstrates rather negative character traits in that he betrays other children or fabricates lies about them in his testimonies, which in some cases leads to a child's later doom. Yet Mitterer is nonetheless able to arouse our pity for him, as Veit, too, is a neglected child who was constantly maltreated. His slandering other children is but an anxious attempt to achieve a better life for himself at the trial's end, though ultimately his only reward is not the coveted "better life," but merely the favor that "you will…not be burned despite your horrible crimes—you will be strangled to death beforehand."[22]

Born in Tyrol, Mitterer grew up in an environment and a society strongly influenced by the structures, institutions, and thoughts of the Catholic Church. Without adhering to a specific religious confession, Mitterer is nonetheless a deeply pious man insofar as he believes that the Creation, and in particular the fate of a human being, is guided by a benevolent power. Through his authoring for his stage plays a number of deeply religious country characters, Mitterer reveals a deep respect for the religiousness of the country folks as he might encounter them in rural Austria. This not withstanding, he criticizes the misuse of power by the church, e.g. in *"Stigma"* or in *"Children of the Devil,"* and he defends the right of religious freedom in particular in 'Lost Homeland' and *"There's Not a Finer Country."*

'Discord in the House of God' (*"Krach im Hause Gott"*)[23] is a rather important and successful, albeit controversial play, in which Mitterer examines the Bible and in particular the *New Testament* for antifeminist traits. However, this essay shall not deal with it in great detail. Instead, the reader is referred to my article on this play.[24] Here, as in many of his plays, Mitterer espouses women's rights and women's equal status in society. He speaks up for women and often shows the unfair conditions to which, even today, they are at times submitted. The female character in the one-act play *"Jailbird"* from *"Visiting Hours"* (*"Besuchszeit"*), for example, does not even have a name, but is called only *She* to indicate the stereotypical and impersonal patterns of communication that dominate relationships between man and woman. Mitterer's interest in women's rights and his high esteem for women in general are, moreover, demonstrated by his portraying several female characters as superior to man: e.g., the Hind (*Hirschkuh*) in *"Dragonthirst"* (*"Drachendurst,"* 1986), the title character of *"The Wild Woman,"* or the Mother of God (*Muttergottes*) from 'Discord in the House of God.'

Despite Mitterer's efforts to render the delicate topic of criticizing certain aspects of Christian religion acceptable through humorous and ironical treatment, 'Discord in the House of God' has been received with mixed reactions and has caused substantial protest.[25] According to Robert Mitscha-Eibl, Mitterer was even officially charged with mockery of religion.[26] Such debate because of Mitterer's treatment of religious topics had also been caused by earlier plays, for instance his *"Children of the Devil," "Stigma,"* or *"Abraham."* In order to stimulate discussion, Mitterer seems to favor provocation. 'Discord in the House of God' represents Mitterer's theological reflections in the shape of a stage play. The idea that woman or the feminine stood at the very beginning of our universe and that the Christian religion does not reflect that idea appropriately is most fascinating and appropriate for our times.

Depending on the epoch, old age and aging play an important role in all literary genres. Felix Mitterer creates many examples that show the tragic fate of aging human beings. However, being a very optimistic and constructive writer, Mitterer also portrays types of older human beings who might fall into negative categories, but who, despite increasing inner and outer alienation, nonetheless are able to surmount, at least for some time, these categories by overcoming their physical deficiencies, by maintaining a confident attitude toward life, and by influencing their environment in an accordingly positive fashion. In the following, a series of examples demonstrates which characteristics Mitterer attributes in his work to old and aging figures.

Especially often he shows them as outsiders of society, e.g., in his plays *"No Place For Idiots"*; *"Visiting Hours"* contains one-act plays, three of which deal with the topic of old age, namely *"Shunted into a Siding"* (*"Abstellgleis"*), 'One Understands Nothing' (*"Man versteht nichts"*), and *"Wheat on The Autobahn"* (*"Weizen auf der Autobahn"*);[27] *"The Wild Woman"*; 'Lost Homeland'; *"Siberia,"* and *"Munde."* Likewise some of Mitterer's short stories take up aging, e.g., 'Inventory' ("*Inventur*"), 'Konrad, or The Condition of the Führer Has Not Worsened—On The Contrary' ("*Konrad oder Das Befinden des Führers hat sich nicht verschlechtert—im Gegenteil*"), 'The Burglar' ("*Der Einbrecher*"), 'Seppei Is Talking to His Old Man' ("*Der Seppei redt mit sein Votta*"), or the audio plays 'The Language Test' ("*Der Sprachtest*"), 'The Protocol' ("*Das Protokoll*"), and finally the TV series 'Sold Homeland' (*"Verkaufte Heimat"*), and 'The Piefke Saga' (*"Die Piefke Saga"*).

Among the elderly portrayed by Mitterer are old men who lose their position in modern society because they resist so-called progress, or because their physical strength diminishes and they can no longer achieve as much as in younger years, or because they have become a burden to the younger generation instead of being useful to them. Old people are fired, for example, in 'One Understands Nothing' or in *"Munde"*; or they are shoved into an old-age home, as in *"Shunted into a Siding"* and in *"Siberia."*

In the play *"No Place for Idiots,"*[28] the old farm hand Plattl-Hans is the only one who shows understanding and also love for the mentally retarded youngster Mandl. A wonderful pedagogic relationship develops between them that is as beneficial for the old farmhand as it is for the boy. Plattl-Hans is the only one who tries to teach the boy. Mandl in turn is very grateful for that, calls the farm hand "father" (*Dati*), and makes astonishing progress in his development. But when Plattl-Hans in his friendliness takes Mandl along to the village inn, the innkeeper who also holds the office of mayor fears to lose business from tourists because of Mandl's embarrassing presence in the inn. A comically tragic incident has as consequence that Mandl is considered being sexually aggressive and dangerous. The old farm hand defends him to be sure and explains the harmlessness of the incident. In the end, however, the pressure on the authorities, influenced by the greedy innkeeper/mayor who is anxious to attract tourists, prevails: Mandl is taken out of the farm hand's loving care and is transferred into an insane asylum.

With this play, Mitterer sets a touching example how an old farmhand finds a new meaning of life by devoting love and care to a handicapped child. Because of his age, he himself is only an outsider in the rough world of farmers, and thus assumes the care for an "idiotic" child that is considered merely a troublesome nuisance even by his own mother—not because the mother is a bad person, but simply because in the tough, everyday life on a farm there is "no place for idiots." The advantageous pedagogical relationship between Plattl-Hans and the retarded child can be compared to that between grandfather and grand-child. The relationship between Mandl and his parents is especially strained since the parents feel cheated out of an heir who in the future would be able to take over the farm. Mandl, on the other hand, feels despised by the father and hated by the mother and, out of fear, acts especially "idiotic" in front of them, while in the presence of Plattl-Hans he feels at ease and confident, and his condition improves. In the course of the play, Mitterer shows how this advantageous relationship between the young and the old outsider is destroyed by society, and that not because of pressing needs, but merely out of greed for financial gain and because of prejudice against the "being different" of the "idiot" Mandl.

Felix Mitterer himself played the role of the idiot in this play two-hundred-and-fifty times. As he remarked in an interview, he completely identified with this role and also with other characters of outsiders as he continued to portray them:

> 'I can identify so well with children, as for example those who are looked upon as idiots, or also old people. And... after having played these roles in the theater, I have felt very strongly that indeed I am all these people myself. That I am the child and the idiot and the old man.'[29]

In the short story "Rebuilding" ("*Der Umbau*"),[30] conflict arises between an old farmer, already somewhat hard of hearing, and his son, greedy for profit. The son leases out meadows and fields, the livestock is sold, and the old stable is torn down. The farm is transformed into a modern hotel, including dancing establishment and bar. The environment the old farmer is accustomed to disappears more and more, and he himself is marginalized more and more. Perhaps already a little senile, he does not understand what is going on, especially so because the son hardly takes time anymore to talk to his father and, instead, prefers to ride around in his Mercedes—which he bought for seventy trees.[31] When the old father finally realizes that the rebuilding has more or less completely destroyed his farm, it is already too late. Horrified and furious, he attacks his son in public with his walking stick. This, however, has only as a consequence that he is not taken seriously anymore and therefore is removed to an old-age home. However, he is spared this last shock because, when even his pipe is taken away from him, he dies, forsaken by all and in despair. His son then arranges a pompous funeral and uses the father for advertising his enterprise by showing him on a colorful flyer posing in front of the farmhouse that had been rebuilt into a hotel. Thus Mitterer demonstrates how the old man and his old values are first mercilessly repressed and destroyed and then hypocritically idealized for profit's sake. At the funeral, the son says in his crude dialect:

> 'At least we still have a small souvenir of you. The new advertising flyer shows you on the front page in multicolor print. You stand there in front of the hotel that once was a farmhouse and you look so surprised. What a beautiful souvenir! Godspeed, father.'[32]

The lumberjack Elias in the play *"The Wild Woman"* is seventy. Mitterer portrays him with sensitivity and sympathy. Elias often uses rhymes or proverbs when he speaks, which makes for an amiable but also almost comical impression. The message of his remarks is often quite blunt and coarse, albeit somewhat softened by the rhymes. Despite his profession, Elias is a relatively gentle character, and he knows, perhaps because of his age, that one cannot force anything when it concerns love. When it becomes his turn to sleep with the strange woman, he is worried because he has not washed himself since Easter. Yet he then fortifies his courage by drinking and sings affectionate rhymes that translate as follows: "The girl is lovely, now she would like to find a male pigeon, I'd know one for her, a little lovely one."[33] Before he then climbs into the sleeping niche of the woman, he starts reminiscing, an act typical for old age:

> Oh, God, when was it, when was the last time?
> Let me see. Way back then, at the church fair.
> The maid from... aw, can't remember anymore.
> Oh, she was so soft and warm and wet! It's

probably been thirty-five years now! Thirty-five years! Yeah, the good old days! Back then I had all I wanted! On all the high holy days I used to have my little sweets! *(sings)* That I've never fallen down, / I thank God for that! / But I've stumbled quite a lot / Over the Sixth Commandment! After a while your pecker just falls asleep, eh? Just like the monks who pee in their habits. If they don't have a horny housekeeper... *(looks over to the hutch)*. But lately the sap has been rising in the old tree trunk, something's stirring again! Who'd'a thought it! *(Sings:)* Why shouldn't I love a sweet little girl, / The birds do it all the time, / Till the tree branches curl![34]

Then he places a piece of resin in his mouth to freshen his breath, and climbs into the woman's bed.

Quite differently from the other lumberjacks, Mutt, Jock, and most of all Lex—old Elias never violates the woman. In the night before the morning when he dies, it is again his turn to sleep with the woman. When she makes him understand that today she is not ready for copulation, Elias does not react with a coarse: "Com'ere, whore!" as Mutt had just done in the preceding scene. Instead, Elias reacts with the following understanding words to her rejection:

If you don't want, woman, then we can forget about it. We don't have to. Not at all. It's really a treat just for me to be able to lie next to you. You're so warm, woman. So toasty warm! When I'm lyin' next to you, my old bones don't hurt anymore, and I feel like a child, lyin' next to his mother. Never would've thought I'd feel this way again. I'm grateful to you for that, woman....[35]

Old age was perhaps the cause for Elias' becoming more serene and gentle. This is how things should be. Every old human being probably wishes for an easy departure from life. Not everyone, though, is granted this wish, as Mitterer also demonstrates in his works. The example of Elias shows that death can almost be beautiful. On the morning after their lovemaking, Elias lies in bed while the woman, sitting fully dressed next to him on the edge of the bed, is holding his hand. Elias is dying, and he knows it. Nonetheless he keeps up his good humor and produces funny proverbs. Only at the very end does he become serious and ask the other lumberjacks to set the woman free so that matters would not turn into a catastrophe.

"*Shunted into a Siding*" ("*Abstellgleis*") depicts the life conditions of an official in a nursing home. His daughter-in-law has just come for a hasty visit. The old man demonstrates characteristics in the conversation that are typical for an old person. He is bitter, his movements are clumsy, he is tiresome, and almost vicious. Thus he is neither often visited in the home, nor is it a pleasure for anyone to visit him. Hardly ever is it the son who visits him because he has more pressing things to do, for example he "had to fix something on the car;"[36] instead, if anyone at all, it is the daughter-in-law who visits him.

The crown out of gold foil presented to him as a gift by his little granddaughter has a double function. When the old man puts it on it symbolizes very fittingly a fool's crown, as he is treated more or less like a half-witted fool in the home. He is completely deprived of any power. When the aides keep repeating: "Eat up nicely, Grandpa, or you won't get any stewed fruit,"[37] even though he does not even like compote, then this is symptomatic for him being regarded as fool or perhaps as child who needs to be persuaded. Shortly before the end of this one-act play, the old man again puts down his crown, thus perhaps pointing to the second function of the crown, that is, to indicate that the human being in such a nursing home is no longer the crown of Creation, but instead is here bereft of any individuality and dignity. This is illustrated through further 'funny' manners of speaking, such as when the aides say: "So, Grandpa, we're going to eat nicely now, no spluttering, all right? So, Grandpa, now we're going to lie down."[38]

At the end, the old man finds out that his beloved dog Haika was put to sleep. The explanation is: "She was old... half blind. She wouldn't eat anymore. She just stayed put in your old room and whimpered, all the time. And hair all over everything!"[39] One is permitted to put an old dog to sleep; an old human being one can merely shove aside into a nursing home. True, euthanasia—as the old man maliciously remarks to a former Nazi—is out of the question for our times. However, it should give us pause for thought that the existence of an old man in a home as portrayed in this play is hardly more humane.

Old age is also the topic of the dramatic monologue *Siberia*.[40] Curiously enough, the play seems to anticipate some of the nursing scandals as they were discovered later in a senior citizen home in Lainz near Vienna. This inner monologue of a male inmate falls into two parts: the imagined visit with dialogue between father and son, and the imagined visit with dialogue between the old man and the "*Bundespräsident*." —In five act-like sections we learn how the world of the sick old man becomes increasingly restricted and more and more shows characteristics of a prison; the nursing home takes on the traits of a penal camp in Siberia.

The old man in this play resists dying as long as possible. But finally he has to give in. He is sad about having to die, but even sadder about having been condemned to die such a slow and undignified death. In his fantasies he experiences the visit of the President and his wife; when they finally come to the nursing home, he informs them of the pitiful conditions there and asks for their help:

> You know, Mr. President,
> Madame,
> I used to sing every day

> to keep
> my body from shrinking.
> But now I have to admit
> the battle's over.
>
> It's not death,
> but the long, drawn-out process of dying
> that frightens me.
> Dying like this,
> here,
> and now.[41]

Old people, foreigners, minorities can be considered by normal society as "outsiders." In the play *Abraham*[42] Mitterer takes up the "problem" of homosexuality, yet also the topic of "aging," and "old age" plays a significant role. Old age is the time when many people begin to give serious thought to the inevitability of death. However, there are cases when a young individual becomes prematurely "old" so-to-speak by contemplating death. Mitterer portrays striking examples of such premature aging in characters afflicted by AIDS, among them Peter in *Abraham*.

According to reports in the media, homosexuality nowadays may be gradually losing its problematic aspects. One is persuaded to believe that love, respectively sex, between adults may someday be acceptable in all its variants. Mitterer, however, shows us, that in reality such tolerance is still sorely lacking, especially in small towns and villages, in country inns, and in sermons at country churches.

Max is a widowed contractor in a village. His son, Peter, is an architect in the city and single—soon the entire village learns that Peter is gay. Peter has to learn in the course of this play that his kind of love is not permitted in his homeland, that a man must not love men, that it is not permitted to have a friend who is more than just a friend, namely a partner in life and a lover. Peter is pushed into the tragic situation of being an outsider. As for the father, now sixty years old, he is not able to accept his son's homosexuality for several reasons: people in rural settings are, in general, more tied to traditions; the father has counted on his grandchildren to carry on his contracting firm; the father demonstrates the rigidity so typical for old age. Max does attempt to forgive his son, yet his forgiveness is tied to Peter's turning away from his lover George, or at least to Peter's behaving so that, at the very least, the appearance of normality can be preserved.

The threat of death gains power with increasing age; to a certain degree aging can be seen as a preparation for death. In *Abraham*, we become acquainted with a number of young people who suffer from AIDS. A young person seeing him- or herself suddenly confronted with death can try to ignore the situation, can rebel against it, or can become serene in a way similar to some old people fully aware of their impending demise. Judy, Charly, and also George, afflicted by AIDS, cling to life until the very end and seem to become more serene or wise only to a limited extent. George undergoes some kind of reformation insofar as he assures his lover Peter in the scene at the AIDS-station that he has discontinued intimate relations with Werner. Furthermore, George's thus purified love is indicated in Peter's dream (scene 9). Likewise one may interpret Peter's and also George's friendliness toward Judy as a form of increased serenity.

Peter, however, is the character who most clearly demonstrates a development toward serenity and wisdom. He recognizes his "guilt," even though homosexuality as such cannot be considered to be wrong in our modern times. Peter feels guilty nonetheless, as he had expected something impossible from his father, namely understanding and support for a lifestyle that his father could not accept because of his age, his education, and his ties to his traditional past. That his father was not able to live up to his son's expectations is certainly a weakness of the father. However, that Peter is in the end able to realize that he had expected too much of his father shows Peter's growing humanity, shows leniency and serenity as they are normally only to be found in an older person, and even then only in ideal cases. When his father implores him to get out of his sight, Peter apologizes and fulfills the father's request, even though he desires nothing more than to be with his father. In the last scene at the garbage dump, Mitterer assigns Peter the role of a kind of saint, as both the corrupt Erich and the weak pastor confess their offences to a dying Peter and ask him to forgive them.

Through his homosexual love and the illness resulting from it, Peter becomes a tragic outsider and already during his youth suffers loneliness and death, normally the fate of old people. Peter loses first his homeland and is then driven to the aggressively gay scene in the city. Drug addicts, types in hip leather outfits, male streetwalkers come into his life. At home, the desperate father, Max, tries to cure Peter of his homosexual preferences by procuring a whore who is to bring his son back onto the "right" path.

The father, on the other hand, shows his old age with his inflexibility and his lack of understanding. He finally ends up marrying a Philippine girl—considerably younger than he and ordered through a catalogue. One might interpret this positively as sign of vitality; interpreted negatively, it would mean that Max applies a different standard to himself than to his son. It is certainly as unusual to order a young girl from a mail catalog as it is to maintain a homosexual relationship. Moreover, Max's marrying such a young girl might be seen as a futile attempt to ignore the beginning of old age.

Only the village vicar—at 60, Max's contemporary and thus also at the threshold of old age and at the outset as inflexible as the father—overcomes his limitations after a long period of silence and exhibits Christian charity and brotherly love toward Peter; critically ill, Peter is being protected and somewhat comforted by the vicar. Peter, now living at a garbage dump, has been betrayed and expelled by his homeland. In the final scene, his father does forgive and embrace him. Yet Peter cannot be helped anymore. At the end of the play, Max sacrifices his son as Abraham did: the father shoots the son, thus releasing him from his pain, yet also releasing himself from a problem that he was not able to overcome. Peter is the victim of prejudice, injustice, intolerance, and a misinterpreted Christian lifestyle.

Mitterer's plays abound with characters that fall into the category "the aged." From his play *"There's Not a Finer Country,"* three elderly characters attract our attention: Rosa, 70 years old, the parish priest's sister and housekeeper; the priest himself, Franz Gruber, 60 years old; and the cattle-dealer Stefan Adler, 55 years old. The play is set in the time period from 1933 to 1945, thus stretches over twelve years—one might assume that the ages of the characters as indicated in the cast of characters refer to their ages in 1933 and that by the end of the play, in 1945, the characters are twelve years older, thus even more distinctly falling into the category of "old age."

The fate of the livestock dealer Stefan Adler stands in the center of the play's action. In the beginning, Adler, as many others in the village, sympathizes with the Nazis. However, when his proof of ancestry is established, he finds out that he is a Jew; in the course of the play he has to come to terms with that.[43]

Rosa is a most interesting character not only because she is the oldest of all, but also because she is female. She demonstrates a tendency towards exaggeration, as perhaps is the case with many older women whose lives lack interesting experiences. When young Nazi-sympathizers damage a window with flower pots at the vicarage, she reports with excitement: "They blew me to bits! The Antichrists!"[44] In the second scene, Rosa is horrified because two members of the Hitler Youth have torn the Christ-figure from a wayside cross and smashed it to pieces. Rosa reacts courageously and dares to express her revulsion about this unworthy prank in front of the head teacher Hopfgartner who is also the local Nazi branch leader: "God will punish you, you Nazi pigs! Just wait!" When Hopfgartner then calls her "an old bitch" and threatens her with deportation, she answers: "Yeah, do you think I'm afraid of you, you old windbag of a teacher?"[45] She appears even braver in the 9th scene by advising Maria to poison that fanatic Nazi: "You have to poison somebody like that! The Lord God understands that!"[46] In addition, she beats up one of the Gestapo men who take away her brother, the parish priest. Her resistance, however, is futile.

At the beginning of the play, the priest is a Nazi-sympathizer who even stirs up hatred against Jews; later, however, he recognizes the criminal development of the Nazi movement and cautiously attempts to distance himself. Finally, a sermon in which he criticizes the cruel practices of the Nazis leads to his arrest. The priest takes a very pragmatic standpoint towards Stefan Adler: since Adler as an individual can achieve nothing against the Nazis, the pastor advises him to flee, though Adler refuses.

By the end of the play, the pastor visits Stefan Adler to ask for his pardon. He feels guilty because he has contributed to Adler's ruin by having supported the Nazis in the beginning and also by always having said malicious things against Jews. Upon hearing this apology, however, Adler begins to laugh sarcastically: 'So did I! So did I, pastor. I, too, was an anti-Semite! Can you imagine that? (*His laughter suddenly breaks off; very gravely:*) I shall be cursed![47]

In his introduction, Mitterer writes:
'Thus this is a story about opportunism, cowardice, mass society, egotism, and political blindness. The victims are the 'others.' These 'others' constitute a continuous theme of my literary work. A great part of mankind lives in constant fear of the 'others,' harbors constant aggressions against them, no matter what kind of otherness they represent (indeed it begins per-

fectly harmless): different hairdo, different dress, different behavior, different likes, different views, different language, different skin color, different religion, different customs and traditions. Thus even the most absurd happens, namely that in a total reversal a fellow citizen, hitherto popular, respected and meritorious, is suddenly branded as a scoundrel and a national pest, and is finally murdered, because it turns out that he is a Jew.'[48]

Many of Mitterer's older characters uphold moral values that have gotten lost in modern times; this also contributes to their becoming outsiders in our society. The feeling of loneliness—which so often accompanies other symptoms of aging—is not so much caused by physical isolation through the decreasing number of contemporaries; instead, the feeling of loneliness is mostly caused by an inner estrangement that very often comes unavoidably with aging. Mitterer attempts to use his plays to create an easing of the generational conflict, thereby depicting many older figures in ways that encourage us to feel compassion for them and thus take part in their fate.

Aging can also be considered a path to otherness. Becoming other is at the same time also a becoming estranged, as Jean Améry and others point out. Human beings see themselves differently from the way they saw themselves during their youth. Furthermore, their fellow human beings see them differently from the way they saw them during their youth. Not only young people see them differently, but also old people see that they have become old, whereas they might tend to overlook their own aging. At the same time, aging human beings develop a certain rigidity by trying to hold on to existing conditions, while in reality the world is constantly changing and evolving. The result is a growing discrepancy between the formerly habitual cultural surroundings and those that newly develop. This also contributes to becoming "different" and estranged.

In Mitterer's works, we find numerous old and aging women, yet they are most often assigned minor roles. However, the play *"Die Frau im Auto"* ('The Woman in the Car')[49] features an old woman in the leading role. In this play, Mitterer adopts a rather pessimistic tone. As is often the case, this play owes its conception to a specific event: in 1982, a son led Mitterer to his mother who had gone on a hunger strike in a small village of the upper-Inn valley. This woman slept for 200 days on the reclined passenger seat of a car and consumed nothing but Fanta, a soda pop. Then she was taken to the hospital. Very often, Mitterer shows in his plays 'rescue from danger and punishment of evil.'[50] But there are exceptions: Already in *Siberia*, the complaints of the old man are not being heard; in 'The Woman in the Car,' Mitterer also shows 'how sometimes law and order have very little in common with justice and how easily it can happen that someone—uninformed and helplessly lashing out—perishes in the battle with the authorities.'[51]

'The Woman in the Car' is a story of resistance. A single woman tries to oppose the ruling system of the village. Hedwig Lamprecht is put out into the street in the middle of winter by her older son Hermann; he expels her from the house that she built after the war with her own hands and under enormous personal sacrifices. Therefore, the house means more to her than anything else. The younger son, Robert, puts his car at her disposal because she wants to stay near her house and property. Hedwig finally begins a hunger strike that leads to her death on New Year's Eve, almost a year after Hermann had pressured her out of the house.

In this play, Mitterer takes up a number of highly explosive topics: Hedwig's senile inflexibility, petit bourgeois narrow-mindedness, the violence of the older son against his wife, the corruption of politicians, and the excessive power of the media. Hedwig demonstrates stubbornness to such a relentless degree that the spectator almost loses compassion for her in certain passages. It is a so-called "*Sympathisant*" who instigates Hedwig's hunger strike and who encourages her stubbornness: his name is Brandstätter, which fits well with his arsonist activities, since its meaning is just that: 'he who produces a burnt patch.' He incites both the old mother and the younger son with Neo-Fascist ideas and causes her private affairs to become a political issue.

Mitterer succeeds in portraying all sides very convincingly. The mother's obstinacy appears at times as repulsive as the complete incomprehension of the people around her. Only at the very end of the play does Mitterer again follow his inclination towards empathy and show the woman in a somewhat more favorable light by representing on stage one of Hedwig's phantom illusions. In her dream caused by a fainting spell, Hedwig meets her husband Simon who was killed in the war. He is one of those daring Germans who followed Hitler's call enthusiastically and unscrupulously. She also meets her lover Slawomir, a very humane "forced laborer" from Poland. It turns out that Hermann is the son of Hedwig's husband Simon, whereas Robert is the son of Slawomir. Hermann accidentally has found out these facts from letters and has held a bitter grudge against his mother since that time.

Hedwig Lamprecht is a person who had a very hard life during the war. Through her wartime experiences she has become very hard herself, hard as nails so-to-speak. She demanded rent from and eventually went to court against her own mother: the house that she was able to acquire under enormous effort and sacrifice is therefore more important to her than anything else in her life. It is more important to her than the two men in her life and more important than her two sons, Hermann and Robert.

The play *Johanna oder die Erfindung der Nation* ('Joan or The Invention of The Nation')[52] appears to be rather complex and permits more than just one interpretation. Mitterer needed a modern twist, since the topic of Jeanne d'Arc has been taken up by many prominent writers, e.g. by Schiller, Shaw, Brecht, and Anouilh, among others. Mitterer's introductory remarks indicate his attempts to arouse interest in the modern audience for this personality from the 15th century: '2 Ladies and 7 Gentlemen play 24 roles;' 'The play takes place in the years 1429-1431, as well as today and tomorrow.' To assign more than one role to an actor brings down the costs of a production, yet artistically, such double or multiple casting might produce an interesting psychological effect so that the different figures appear as possible spin-offs of but one character. On closer examination, we discover that 'Joan or The Invention of The Nation' could be classified as a psychodrama for several reasons—after Johanna is no longer useful in politics, she ends up in a psychiatric ward, suffering from a trauma that causes her to hate foreigners: a young foreigner has sexually violated her. This young foreigner is Gilles de Rais, a mass murderer who delights in killing boys and who dedicates his 170 murders to the androgynous-looking Johanna. In the role of TV chef, he transmits to Johanna the message of resurrection and in the end administers the injections to Johanna. At the same time Gilles de Rais might be considered an off-spin of Johanna's own personality. As he himself puts it: 'Holiness and devilishness is one and the same thing.' This play is very complex with its messages. It criticizes nationalism, and our sympathy is once more aroused for foreigners.

In the afterword to the play, Sylvia Tschörner describes Mitterer as an attorney among writers, defending the weak. It is almost surprising that he did not discover the topic of Saint Joan a long time ago: a 17-year-old farm girl from France who believes to hear the voice of God, who goes to war against the English, who is worshipped as a saint by the people, is exploited by the ruling powers, and is finally burnt at the stake. This is a human fate destined to be treated by Mitterer: worshipped and degraded, raised up high and thrown down deep, a female personality who has to stand up all on her own, and who nonetheless remains imperturbable. A typical Mitterer theme.

Notes

[1] See "No Place for Idiots," in *Anthology of Contemporary Austrian Folk Plays*, translated by Richard Dixon (Riverside, CA: Ariadne Press, 1993), 269ff.

[2] The two major anthologies of Mitterer's plays in English translation to date are: *Siberia and other Plays* (including "Siberia," "Stigma," "Visiting Hours," "Dragonthirst," and "There's Not a Finer Country") (Riverside, CA: Ariadne Press, 1994), and *The Wild Woman and other Plays* (including "The Wild Woman," "Home," "Children of the Devil," "One Everyman," and "Abraham") (Riverside, CA: Ariadne Press, 1995). For the original German versions, see Felix Mitterer, *Stücke, in 4 Bänden* (Innsbruck: Haymon, 1992/2001/2007).

[3] Mitterer also produced a number of TV series, e.g. *"Schießen"* ('Shooting'–ORF, 1977), *"Die fünfte Jahreszeit"* ('The Fifth Season'–ORF, DRS, NDR, 1983-86), *"Erdsegen"* ('Blessing of the Earth'–ORF/ZDF, 1984/1985), *"Die Piefke-Saga"* ('The Piefke Saga'–NDR/ORF, 1989-1992), *"Verkaufte Heimat: Eine Südtiroler Familiensaga von 1938 bis 1945"* ('Sold Homeland: A South Tyrolean Family Saga'–ORF/NDR/BR/RAI, 1988/89). I do not discuss these scripts in detail here, but refer the interested reader to Jutta Landa's essay "*Heimat* Sold Out: Felix Mitterer's Television Plays," in *Felix Mitterer: A Critical Introduction*, edited by Nicholas J. Meyerhofer and Karl E. Webb (Riverside: Ariadne Press, 1995), 101-119.

[4] *Meyers Großes Universallexikon*, Bd. 6 (Mannheim: Meyers Lexikonverlag, 1982), 386.

[5] *Felix Mitterer: A Critical Introduction* contains two essays on "homelessness," Jennifer Michaels' "Confronting the Past: Felix Mitterer's *Kein schöner Land* and *Verkaufte Heimat,"* 67-87, and Bernd Fischer's "Ethnic, National, and Regional Identities in Felix Mitterer's *Verkaufte Heimat*," 89-99.

[6] See also Jutta Landa, "*Heimat* Sold Out," 106.

[7] "The Wild Woman," translated by Todd C. Hanlin, in *The Wild Woman and other Plays*, 7.
[8] Cf. Gerlinde Ulm Sanford, "Onward or Downward? The Eternal-Feminine in Felix Mitterer's Play *Die Wilde Frau*," in *Felix Mitterer: A Critical Introduction*, 131-145, and her "Brutalität und Zärtlichkeit in Felix Mitterers *Die Wilde Frau*," in *Modern Austrian Literature*, 26 (1993), 167-181.
[9] "The Wild Woman," 10: "I bet you she's Italian!" (*"Des is sicher a Walsche!"* – *Stücke I*, 268).
[10] "The Wild Woman," 58.
[11] "There's Not a Finer Country," translated by Robert Acker, in *The Wild Woman and other Plays*, 275-365. Also "*Kein schöner Land*," in *Stücke I*, 303-362.
[12] My translation. "*I hab gnuag von Europa, des sag i enk! Ihr machts uns kaputt! Meine Glauben hab i abgstritten, daß i enk gfall! Daß i enk nit fremd bin! Hab i Bier trunken, und gsagt der Frau, sie soll an kurzen Rock anziehn und des Kopftüachl wegtun! Aber alles nit! Alles nit! Wia sie gsagt hat, sie will arbeiten gehn, da hab i gwußt, Memet, jetzt muaßt aufpassen! Wollt sie in Büro gehn, zu Chef, putzen gehn wollt sie! Und hätt sie gnommen, Chef! Hätt sie ihm gfallen, ja, dem Chef! Nix! Nix! I bin schon kaputt, du gehst mir nit kaputt, hab i gsagt! I bin mir selber schon a Fremder, verstehts ihr des? I kenn mi nimmer! Nacha hat sie gsagt, sie haltet des nit aus in Wohnung, kimmt nit unter Leut, da muaß sie immer an dahoam denken! Da geht sie liaber hoam! Guat, hab i gsagt, gehst hoam! Gehst hoam mit die Kinder! Und arbeit i, und arbeit i, und tua viel sparen, und dann geh i a wieder hoam, da wo die Sonn scheint, und jeder tuat auf sei Herz und sei Haustür, und du kannst überall einigehn und bist aufgnommen!*" – *Stücke II*, 267.
[13] "*Pfiat di, Moaster! Bist sicher gut aufgehoben in Abrahams Schoß!*" –II, 271.

[14] *"Home,"* translated by Heidi L. Hutchinson, in *The Wild Woman and other Plays,* 61-110.
[15] *"Home,"* 106.
[16] *"Home,"* 109.
[17] Richard B. Reich, "Ein Heimsucher," in *Felix Mitterer: Materialien zu Person und Werk* (Innsbruck: Haymon, 1995), 98.
[18] "Eine entwickelte Gesellschaft muß den Staat zur Heimat für alle ausbilden." Martin Walser, "Heimatbedingungen," in an Essay for a radio broadcast on the topic: *"Wie heimatlos ist die Linke heute"* ('How Homeless is the Left Today?') in Martin Walser, *Wie und wovon handelt Literatur? Aufsätze und Reden* (Frankfurt am Main: Suhrkamp, 1973), 89 ff.
[19] "Children of the Devil," translated by Todd C. Hanlin, in *The Wild Woman and other Plays,* 111-245.
[20] "Children of the Devil," 113.
[21] "Children of the Devil," 245.
[22] "Children of the Devil," 238.
[23] Mitterer, *"Krach im Hause Gott"* (Innsbruck: Haymon, 1994).
[24] Gerlinde Ulm Sanford, "In the Beginning was the Word–And before That? Theological Problems in Felix Mitterer's *Krach im Hause Gott,*" in *Postwar Austrian Theater: Text and Performance,* edited by Linda C. DeMeritt and Margarete Lamb-Faffelberger (Riverside, CA: Ariadne Press, 2002), 191-212.
[25] Compare e.g., Martin Larcher's and Robert Mitscha-Eibl's remarks as quoted in *Felix Mitterer: Materialien* (Innsbruck: Haymon, 1995), 113-114.
[26] *Felix Mitterer: Materialien,* 113.
[27] "Shunted into a Siding," "Wheat on the Autobahn," translated by Udo Borgert, Gertraud Ingeborg, and David Ritchie, in *Siberia and other Plays,* 149-202.
[28] In *Stücke I,* 9-58. The stage play premièred in 1977.
[29] *"Ich kann mich auch so gut hineinfühlen in Kinder zum Beispiel oder in solche, die als Deppen angeschaut werden, oder*

in Alte. Und... nachdem ich selber am Theater gespielt hab, hab ich das so stark gespürt, daß ich es wirklich auch bin. Daß ich das Kind bin und der Depp bin und der Alte bin." In *Felix Mitterer: Materialien*, 46. My translation.

[30] In *Am Rande des Dorfes: Erzählungen* (Innsbruck: Haymon, 1997). This story was first published under a title in dialect "Da Umbau," in *Tiroler Kulturzeitschrift das Fenster*, Heft 22, (Innsbruck: Tyrolia, 1978).

[31] "*Der Umbau,*" 85: "*dena si kauft hod um a siebzg Bam.*"

[32] "*Der Umbau,*" 87: "*Wenigstens an kloans Ondenkn on di gibts no. Aufn noin Fremdnverkehrsprospekt bist vorn drauf, im Vielfarbendruck. Do stehst vor dein umbautn Haus, des amoi a Bauernhof wor, und machst große Augn. A schöns Andenkn, wos? Pfiat di Voda.*" My translation.

[33] "*'S Dirndl is sauber, jetzt möchts gern an Tauber, und i wissert ihr oan, recht an saubern, an kloan!*" – 279. My translation.

[34] "*The Wild Woman,*" 28.

[35] "*The Wild Woman,*" 50.

[36] "*Shunted into a Siding,*" 151.

[37] "*Shunted into a Siding,*" 151.

[38] "*Shunted into a Siding,*" 157.

[39] "*Shunted into a Siding,*" 158.

[40] "*Siberia,*" translated by Margit Kleinman and Louis Fantasia, in *Siberia and other Plays*, 1-63. Originally in Felix Mitterer, *Stücke II* (Innsbruck: Haymon, 1992), 175-229. For a more detailed interpretation, see Gerd K. Schneider's essay "Timely Meditations or Not Yet! Social Criticism in Felix Mitterer's *Siberia*," in *Felix Mitterer: A Critical Introduction*, 195-205.

[41] "*Siberia,*" 62.

[42] "*Abraham,*" translated by Heidi L. Hutchinson, in *The Wild Woman and other Plays*, 351-421. See also Felix Mittterer, *Abraham* (Innsbruck: Haymon, 1993).

⁴³ Interestingly, Mitterer based the character of Adler on the true story of Rudolf Gomperz that he discovered from an article in the community newspaper of the village of St. Anton in Tyrol.
⁴⁴ *"There's Not a Finer Country,"* 283. (312).
⁴⁵ *"There's Not a Finer Country,"* 305.
⁴⁶ *"There's Not a Finer Country,"* 359.
⁴⁷ "*I doch a! I doch a, Pfarrer! I war ja auch Antisemit! Kannst du dir des vorstellen? (Sein Lachen bricht plötzlich ab; ganz ernst:) Verfluacht soll i sein!*" – 352. My translation.
⁴⁸ "*So ist dies eine Geschichte über Opportunismus, Feigheit, Mitläufertum, Eigennutz und politische Verblendung geworden. Die Opfer sind die „Anderen." Und diese „Anderen"—die Außenseiter, die Ausgestoßenen—sind ein durchgehendes Thema meiner literarischen Arbeit. Ein großer Teil der Menschen hat ständig Angst vor „den Anderen," hegt ständige Aggressionen gegen sie, ganz gleich, auf welche Art sie anders sind (und es beginnt ganz harmlos): andere Frisur, andere Kleidung, anderes Gehabe, andere Neigungen, andere Ansichten, andere Sprache, andere Hautfarbe, andere Religion, andere Sitten und Gebräuche. Und so geschieht selbst das Absurdeste, daß nämlich im Umkehrschluß ein bisher beliebter, geachteter und verdienter Mitbürger plötzlich zum Schurken und Volksschädling gestempelt und zuletzt ermordet wird, weil sich herausstellt, daß er Jude ist.*" In Felix Mitterer, *Stücke I*, 306. My translation.
⁴⁹ Mitterer, "Die Frau im Auto" (Innsbruck: Haymon, 1998).
⁵⁰ "Die Frau im Auto," 110. My translation.
⁵¹ "Die Frau im Auto," 111. My translation.
⁵² Felix Mitterer, *Johanna oder die Erfindung der Nation: Theaterstück*, mit einem Nachwort von Sylvia Tschörner (Innsbruck: Haymon, 2002).

GLORIA KAISER
Courtesy of Residenz Verlag
im Niederösterreichischen Pressehaus

Gloria Kaiser: From Provincial to International Author

by Donald G. Daviau

The aim of this essay is to examine the question whether Austrian authors who are not centered in Vienna write differently than those writers who reside there and are known as Viennese authors. The question has been posed before, primarily by the renowned literary scholar Josef Nadler, who made it the central thesis of his massive four-volume literary history, 'History of German Literature according to Tribes and Landscapes'[1]. In his view, a writer is so influenced by the environment of his homeland that his or her writings bear its unmistakable characteristics. Hence a Tyrolean writes differently than a Styrian, and all authors from different provinces are distinctive from each other and from Viennese writers. Certainly no one would confuse the writings of the Styrian Peter Rosegger with any contemporary writer from Vienna. Up to the post-World-War-II period, provincial writers, who normally did not travel extensively, concentrated on local themes reflecting the life and society of their towns and villages, while the Viennese authors such as Schnitzler and Hofmannsthal dealt with larger issues of sophisticated upper-class and aristocratic Viennese society as well as political and philosophical matters. In 1897 the Upper Austrian Hermann Bahr from Linz, who was endeavoring to unify Austria by eliminating this schism between Vienna and the provinces, featured a series on provincial writers in his newspaper *Die Zeit* (The Times) under the title 'Discovery of the

Province' ("*Entdeckung der Provinz*") to call attention to the worthwhile literature being produced by provincial authors while being totally ignored by Viennese readers.

In the postwar period, however, Austria became much more open to the world, and through the Four-Power occupation, radio, television, Internet, e-mail and travel, this difference between provincial and Viennese writers has gradually eroded, until at present it has been completely effaced, rendering Nadler's conception (based on a bygone social model) completely irrelevant today. With the development of the European Union and the expansion of globalization along with the availability of information through the media, television and the Internet, writers everywhere share the same unlimited horizons and the same access to world events, wherever they may live and work. Provincial authors as such may still exist as a matter of personal choice, but one can also live in the provinces and belong to the new trend, which is to go beyond national borders, to become European and even an international or global writer. Indeed, for two years Austria has awarded a prize for the best European novel by an Austrian, and with the Austrian penchant for awards perhaps there will soon be one for the best international novel. The process of homogenization is also advancing in the European Union; though founded on the premise that each nation would retain its own language and culture, the EU is now promoting the idea of a European identity.

As a model exemplifying this transition of a provincial author to a new international outlook, I have selected Gloria Kaiser, who began her literary career as a local Styrian writer, describing the life and conditions of the small-town environment in which she grew up, until a stroke of fate expanded her horizons and transformed her into the successful, internationally recognized author that she is today.

Gloria Kaiser was born in 1950 in the relatively small town of Köflach, Styria (population 15,000), a minor manufacturing town populated with many foreign workers employed in the glass, shoe, and porcelain factories; her father worked in a glass factory. At the age of 14 she was able to enter business school in

Graz. After her mother died, the family went through a difficult period, and Gloria worked summers at a conveyor belt in a factory to earn enough money to pay her school expenses. In 1969, at the age of 19, she graduated with a diploma in accounting and began her career in the business world as a bookkeeper and tax consultant. Over time she advanced to the position of tax advisor.

The transition to a literary career as a freelance writer was not the result of any sudden change but, typical of Gloria Kaiser's conservative nature, evolved gradually over a fifteen-year period. During her difficult childhood years, Gloria often sought refuge in her fantasy, creating stories for herself. In addition, at the age of eight her mother taught her to keep a diary, a practice, which, unlike most contemporary authors, she still maintains today.[2] Writing for her diary sharpened her eye for selecting events and also taught her how to compress her language by giving great care to the choice of words. From the diaries she moved on to writing stories, some of which she could publish as feuilletons in newspapers or magazines and also present in readings on ORF, the Austrian Radio Station. Her writings enabled her to escape the mentally confining professional world of numbers and allow her fantasy free reign. Her projects grew more and more ambitious and so did her success. Her first novel *Selbstgespräche einer Unbekannten* ('Monologues of an Unknown Woman,' 1980) was broadcast on Saarland television in 1980, and the radio play *Alltägliches* ('Everyday Life,' 1981) was aired in Germany in 1982, as was *Grenzlandfahrt* ('Border Trip,' 1985). In 1986 the novel *Grenzland* ('Borderland') was published as a serialized novel in the *Tagespost* and in the literary journal *Panorama.* The two narratives were broadcast on ORF and Southwest Radio, Baden-Baden, Germany. In 1986 another tale, "*Pokorny—Ein Begräbnis"* ('Pokorny—A Burial'), was broadcast on ORF.

In 1984, after fifteen years of a life divided between her business profession and her desire to be a creative author, the inner conflict grew to the point that she had to make a choice. Though successful as a businesswoman, she had tired of the impersonal nature of her work with its cold language and its sole reliance on numbers that had to be accurately balanced. The lives and fates of the people represented by the numbers were left out of account in her chosen profession and so was nature, both features of the world that had attracted her from early youth. It was nature and people with all their flaws and imperfections that she found so fascinating and that had attracted her to become a writer in her spare time. The strength of the call to literature finally impelled the conservative but strong-willed accountant to take the risk of becoming a freelance writer. She did hedge her bet at the beginning by continuing to serve as tax advisor to a sufficient number of clients to be able to support herself while she was in the process of establishing herself as an author. She was able to sell radio plays and also videos, in addition to reading her stories on ORF as well as publishing them in newspapers and magazines. Only after three years did she receive the first of a succession of monetary awards and other prizes in recognition of the talent she displayed in her early works.[3]

Kaiser joined the Graz Authors' Group when it was founded in 1973 and still remains a member, but she never became an activist and never entered into the politics either of the group or of the country. As a practical, no-nonsense individual, she, like many of her women protagonists, simply worked industriously and quietly and followed her own independent way as she still does. She never joined cliques and did not form close associations with other Austrian writers, although she does single out Hans Weigel as instrumental in reviving Austrian literature in the postwar period and helping so many writers by serving as a mentor and opening the doors of the Styria Publishing House for her. Styria, in Graz, remained her publisher until the firm gave up publishing literature in 1997. There is no discernible influence of other authors on her writings, although she may have become interested in historical biographies through Stefan Zweig, whom she greatly admires and often discusses in lectures. However, the similarity can only be the form. As a true individualist, she developed her own style and technique and pursued her own themes, which make no concessions to readers and do not follow the popular trends of Austrian literature in the last 25 years. One distinguishing feature that sets her apart as a serious author is her effort to write lasting works of literature and not simply ephemeral entertaining works (*"Modeerscheinungen"*) to achieve commercial success.

Following the old adage of writing what you know, Kaiser at first dealt with the small-town world in which she grew up and knew at first hand. Most impressive of these early writings is *Monologe einer unbekannten Frau* ('Monologues of an Unknown Woman,' 1989), which consists of the revelations of a woman whose life unravels before our eyes like a ball of string. Every aspect of her existence fails her, from her husband, her career, her friends and associates, down to and including nature. In brief monologues she examines each facet of her existence and then dismisses it, in each instance further weakening her hold on life. When she has exhausted every reason to go on living, she makes preparations to depart this world. This is a dark, tragic text, based on the life of a real person, which shows in mirror image what a human being needs for life. At the same time this beautifully written, mature novel demonstrates that Kaiser is a serious, talented author as well as a first-rate stylist with a gift for language.

Equally dark is the novel *Ein Opfer ohne Bedeutung* ('A Victim of No Importance,' 1990), which is also based on a real event. In this combination crime story and social novel, Kaiser used the experiences gained in growing up in Köflach to portray what life is like in a small provincial town that suffers from stagnation after having lost its industry and hence its economic base. The town declines and the people degenerate. Those who were still vital and energetic abandoned the no-longer viable town, leaving behind the inert people who, cut off from economic support, succumb to lethargy and merely continue the routine of their pitiful lives without aspirations or dreams in the gray, dismal backwater. As in all small towns, everyone knows everything about everyone else, as gossip is the staple of all conversations. In this way the reader gets to know a number of these people and the dreary lives they lead. The main setting is the inn, run by a woman who knows the skeletons in every closet and thus has a hold over everyone and some power in the community.

The central event that provides the basis for the conversations is a murder—actually the second of two murders that are related. The primary victim is Berta Hoisnik, a slightly handicapped older woman whom the innkeeper feels obliged to support and protect by employing her to assist serving food and drinks. The first victim is Schorsch, a handicapped man, whom Berta has befriended and tries to help. Both are regarded as worthless in the community, and thus their deaths cause no stir in town. The chief of police and the local magistrate consider these cases a nuisance since they are required to carry out an investigation, in the course of which we learn more about this town and its residents. Ultimately they will concoct a report for the files, and the case will be buried and forgotten. Justice will not be served, a final indication of the morally bankrupt conditions that prevail.

The novel is divided into three chapters: *"Die Wirtin"* ('The Innkeeper'), the person who discovers Berta's dead body; *"Kogler,"* a factory supervisor who falls into disgrace because of his dissolute, eccentric behavior after his wife and son leave him; and *"Guster,"* the police chief in charge of the investigation. In each case the sections are written as virtual monologues with the sentences connected primarily by semicolons, a technique which Kaiser developed and likes to employ. The innkeeper pours out a torrent of language, badgering the police and other officials demanding justice for Berta and, at the same time, providing a pitiless portrayal of the town and its inhabitants. Guster has no illusions left about justice or anything else, but because his assistant Windisch is pressing for his job, he has to give the appearance of carrying out a thorough investigation. Windisch is the only character who has not lost all his energy and succumbed to resignation; he has been taking classes and is preparing to move elsewhere. His inadequate life and job keep him filled with such aggression that he killed the handicapped Schorsch one day simply because he had the opportunity to do so. Later he has to kill Berta because she witnessed the murder and is threatening to reveal him. He will not be caught because Guster has no real interest in finding the perpetrator. Rather, he plans to write his report and then let the case just fade away, as he knows it will. Windisch will simply start life anew elsewhere, while the town continues to deteriorate and decay.

In describing in unsparingly realistic terms the results of economic deprivation on the people in a town that was prosperous during the postwar economic miracle and then suffered a recession, Kaiser—who characterizes herself as a realist in life and in her writings—does not agitate or take sides, but merely reports. She knows these people, vegetating in a stagnating environment, and conveys a sense of what the people and their lives are like. Her command of language enables her to create characters that ring true. She does not judge these people—they judge themselves, for Kaiser uses a technique perfected by Karl Kraus of allowing the characters to reveal their true natures through their speech. Another strength of the novel is the artful way she employs the crimes as a means of maintaining suspense while she carries out her main purpose of portraying the dreary existence of the people in this town. The result is a powerful social document, showing the demoralizing effect that the loss of industry can have on the inhabitants of a small provincial town. The residents have lost their vitality and with it their character, their decency, and their humaneness. In all respects this town represents the polar opposite of the normally cheerful, harmonious atmosphere and happy ending of the typical regional novel or film.

If she were a social activist, she would try to assess blame or suggest a solution to the problem. As a realist, however, she merely presents the dilemma convincingly and leaves it up to the reader to continue to mull over the problem and come to his or her own conclusions. Kaiser achieves her aim of provoking thought, and it is this quality that marks this novel as a work of literature and the author as a serious writer.

If up to this point Kaiser's literary life and writings fit into the typical pattern of a budding Austrian provincial author in terms of subject matter, if not in style and technique, her life and work underwent a radical shift in 1988 when she took a pleasure trip to Brazil, an event that illustrates the important role of chance in life. Just to engage in something completely different from her rigid business profession, she began to study Portuguese in the late 1970s at a private school; when she enrolled, the class consisted of three students. In 1986 she wanted to try out her linguistic skill in a real situation and decided to travel to Brazil. Her ticket brought her to Rio de Janeiro and then allowed her to visit four other cities. The last stop was Salvador, a large northern coastal city of three million people, heavily populated by descendants of the 3 to 4 million African slaves the Portuguese imported over three centuries to work on the sugar, coffee, and rubber plantations, as well as in the mines. While on the beach one day, Kaiser by chance met Celeste Aida Galeao, who not only turned out to be a Professor of German at the University of Salvador, but also an enthusiast of Austrian literature which she was eager to teach, but needed texts for her classes. Thus began a friendship and a productive working relationship that continues to the present day.

When she returned to Vienna, Kaiser reported this interest in Austrian literature and culture to the Ministry for Education and Art, and was given an appointment to create an organization for cultural exchange. Thus, in collaboration with Professor Galeao and Professor Ewald Hackler, an internationally known theater director, the Austrian/Brazilian Cultural Initiative was born. Later the Hispanic Division of the U.S. Library of Congress, where Kaiser has become a familiar, highly regarded figure through her research visits and her almost annual lectures and readings, joined the group. From the founding in 1989 up to the present, Kaiser has been spending months each year in Brazil, actively arranging annual events. She has brought the Austrian Library and continues to sponsor increasingly ambitious literary and musical programs as well as exhibits. Kaiser herself has given a number of lectures as well as readings from her works, which are now all available in Portuguese. In recognition of her cultural contributions to Brazil, Kaiser has received a number of honors over the years, the latest being two awards in December 2005 and being named a Corresponding Member of the Bahian Academy of Letters in 2006.

Kaiser loves Brazil and considers it her second homeland. During her stays she not only actively promotes Austrian culture, but also researches the earlier Austrian-Brazilian connections, specifically the important role that the Habsburgs played in the development of Brazil in the 19th century. Thus, this discovery of Brazil not only vastly broadened Kaiser's horizons and gave her a cultural mission, but most importantly this new world also opened an entirely fresh direction for her writing, one she has been pursuing diligently, enthusiastically and profitably ever since.

Brazil first appears in *Oktoberfrühling* ('October Spring,' 1991), an ambitious generational novel that juxtaposes a critical examination of the effects of the postwar economic miracle on a typical Austrian family with the promising life offered by Brazil. As in her previous novel, Kaiser divides the text into three chapters, focusing in turn on the three principal characters: "*Weger*," the patriarch of the family; "*Günther*," his oldest son and heir; and "*Oskar*," the black sheep of the family who finds a new independent life in Brazil. The title reflects the fact that when it is fall in Europe, it is spring in Brazil, and indicates in metaphoric terms that, in Kaiser's view, Europe is weary and declining, while Brazil is burgeoning with life and opportunity.

Weger, whose 80th birthday celebration serves as the focus of the first chapter, represents the postwar generation in general. Because of his difficult youth and the deprivations suffered during the war, he has driven himself to succeed in business and demands the same commitment from his three sons. This monomaniacal ambition to achieve wealth takes a high toll on the family, for Weger's financial success is achieved at the cost of his humanity. Despite material prosperity, the family is at odds and unhappy, because Weger has alienated everyone by his dictatorial manner. His wife leaves him, and when he suffers a heart attack, his oldest son Günther forces him out of the business so that he and his brother can run it in their own way. When he cannot break Oskar's spirit of independence and force him to obey his will, Weger gives him money and disowns him. His mother and siblings reveal their character when they agree to ejecting Oskar, because this will mean a larger inheritance for them. It is a shock when a letter arrives for Weger from Oskar in Brazil. He delays opening it, so it becomes a matter of suspense, causing great speculation and nervousness in the family about what it might contain. Is Oskar planning to return to claim his inheritance?

To add further complexity, Kaiser inserts another major figure named Hoffmann who represents the diametrical opposite of Weger and takes a counterview to everything his friend stands for. Whereas Weger is an overachiever, devoting his life to accumulating wealth, Hoffmann drops out of the rat race entirely, quitting his job in order to live a modest life according to his own wishes. He is a true original, and Weger admires him and relies on this alter ego as the one sympathetic person in his life. Hoffmann is considered as something of a philosopher who continuously defends others from criticism by stating that they have "a certain philosophy," that is, their own point of view, an innocuous refuge which is never explained or challenged. Most of his pronouncements are platitudes, which are taken for profundities in these circles. Hoffmann's passion is Beethoven, especially the Fifth Symphony. It becomes a *leitmotif* when he repeatedly attributes most of the ills of the Western world to the fact that musicians always play the Fifth Symphony too fast. One day, to Weger's shock and dismay, Hoffmann disappears. He surfaces later in Brazil, where he meets Oskar. He lives a penniless life, barely surviving, until one day Oskar learns of his death. At first it appears that this eccentric original will figure importantly in the novel, but in fact he is never really developed and, beyond a little bemusement over his repetitive diatribes, his appearance is not sustained. Beyond offering a contrast to Weger at the beginning, Hoffmann plays no intrinsic role in the novel.

Although he is also a free spirit who revolted against the family system, Oskar wants to succeed, but on his own terms, with his own dreams and aspirations. His efforts to integrate into

Brazilian life enable Kaiser to portray the social situation with all its promise as well as the negative aspects such as thievery and corruption at every level, the exploitation of the poor, and the disregard of their human rights. Oskar attempts to fit into this new life, but becomes the victim of a well-connected, crooked lawyer who bilks him out of his money, has him beaten up, robbed of his passport, and thrown in jail. His luck turns by chance when a stranger takes interest in him and gives him a job as a designer. This new friend and benefactor obtains papers and a building permit for Oskar, whose future now brightens. He had always dreamed of building a terraced city, but his pragmatic father, who with reason had no confidence in Oskar at that time, had only scoffed at such a ridiculous fantasy. Now after the hard trials he has endured, he will have the opportunity at last to prove himself, illustrating the theme of the novel that what was not possible in fading Europe is achievable in growing Brazil. Oskar is able to marry and look forward to a happy, productive life. His letter to his family reports his success and puts everyone at ease by stating that he will never return for his inheritance but will make his future in Brazil.

Kaiser believes that Austrians harbor many misconceptions about Brazil,[4] and her subsequent books all further the aim of her Cultural Initiative to bring better understanding and closer rapprochement between the two countries. This is also the purpose of her series of four youth novels, which were written to give young Austrian and German readers accurate information about the lives of children their age in Brazil: *Julchen und Kasimira* (1991), *Violetta* (1993), *Maurice und Violetta* (1995) and *Arnoldo. Ein Strassenkind in Brasilien* ('Arnoldo, A Street Child in Brazil,' 1996). She concentrates on the children of the lower classes, depicting with her usual realism the difficulties they face. They have to begin working at a young age, often at more than one job a day to help support their parents, usually only a mother. And because of their inexperience, they are generally exploited and cheated at every turn. They have no time or money to go to school; indeed, some of the parents are so poor that they cannot afford the cost of registering their births.[5] Thus they have little chance of getting the education that would enable them to break out of the vicious cycle of poverty. Brazil does have a law against child labor, but it is not enforced.

The families live in makeshift huts without running water or electricity in unauthorized areas, which the police raid and raze on a regular basis. There is no health care, sanitation is poor to non-existent, and disease is prevalent. Crime is endemic, and the tougher elements form gangs that coerce and rob other young people who are trying to earn money from various independent ventures such as street stands or parking cars. Those who do not join the gang or pay for protection either have to flee elsewhere or are severely beaten or killed. Life is cheap among the impoverished in these settlements.

Despite this dismal situation, Kaiser shows the positive attitude of the young people whose lives she describes, the warmth and happiness they can find amidst the squalor of their living conditions, so much so that when one has an opportunity to find a better life with one of the upper-class families he or she works for, it becomes a difficult decision to leave home. Like her countryman Stefan Zweig, who glorified the country in his book *Brazil: Land of the Future* (*Brasilien: Land der Zukunft*, 1941), Kaiser is clearly smitten with her second homeland. Because of the potential and promise she sees in this fertile land of abundance, she is able to look beyond the squalor, the oppression and exploitation of the poor by the wealthy, and the seemingly hopeless predicament of the poor who, only with extreme difficulty, can ever hope to break out of their life of poverty. Because of her honesty as an author, her books report all of these circumstances in detail; but ultimately she focuses on the positive qualities, the strength and the joyous spirit of the people, their warmth and openness, and their receptiveness to nature. These books, which are suitable and informative for adults as well as teenagers, have been well received both in Europe and in Brazil.

To further her efforts to develop an Austrian-Brazilian connection in terms of her Cultural Initiative, Kaiser could not have found a better topic than the life of the young Habsburg archduchess Dona Leopoldina who in 1817 was given in marriage to Dom Pedro de Braganca, the young king of Brazil for the express purpose of forging an alliance between the two countries. Actually, Austria had little interest in Brazil per se but a great deal in the importance of the Braganca family in Portugal, ruled by Pedro's father John VI. On the basis of Leopoldina's letters, diplomatic correspondence, and diaries, as well as her knowledge of Brazil and Brazilian life, Kaiser produced the biographical-historical novel *Dona Leopoldina: The Habsburg Empress of Brazil (Dona Leopoldina: Die Habsburgerin auf Brasiliens Thron,* 1994),[6] initiating an impressive series of historical-biographical novels linking Brazil with Austria and with Europe which is still continuing today. Kaiser prefers the novel form to a straight biography, because the literary as opposed to a philological work allows her the latitude to fill in the areas not covered in the meager existing documents, while also allowing her the freedom to recreate in her own manner the inner life, feelings, and thoughts of her protagonist. To add a tone of authenticity, she quotes from Leopoldina's letters and diaries in the original orthography. She continues to use the novel form in all of her subsequent biographies.

In arranging the marriage, neither her father Emperor Franz I or Chancellor Metternich gave any consideration to Leopoldina's feelings; but, in fact, she was attracted to Pedro, who looked so handsome and dashing in his pictures. From the day that the agreements for the wedding were arranged, her existence became a crash course in learning Portuguese and about the life and customs of her new country. Although she was an apt and willing student, little that she learned prepared her for the life and the husband that awaited her in Brazil. The archduchess Leopoldina, daughter of Emperor Franz I and grandniece of Empress Maria Theresia, was married by proxy to Prince Pedro von Braganca in 1817 and met her husband in person only months later in Brazil. At first she was enchanted with her new country, especially with the exotic landscape and with the friendliness and spontaneity of the people she met, in contrast to the strict formality of the Austrian court.

Leopoldina was an intelligent woman with many interests, but none stronger than her attraction to nature. In Vienna she had already made plans to collect specimens of the flora and fauna, and her retinue included botanists as well as the painter Thomas Ender, who created more than 800 aquarelle paintings of the landscape. He also assisted Leopoldina in collecting chests full of plants, flowers, insects, and minerals which were sent to Vienna. Ender's decision to return home a few years later deeply saddened her, for he was her major contact with her homeland. Although she wrote letters continuously to Vienna, neither her father nor Metternich nor any other members of her family saw fit to respond. She suffered terribly from homesickness, but even her pleas to be allowed to visit for a short time were ignored. Brazil did not rank high on the list of Austrian priorities, so Leopoldina was left to her fate without family support to help sustain her. The one exception was her sister, Maria Louise, who became her main confidante and sympathetic listener. Maria Louise had been similarly married off to Napoleon and therefore could empathize with her sister's plight. Leopoldina's principle source of strength and support was the radical priest and important statesman, José Bonifácio de Andrade, who was employed to continue her education. This important figure in Brazilian politics served as her advisor, mainstay, and bulwark in Brazil through the most difficult and perilous times to which she was subjected, including saving her children unassisted during the revolution. Because he instilled her with courage and filled her with ideas about social improvements, Pedro had Bonifacio banished to end his influence. Leopoldina still managed to seek his advice, and they became lovers.

After the promising beginning, Leopoldina's life became much more complex and difficult than she could have ever dreamed. After basking in the natural splendor of the landscape, she soon discovered the reality of life for her subjects in Brazil: the slavery, the exploitation and cruel treatment as well as the sickness and misery of the poor, the slum housing and lack of proper sanitation, the child labor, making it impossible for the children to attend school—all of which aroused her compassion. Personally, she had to endure constant political intrigues as well as the ill treatment of her boorish, inconsiderate husband, who made her life miserable with his inattention to his duties and his flagrant philandering. Pedro de Braganca, poorly educated and afflicted with epilepsy, was by no means capable of ruling Brazil, any more than Emperor Franz' handicapped son Ferdinand could rule Austria. Pedro I succeeded to the throne when his father King John VI found it safe to return to Portugal, which controlled Brazil politically and economically. Although he was not attracted to her, Pedro kept Leopoldina pregnant with seven children in 10 years, only five of which lived. She suffered continuously from her weakened physical state. Pedro was incapable of loving Leopoldina and forced her to accept his life with a greedy mistress who exploited this affair to the maximum. While he kept Leopoldina without money, he lavished expensive gifts on his mistress and provided for all her relatives. Leopoldina's last pregnancy killed her. She was so worn down mentally and physically from the years of her hard life—which she accepted as her fate and above all as her duty, despite the fact that she received neither support nor sympathy from her family in Austria and only hostility from her husband and his ministers. Drained mentally and exhausted physically, she died in 1826 at the age of 29, one week after delivering yet another stillborn child.

What makes this biographical novel so remarkable and compelling is the gripping way that Kaiser portrays the character of Leopoldina with her extremely strong sense of duty. When she was denied any possibility of a visit home, Leopoldina accepted her fate and determined to become Brazilian and work to improve the lot of her suffering people. To implement her social ideas, most of which she gained from her mentor José Bonifácio, she had to overcome her homesickness (or *saudade,* as the Brazilians call it), the disapproval of her family in Austria, the hostility of her husband, and the malicious enmity of many of the ministers and politicians. Despite all these odds, Dona

Leopoldina, with the guidance and encouragement of Bonifácio, accomplished more for the social improvement and betterment of Brazil than her husband, the king, and all of the politicians combined. She demonstrated that she was not only intelligent and compassionate, but that she was also imbued with inner strength, tenacity, and perseverance. When Pedro was summoned to Portugal in 1822, she, acting with full power as regent in his stead, signed a decree declaring Brazil's independence from Portugal. This bold, long-overdue step brought economic independence for Brazil, which could now trade with other nations directly, instead of having to ship all goods to Portugal, which then reaped the profits for itself.

This development angered her father, who thought only in European terms and was not concerned about the betterment of Brazil. Franz I, a reactionary bent on keeping his own citizens ignorant and the country backward, was even less pleased with his daughter, when, again serving as regent, she signed a decree making the children of slaves free at birth.[7] Leopoldina also successfully introduced the idea of bringing in skilled workers and successful farmers from Austria and Germany to teach their crafts and farming methods to the Brazilians. She saw no means of improving the lives of her people unless they had more advanced models to follow. She also initiated a campaign to educate the people about the need to implement more advanced methods of sanitation. Despite her contributions, carried out under the most difficult circumstances, the populace could never accord Leopoldina the gratitude it felt during her lifetime, out of fear of retaliation by Pedro. Only after he was forced to abdicate in 1831 and return to Portugal could the public finally openly acclaim her for her achievements by designating her the "Mother of the Nation."

Kaiser employs a new technique in this novel: instead of proceeding chronologically, she begins at the end, depicting the last twelve days of Leopoldina, as she was in the throes of succumbing to the accumulated debilitating effects of her life. The story is told as it unfolds in her feverish mind, that is, with a jumbled time sequence that forces the reader to stay alert to the sudden leaps from present to past that occur without any transition, exactly the way a dreaming or hallucinating person's mind can flit seamlessly through different time sequences. The aim is to convey a sense of the human being that Leopoldina was in all her complexity. History can record her deeds, but they alone do not provide any insights into the inner life of the person, which is the essential feature of Kaiser's literary technique. Only the rich imagination of the novelist can delve into the mind and soul of her protagonists to show the simultaneous forces and pressures at work at any given time, to reveal the inner life, which cannot be verified by existing documents but only captured by a creative, empathetic author. To reflect her goal of capturing the rhythm of the various phases of Leopoldina's life, Kaiser employs musical terminology in the chapter headings: *"Largo," "Tranquillo," "Allegretto," "Animato," "Forte,"* and *"Andante con moto."* Kaiser's approach makes the novel the rich, fascinating experience that it is, and it remains the technique that Kaiser has continued to employ with similar success in all of the following novels. All of her writings that deal with Brazil are creative biographical novels and at the same time historical and educational novels, for in each case the author provides a rich tapestry of the background as well as showing the education of the protagonists and of the nation. Each of the historical biographies presents an imposing historical personage whose contributions to society and sensible, courageous approach to life can serve as a universal model.

    Pedro II, the subject of Kaiser's second biographical novel *Pedro II of Brazil: Son of the Habsburg Empress (Pedro II von Brasilien: Der Sohn der Habsburgerin*, 1997)[8] forms a logical sequel to *Dona Leopoldina*, carrying the history of the country forward and recounting how he continued the programs that his mother had initiated. Of her five surviving children, Pedro II most resembled Leopoldina in character and intelligence, and, as fate would have it, he shared a similar destiny. He, too, had no choice about becoming Emperor of Brazil at the age of five, when his father, Pedro I, because of his negligent and profligate life, was forced to abdicate in 1831 and go into exile in Portugal, where he died in 1834. Like his mother's before him, Pedro II's childhood was devoted to study to prepare him to rule, and at her wish the man chosen to provide his rigorous education was José Bonifácio, who had played such an important role in his mother's life. She could not have picked a better mentor, for Bonifácio was an enlightened thinker whose ideas helped shape Brazil through his strong influence on the Royal Family as well as his service as minister during the crucial period of the revolution. Because he was ahead of his time and his thinking ran counter to that of the ruling class, his intelligent ideas were not always appreciated and neither was his liberal education of Leopoldina and Pedro II. Pedro had banished him to end his support for Leopoldina, and the ministers exiled him a second time in 1833 to isolate and weaken Pedro II. However, the young Emperor continued on the progressive course set by Bonifácio, stabilizing the country and enacting humane legislation. As a result Pedro II during his rule gained the adoration of the people, which his mother never enjoyed in her lifetime but achieved only posthumously

Pedro II resembled his mother in his devotion to duty above all else, as well as in being enlightened and progressive in his thinking. These qualities can be attributed in part to inheritance and partly to the influence of the same teacher. Like his mother, Pedro II possessed intelligence, intellectual curiosity and a love of learning which he satisfied on lengthy journeys through Europe and the United States. It made an important difference that he was accepted as a native Brazilian, not as a foreign interloper, as his mother had long been regarded, and so he did not face the opposition that she had confronted in this respect. Also the son equaled his mother in strength of character and perseverance, but at the same time was endowed with more patience, forbearance, and balance, so that he became known as Pedro the Wise. Above all, he was not afflicted and weakened, as was Leopoldina, by suffering from s*audade*, that particularly virulent and debilitating Brazilian form of homesickness. Finally, he was a courageous man, who, when he could not avoid war, which he hated, led his troops into battle against Paraguay and shared their life in the field. When he survived uninjured, he took that as a sign from fate that he was destined to fulfill his duties and responsibilities.

This biographical novel illustrates once again Gloria Kaiser's intimate knowledge of Brazil, as seen in the myriad descriptive details, portraying not only the history, but also the luxuriant richness and abundance of the exotic landscape with its colorful flora and fauna. Much more is known about Pedro II, and thus there is less need or latitude to create an interpretation. The author's portrayal shows a likeable, capable, resourceful individual, imbued with a strong sense of justice. He felt great compassion for the poor people of his land, including the slaves, and he pursued many of the social and political programs that his mother had initiated but could not complete. He fought for a new constitution for Brazil, one that would free the slaves and abolish slavery, guarantee a free press, freedom of religion and open, direct elections by popular vote of the people. Like his mother, he too was unable to carry out all of his programs.

This novel is also related in flashback, beginning with Pedro II in 1889 preparing to leave Brazil and go into exile in Europe. To avoid civil war, he has abdicated his crown so that the country can become a republic. As always, his duty to his people and his country come before his own preferences. At the same time, he feels relieved at the thought of finally having the freedom to pursue his own interests. He has grown weary of struggling to change the political system in Brazil, which has always disgusted him because of its corruption and fraud. While on the ship during the lengthy crossing to France, he drifts into reveries about his life, which is undergoing a major change now, and in this way the reader becomes intimately acquainted with an intelligent, sensitive, sympathetic man who is well worth knowing. We trace his life through his education, his marriage to Teresa Christina Bourbon, princess of the Two Sicilies, with whom he is at first greatly disappointed, causing him to enter into an active social life and an indulgence of his love for dancing, at which he excelled. However, his sense of duty eventually prevailed, and he became reconciled to his obligations to wife and family.

A high point of his life was the trip of two years, 1875-1877, during which he traveled extensively and met many notables, including the Pope, whose request that the Free-masons be driven out Pedro had to deny. Pedro II always hated to waste time—work and duty always dominated—and he maintained a demanding itinerary and schedule. He traveled to Egypt and Greece, where he encountered Schliemann. He met Pasteur in France and traveled from there to St. Petersburg, Constantinople, and Jerusalem; he avoided Austria. Once he saw Nietzsche on a train but did not talk to him. His itinerary carried him to the United States, where he crossed the country from Cambridge, Massachusetts, to New Orleans and San Francisco. During his travels he met Alexander Graham Bell and, as a result, built the first telephone system in Brazil upon his return home. In summing up his own life, Pedro II felt that his biography lacked anything spectacular and that he had not lived up to his parents. He considered himself an ordinary man, a judgment with which history concurs. However, anyone who reads this engrossing historical biography might come to a different conclusion.

After exploring the connections between Brazil and Austria, Kaiser presents another outstanding figure in *Anita Garibaldi* (2001) that served as a link between Brazil and Europe, in this case with Italy. Anita Garibaldi was the Creole wife of Giuseppe Garibaldi who fought for years unsuccessfully for the independence of southern Brazilians and then led the campaign to protect Rome against the French. While Garibaldi has been and still is widely known and celebrated for his heroic deeds in the cause of freedom, his first wife, Anita, has never received recognition commensurate to the sacrifices she made and the sufferings she endured in supporting her husband's military exploits. She bore Garibaldi three children and sustained the family on her own by her sewing skills, because her husband spent most of his time away from home. Later Anita dressed as a man and marched and fought alongside him on his campaigns. She went to jail for him and finally gave her life's blood for his cause, such was her love and admiration for the Italian national hero who is celebrated and honored throughout Italy with countless squares and streets named after him, while she is almost totally forgotten.

Anita is as unknown as her husband is famous, because she was self-effacing, living for his glory and seeking only to serve him. Little factual material exists about her life, allowing abundant room for Kaiser's imagination to create her own interpretation of what the dark-skinned, Creole beauty, Ana Maria de Jesus, the daughter born in 1821 to affluent parents in Laguna in northern Brazil, might have been like. Because of her independent spirit, Ana at the age of five was shunted off to a convent, where she benefited greatly from the exceedingly rare opportunity at that time for a girl to receive an excellent education. She also developed a friendship with the priest Augusto, who remained her mentor throughout her life, similar to the role that José Bonifácio played in the lives of Leopoldina and Pedro II. At sixteen Ana married a wealthy businessman in Rio de Janeiro and lived a life of luxury. However, when by chance she heard the exiled Italian Garibaldi speak one evening in 1839, her fate and her future were determined. She abandoned her husband and children and joined the freedom fighter and his cause and never looked back or suffered any regrets. She died alone near Ravenna, Italy, in 1849 at the age of twenty-eight, possibly from an attack of malaria, following Garibaldi's defeat of the French troops that were attempting to take Rome.

The background in Brazilian history acquired in writing *Dona Leopoldina* and *Pedro II* served Kaiser well in fleshing out the details in this novel and portraying the people and the country in a vivid manner. Her expressive language enables the reader to see and feel the situations describing the life of the people in the full spectrum, from the exceedingly wealthy to the oppressed and exploited lower classes at a time when slavery flourished in Brazil. Kaiser introduces one change of technique here in that the biography proceeds chronologically rather than being told in flashback. To allow Anita to express her inner life and feelings, the author uses monologues as well as the letters she writes in her mind to her mentor Augusto. Two things help sustain her through all her tribulations: her dream home, which she builds brick by brick and room by room in her imagination; and her headband of beads, which the seller promised would last her to her death. When she is lying on her deathbed, Anita completes her home in her feverish reverie, and her headband is down to the last bead.

This blend of fact and fiction results in a highly readable, engrossing tribute to an extraordinary woman. The author admires Anita's courage and spirit of independence—like Leopoldina, she could be considered an early feminist seeking her personal fulfillment on her own terms—and has presented her protagonist in completely positive terms. The book is based on thorough research and is accurate in its historical details; because of the sparseness of materials, the portrayal of Anita is ultimately Kaiser's own interpretation, the same technique employed in all of her biographical novels based on historical characters and events.

With *Saudade: The Life and Death of Queen Maria Gloria of Lusitania* (*Saudade: Leben und Sterben der Königin Maria-Gloria von Lusitanien,* 2003),[9] Kaiser continues the history of the Braganca family. Maria Gloria, the first-born child of Pedro I and Dona Leopoldina, was seven years old when her mother died in 1826, nine when her father was forced to renounce his throne in 1831 and go into exile in Portugal, and barely fifteen when she was compelled to take the throne and serve as Queen of Portugal. Like her mother, Maria Gloria suffered terribly from homesickness and melancholy, "*saudade*," a complex and particularly malevolent and debilitating form of suffering caused by being uprooted from one's homeland. Dona Leopoldina spent years of her life pining for Austria, until she finally accepted her fate and determined to become Brazilian. Her son Pedro II, who had to ascend to the Brazilian throne at the age of five, also suffered *saudade* for Brazil when he went into exile in France in 1889. But he was much older, more mature, and a world traveler, so the effects were not as severe for him. Strangely, since she left Brazil at the age of nine, Maria Gloria suffered from this crippling malady the most severely and the longest; indeed, she never overcame it. Weakened physically from eleven pregnancies, exhausted mentally from the constant political struggles, and weary of soul, she literally willed herself to death during childbirth on her mother's name day, November 15, 1853, at the age of 34.

While her mother and brother were able to make productive contributions and could gain the admiration of their subjects, if not of the politicians and farmers who fought against their social innovations, Maria Gloria, who was supposed to revive Portugal after years of mismanagement by the authoritarian Miguel regime, could never accomplish the social programs needed to improve the lives of her people, and thus she could not win their respect or their hearts. Kaiser portrays not only the vicissitudes of Maria Gloria's life, but she also juxtaposes the life of her Brazilian servant, Graca, who likewise and with more reason suffers from *saudade,* for as a slave she had no more choice about being uprooted than her mistress did. Graca narrates tales of what she has lost, as well as describing the hardships of the victimized and exploited lower classes, of the slaves who have no control over their own lives. Through these parallel lives the novel conveys the full spectrum of social life at this time. Ultimately, Graca's fate was kinder to her than to Maria Gloria. When her mistress died, Graca was able to return to Brazil, where she married and raised a family.

Maria Gloria had ample reason to be unhappy in Portugal beyond *saudade*, for she was always regarded as an outsider, and throughout her reign was rejected by the people she was trying her best to help, while being openly opposed by her ministers. Despite this unpopularity, she was not daunted, but displaying the same qualities of fulfillment of duty, perseverance, and tenacity as her mother and brother, she managed to make some significant, lasting social, cultural, and educational contributions for the betterment of the country. She introduced mandatory schooling and, like her brother, founded schools such as an Academy of Fine Arts, Institutes of Chemistry and Pharmacy, and established an Observatory in Lisbon along with the Royal

Library. She also established the first newspaper *O Pais* in 1835. For these achievements she became known in time as Queen Maria II, the Educator.

Maria Gloria did not have the advantage of learning from an educator of the stature of Bonifácio. Instead, she and her servant Graca had to seek solace and guidance from the writings of a Brazilian priest from an earlier century, Antonio Vieira. However, even his wisdom could never reconcile Maria Gloria to her life in Portugal, any more than could two husbands and a love affair with one of her ministers. What she gained from Vieira's writings was a sense of the value, of the necessity of education for herself, for her children, and for her nation, just as Bonifácio had instilled this principle in Leopoldina and Pedro II. All three family members believed in enlightenment and progress, and all three were ahead of their time in the countries they were trying to lead.

In her most recent novel, *Die Amazone von Rom: Das abenteuerliche Leben der Christina von Schweden 1626-1689* ('The Amazon of Rome: The Adventurous Life of Christina of Sweden 1626-1689,' 2005),[10] Kaiser continues her examination of outstanding, intelligent, educated women who play an important role in their lifetimes as cultural pioneers as well as social and political activists, and serve as models of a liberated woman at a time when most females at all social levels were repressed in their patriarchal hierarchies. Like the Habsburg rulers a century later, Christina of Sweden, who was born in 1626 as the daughter of King Gustav II (killed in 1632 in the Thirty Years' War), was subjected to a rigorous, almost cruel upbringing to prepare her to be Queen, a duty she never wanted to fulfill. She devised a clever way to survive her ordeal: she obediently fulfilled every demand made of her, while mentally fleeing into a second world in which she could feel as free as her outer life was strictly regulated. She became expert at living a dual life, and the synergy of the two endowed her with enormous mental strength, perseverance, and total independence of spirit. She despised hypocrisy and sought truth. This dualism in her life extends to her religion—she was born Protestant but converted to Catholicism in 1655—and to her intellectual curiosity. She accepted her new faith, but never let it interfere with her libertine lifestyle or with her fascination for the budding sciences which were revealing the secrets of nature—up to the 17th century a taboo, subject to church punishment. To prevent freethinking and scientific inquiry was the rationale for the Inquisition.

Christina never intended to become Queen, but she also wanted to end the senseless Thirty Years' War. In 1641 she began to plan her strategy to accomplish her goals. For twelve years she lived a dual life, agreeing to become Queen and marry after the war was concluded, while behind the scenes forwarding money and goods in preparation for fulfilling her own wishes to leave Sweden, convert to Catholicism, and live in Rome. By forcing the end of the war, this young woman with a will of steel changed the entire course of Swedish history. Christina thwarted the plans of the military and the political power structure of Sweden which desired to keep the conquered territories and become the strongest country in Europe. When the war ended in 1648, she kept her part of the bargain and accepted the crown in 1650, only to abdicate and leave Sweden in 1654.

Christina stands out as an early example of a fully emancipated woman who, after discovering that her first great love intended to marry her only to gain political power, determined never to marry but to take lovers as she found them. Even though she was only a civilian in Rome, her presence was so commanding that she was always treated as if she were still queen. She lived in Rome for 33 years and became a good friend of Pope Innocence XI. This made her an enemy of Joanna Orsini, known as the pope maker, who did not want her influence over Innocence weakened. Christina's mentor and longest lover was the Jesuit priest Antonio Vieira, an intellectual and free thinker who had been condemned by the Inquisition and forbidden to preach or speak. At Christina's request the Pope saved his life and allowed him to move to Rome. He was required to live in solitary confinement, but Christina could visit him.

In 1675 the Pope released Vieira from his confinement and allowed him to return to Salvador, Brazil. His departure was a terrible loss to Christina, but he remained in her mind and heart through her copy of his writings, which she treasured. Orsini brought charges against Christina for her affair with Vieira and Ehud de Neto, but in 1684 the Pope, who was greatly in Christina's debt, acquitted her. She had helped the Pope in 1683 by sending money to Johann Sobieski to support him in defeating the Turks when it looked as if they would take Vienna and then Rome. With the Turkish defeat, Rome remained safe as the seat of the papacy.

In gratitude, the Pope gave Christina his blessing to proceed with a bold stroke to become Queen of Naples. To do so, she had to drive out the Spanish and end their control over the papacy. She failed because the plan for a military coup was betrayed to the Spanish by Monaldesco, her second great love, while serving as her counselor and secretary. As an impoverished nobleman, he wanted the crown of Naples for himself to restore his stature. In a frenzy of anger Christine ordered her soldiers to stab him to death.

Christina died as the result of a fall in 1669 and was buried in St. Peter's Cathedral. She had left a detailed will, specifying what was to be done with her large library of 7000 volumes, her 200 original manuscripts on astronomy and alchemy, as well as libretti, plays and opera scores, along with several hundred paintings and sculptures as well as coin collections. She had ordained that this collection should be kept together in the Riario Palace. But with the death of her chosen executor Decio Azzelino six weeks later, the collections were broken up and sold. Centuries later the Swedish government was able to buy back some of the pieces for the Swedish National Gallery.

These five historical-biographical novels, soon to be supplemented by the life of Antonio Vieira, combine to present a detailed and insightful examination of the life and times of Brazil and Portugal from the 17th to the end of the 19th century, written by an author who has both studied her subject matter thoroughly and has adopted Brazil as her second homeland. As novels they present their protagonists as rounded characters, something historians are unable to accomplish. It is not just what these protagonists accomplished, but how they managed their achievements and at what cost in personal terms that provides the richness and complexity of these works and makes them valuable resources for understanding this period at a depth that a straightforward historical recitation of facts can never accomplish. History with its reliance on accurate facts can represent a documented surface truth that appeals to the mind, while literature with its possibilities for the unlimited imagination of the novelist can divine the higher truth that grips and moves the heart.

Like Zweig's biographies, Kaiser's works are literary contributions, intended among other things to educate readers about fascinating historical personages and political interconnections that are not as well known in Europe as they should be, to help overcome prevailing misconceptions. Also, like Zweig, she has written works that are timeless, not merely entertaining trivial literature for short-term diversion. These writings, which up to now have proved to be more popular in Brazil than in Austria or the U.S., will retain their interest and engage readers as long as publishers keep them in print. For they not only deal with outstanding subjects, but they are also narrated in a manner that makes them as enjoyable as they are informative.

Clearly Gloria Kaiser has moved from her provincial beginnings to become an international author and cultural mediator of note. Her experience demonstrates that if one remains a provincial author today, then it is by personal choice, not by necessity, as was the case up to the 20th century.

Notes

[1] Josef Nadler, *Geschichte der Deutschen Literatur nach Stämmen und Landschaften* (Regensburg: J. Habbel, 1912-1928).
[2] Many of the details in this article are attributable to an interview with the author and to subsequent correspondence. Her openness and willingness to supply materials and answer questions have made it possible to write this article and are greatly appreciated.
[3] For a list of her early prizes, see *Leseprobe, Gloria Kaiser* at <http://www.literaturhaus.at/buch/buch/rez7gloriakaiser/bio.html>
[4] Quoted in "Gloria Kaiser, vorgestellt von Renate Welsh," in *Autorenporträts*, <http://www.plautz.atautoren/13kaiser.htm>
[5] Gloria Kaiser, "Hauptberuf Schüler," in *hpt Magazine*, 2 (Vienna: 1995), 14.
[6] The English version, *Dona Leopoldina: The Habsburg Empress of Brazil*, was published by Ariadne Press in 1998 in the translation of Lowell A. Bangerter, with excellent Afterwords by the author and by Ernestine Schlant.
[7] The flourishing African slave trade was not finally abolished until 1888 by Isabella, the daughter of King Pedro II and heir apparent, who signed the decree while ruling in the absence of the king. For her bold action she became known as Isabella the Redeemer.
[8] The English version, *Pedro II of Brazil*, was published by Ariadne Press in 2000 in the translation of Lowell A. Bangerter, with Afterwords by the author and by the translator.
[9] The English version, *Saudade: The Life & Death of Queen Maria Gloria of Lusitania*, was published by Ariadne Press in 2005 in the translation of Lowell A. Bangerter, with Afterwords by the author and by the translator.

[10] Cf. the excellent review by Werner Krause, "Ein Schicksalsbild, in Worten gemalt," in *Kleine Zeitung*, 24 (December 2005), 80.

ELISABETH REICHART
Courtesy of Otto Müller Verlag

Elisabeth Reichart's *Komm über den See*: Upper Austria and the Excavation of Its History

by Felix W. Tweraser

Elisabeth Reichart's short novel *Komm über den See* ('Come Across the Lake'),[1] persuasively links its protagonist's protracted memory work to her experience of physical space: the novel recounts Ruth Berger's relocation from Vienna to the Salzkammergut resort town Gmunden and her fruitful efforts to find out about her own past and its connection to the anti-Nazi resistance in the region. Leaving behind a twenty-year career as a translator in Vienna—and, the novel implies, social status bought at the price of conformity—Ruth becomes a history teacher and accepts a one-year appointment to the *Gymnasium* in Gmunden; thus begins her simultaneous journey of self-discovery and an investigation into Austria's Nazi past, with a scholarly focus on resistance by the region's women. Ruth's personal history, as she gradually discovers, begins in Gmunden and the Salzkammergut in these same resistance circles. As Ruth achieves physical distance from the comforts of her life in Vienna, she begins to cast off the denial and rationalization that had prevented her from a more reflective engagement with the world around her; as she gathers more information about her own past as the daughter of a Nazi-careerist father and resistance-fighter mother (and how the primal experience of parental abandonment has influenced her own adult relationships) she is able to contextualize broader historical narratives in Austria. This process of finding her own language is suggested by Reichart's narrative technique, which posits contradictory interior voices within Ruth's consciousness. Perhaps in a nod to the tradition of the Bildungsroman, Ruth's journey away from the Viennese center corresponds to a more nuanced look within: self-knowledge and knowledge of the society around her correspond to relocation to an assumed periphery, one that is not so peripheral upon closer examination. As a trained historian, Reichart herself is attuned to the intricate relationship between personal experience, socialization, and political interests; in the Austrian postwar context, all these found their expression in a conspiracy of silence with respect to the Nazi past, and it is this dialogical nexus that the novel's protagonist sorts out.

Reichart's major works from the 1980s, *Februarschatten* (*February Shadows*)[2] and *Komm über den See*, reflect in many ways the author's socialization—education, religion, family life—in the province of Upper Austria during the 1950s and 60s. Born in Steyregg, a suburb across the Danube from Linz, Reichart grew up in a region and time that had a problematic relationship with the legacies of the Nazi past. *February Shadows* recounts the grisly murders of hundreds of Soviet prisoners of war at the hands of the local populace after they had escaped from the nearby Mauthausen concentration camp, an event that has come to be known as the 'Mühl District Rabbit Hunt' (*"Mühlviertler Hasenjagd"*). The novel documents the memory work of its central character, Hilde, someone who witnessed the murders but did nothing to stop them, a fairly typical attitude in the war's aftermath. In these novels Reichart foregrounds many of the concerns that animated her dissertation research at the University of Salzburg on resistance to Nazi rule in Upper Austria. In an interview, Reichart grouped these two novels together as an act of personal creative liberation, one tied to the long-suppressed memory of the victims of Nazi terror and those who actively resisted it:

'My development is actually one of liberation. Perhaps that sounds strange, because the war has always been there. But with *February Shadows* and 'Come Across the Lake' I still had the feeling that I needed to do right by someone. In *February Shadows* it was the murdered escapees, and in 'Come Across the Lake' it was the women resistance fighters. That was quite a burden while I was writing, because I felt like I not only could write what I wanted to, but that I also had to be careful to do honor to these people.'[3]

In the following remarks, I argue that Reichart contrasts the ineffable qualities of individual memory to the individual's inquiry into the historical record—here the protagonist Ruth's investigation of women who actively resisted Nazi rule—and how these are inextricably linked to self-reflection, personal growth, and social integration. Reichart's novel becomes a close examination of the silent agreements and codes that prevent an honest engagement with the past, one in which Ruth simultaneously uncovers long-suppressed evidence about the Austrian past, finds out the truth about her own personal history, and, in so doing, becomes a more effective and reflective professional and citizen.

The novel's plot may be quickly summarized: Ruth Berger, at age forty-five, accepts a one-year appointment to teach English and History at the *Gymnasium* in Gmunden. Over the course of the year, Ruth confronts a rigidly hierarchical school, in which the director and senior colleagues try to intimidate her into conforming to its standard practices. Nevertheless, she employs some innovative methods to get her students to investigate the Salzkammergut's past. Ruth finds one friend and colleague at the school, Susanne, with whom she travels in the area and shares interests and world-view. Ruth has two brief affairs during the year, one with Christian, a freelance investigative journalist whose critical work about Gmunden—he has exposed the current

212 Beyond Vienna

city fathers' commemoration of the "Night of Broken Glass" ("*Kristallnacht*")—is rejected by Austrian public television (ORF), and one with Heinz, Susanne's son, an architecture student in Vienna. Ruth's most important new acquaintance is Anna Zach, a former anti-Nazi resistance fighter who lives alone in Gmunden. Through Anna, Ruth finds out that her own mother was also in the resistance, but that she had, under torture and the threat of losing her daughter, betrayed Anna to the Gestapo; she also finds out that her parents had originally named her Brigitta. In the novel's final ironic twist, Ruth's contract is not renewed because the school's director considers Anna a criminal, due to her involvement in the Gmunden milk-revolt of 1947 and subsequent imprisonment by American occupation authorities, so Ruth's consorting with such criminal elements is deemed unacceptable.

Historical Background

The appearance of 'Come Across the Lake' was part of a gradual loosening of the self-serving mythology crucial to the founding and, indeed, success of the Second Republic. The broad consensus that prevailed in Austrian political culture, at least until 1986, the year of the Waldheim affair and Jörg Haider's assumption of power in the Freedom party, had been reinforced by certain foundational historical narratives that bound various constituencies across party lines, chief among these being official Austria's assertion of victim status during the period 1938-1945—incidentally a policy promoted by the allied occupation powers—the less-than-forthright official and private confrontation with shared responsibility for the Nazi period, and the subsequent rapid reintegration into the Western sphere of influence during the Cold War. As new generations of opinion leaders have come upon the scene, these foundational myths have had less and less force; the truth-seeking and truth-telling that became the unintended consequences of Kurt Waldheim's presidential campaign in 1986 and the changing geopolitical situation have opened up previously unexplored avenues for dialogue with regard to the past. The political and social realignments that have taken place in Austria since the 1986 Waldheim affair, while amply described and reflected upon in print media, also have symbolic and visual analogs in public space: in the ephemeral interventions attached to demonstrations, temporary art exhibitions, and performance that have characterized the last two decades; and the more permanent changes in the physical commemorative landscape, which provide more opportunities for introspection, reflection, and expiation, all activities pursued by Ruth Berger in 'Come Across the Lake.'

The visual and physical commemorative analog has become particularly important because it anchors memory to something concrete and documentable, that is, the tangible qualities of artifact and property offer different access to historical memory, so as eyewitness accounts—such as Anna Zach's in 'Come Across the Lake'—fade and narrative accounts, both fictional and non-fictional, proliferate, the symbolic terrain of the visual takes on special importance. While the phrases of commemoration do not necessarily support the preservation of historical memory—and are subject to instrumentalization for various political ends—the interrogation of property rights and the interventions in the physical landscape may promote historical memory in qualitatively different and more permanent ways.[4]

Why such memory work skipped two generations in Austria has been the subject of numerous theoretical reflection coming from the cultural critics of postwar Austria. Robert Menasse's analysis of the 'aesthetics of social partnership' (*"Sozialpartnerschaftliche Ästhetik"*), in which he argued that cultural production was subordinated to the goal of building broad, even undemocratic, political consensus, was complemented theoretically by Joseph Haslinger's assertion of a uniquely Austrian 'politics of emotions' (*"Politik der Gefühle"*), in which public pronouncements of *"Vergangenheitsbewältigung"* (or 'coming to terms with the past') did not match the private and unofficial versions of this same historical narrative.[5] Such privately held opinions, brilliantly satirized by Helmut Qualtinger's "Herr Karl," did not really crystallize in public until the Waldheim affair, the reactions to the commemorative practice of the *Bedenkjahr* 1988 (for instance, the rampant demagoguery surrounding the staging of Thomas Bernhard's *Heldenplatz* at the Burgtheater)[6] and the crumbling of the Iron Curtain and the ideological cover it had provided. Menasse identified correctly the antidemocratic aspects of the *Sozialpartnerschaft* and other extra-parliamentary conflict-resolution practices, and indeed a broad constituency emerged that began to tire of such behind-the-scenes patronage; it was to this constituency that Haider spoke, offering relatively facile solutions to complex problems, but also hitting a broad vein of resentment towards such corporatist arrangements. Haider also spoke the coded language of the privately held versions of the past, a political ideology promoted most potently by the daily newspaper, "*Die Kronen Zeitung,*" and unofficial, more local organizational forms. The force of these private opinions with respect to public institutional practice is personified in 'Come Across the Lake' by the school director, who labels the resistance fighter Anna Zach a criminal, and by her colleague Knapp, who insists on exclusively teaching so-called 'finer literature' ("*schöne Literatur*"), eliding anything politically critical such as works by Borchert or Brecht.

How are such aspects of political ideology mapped onto the physical world around us? Heidemarie Uhl argues very persuasively that the official policy towards the commissioning of public army ("*Wehrmacht*") veterans' memorials in the 1950s and 60s—be this at the federal, state, or local level—perpetuated a kind of historical amnesia that has only slowly eroded. While such memorials are common in Austria—here a confluence of local patriotism and Cold War ideology can be seen—there were hardly any monuments, even up until the most recent years, that honored the victims of Nazi persecution in any but vague terms. Uhl, like Haslinger, argues that a certain type of double-speak evolved, in which public declarations of solidarity with the Nazis' victims were kept vague, when, uttered at all, while a private language and commemorative practices emerged that could emphasize continuity with the Nazi past without getting into specifics.[7] In 'Come Across the Lake,' Anna Zach's rejection of the label victim and her metaphorical insistence that she is but a droplet in a sea of forgetting (yet one droplet that can turn the tide), speak to one person's defiance of this dominant mode of historical memory. More recently in Austria, though, there is more local initiative to correct such omissions in historical memory, witness the numerous new memorials to the victims of Nazism and the renovation and re-opening of the synagogue in Graz, as a majority of Austrians seems to be initiating a re-evaluation of commemorative practice. The public discussion of "*Vergangenheitsbewältigung*" has itself become more messy and pluralistic in Austria, but is arguably merely a reflection of the increasing public—and now private, as well—honesty with regard to this past; a different type of consensus has emerged, one in which a more open, democratic society breaks certain taboos that prevailed for many generations. Reichart's work is an important part of this process, as Ruth Berger's story links personal history with collective memory in a landscape most resonant with allusive locations.

To illustrate this movement towards more nuanced commemorative practice, one may compare the composition of two public monuments in central Vienna: Alfred Hrdlicka's monument to the victims of Fascism on the Albertinaplatz, unveiled in 1988; and Rachael Whiteread's monument to the Jews of Austria who perished at the hands of the Nazis, unveiled in 2000. Hrdlicka's is an ensemble of marble and bronze sculptures on mostly a grand scale; it gave specific form to many of the foundational myths of the postwar era in Austria. Victims of aggression associated with war and fascism are leveled: the allied bombing raids take a prominent place in the ensemble, while the miniature bronze figure of the kneeling Jew—an image taken from the time immediately after the "*Anschluss*," when Jews were forced to clean off the painted slogans from the pre-empted referendum on Austrian independence—in its scale relative to the ensemble's other pieces and its depiction of abject victimization, actually perpetuates the prevailing attitudes.

    The more abstract artistic vocabulary of Rachael Whiteread's composition, is, by contrast, able to express the void of this history in compelling ways. Whiteread's concrete is sparse in its references: a rectangular structure depicts an inverted library, the books' bindings are hidden and that they face outward implies a void within the interior space of the monument. Whiteread engraves the monument with the names of the concentration and extermination camps where 65,000 Austrian Jews perished. The void at the center of the monument is an apt, indeed profound, symbolic rendition of the void left by the annihilation of this part of Austria's past; the monument invites the viewer's reflection on the ultimate implications of such empty space. (How was this empty space filled in the immediate postwar years? Not with honest confrontation, expiation, symbolic expressions of solidarity, or even the commission of a commemorative monument, in fact, quite the opposite.) Whiteread's monument speaks eloquently to both the actual void left and its implications for subsequent generations. The enigmatic composition is open-ended, allowing the viewer to imagine how the cityscape might be different if the library were not inverted, if the void were not so ever-present. The monument has become a place of private expiation and mourning in public space. The city's decision to turn this plaza into a pedestrian zone has reinforced the opportunity for this to become a place of reflective contemplation. Such changes in the Austrian physical landscape are indicative of recognition that commemorative practices are an important indicator, however symbolic, of a society's ability to more honestly interrogate its shared heritage.[8]

Vienna to Gmunden: Space, Distance, and Reflection

The novel begins with a compact description of Ruth's life in Vienna during the summer prior to her appointment to Gmunden: she is in professional limbo, waiting for word from the education ministry whether or not she has received a teaching assignment. She is trained as a translator, due in part to having inherited her actor father's linguistic talent, but it becomes clear that in her own language she is blocked by gaps in her memory. Her life in Vienna is at a standstill, as she withdraws from the world and any personal intimacy. When Ruth finds out that her teaching position is in Gmunden, her reactions run the gamut:

> 'For a moment only joy, an almost forgotten clarity of feeling. Then came disappointment, against which Ruth fought, but how do you fight against yourself when one voice, indeed your own, reminds you of your forbidden hopes while another resists leaving Vienna to go to this small town, Gmunden. Ruth tried to imagine Gmunden. She sought help from Peter Altenberg, read: "to enjoy most deeply with my eyes the forested shores of this beloved lake!"—and saw the lake and the forests, saw Gmunden, saw everything pictured on many postcards that had spilled out of a box, lying on the floor, but she no longer knew where she had held the box in her hands.'[9]

In this passage, Reichart re-emphasizes the competing voices that inhabit Ruth's consciousness and suggests the vague feelings of déjà vu that are to accompany her in Gmunden. There is also an assumed dichotomy between center and periphery set up in the two voices that, taken together, express Ruth's ambivalence about the move.

Initially, Ruth experiences aspects of life in a small town that conform to her own (and perhaps readerly) expectations. Everyone seems to know about everyone else: when Ruth makes a trip to the druggist to combat a skin rash prior to her first day at school, the druggist knows who she is, and, in turn, the school's director knows about the visit on the first day of school. There is a lack of privacy in personal matters: the school director, in introducing Ruth to the staff, openly states that she has been chosen because of her father's fame and social status; Ruth's affair with Heinz becomes the talk of the town; and, perhaps most significantly, Ruth's association with the former resistance fighter Anna Zach leads to her dismissal at the end of the year. There is a lack of intellectual curiosity in the institutions meant to foster such inquiry: in the *Gymnasium*, authority is patriarchal and administered through intimidation and fear, while the curriculum discourages creativity and, in literature, forbids teaching such "controversial" authors as Borchert and Brecht. And yet, as Ruth discovers, rendered in extended sequences of interior monologue, these same obstacles to human creativity were present in Vienna. Indeed, the experience of being an outsider in Gmunden—and the object of innuendo, snap judgment, and ostracism—is precisely what Ruth has enacted in Vienna with respect to anyone who had tried to establish a close relationship with her, from her ex-husband Walter to her college roommate Eva, who commits suicide, to her colleague Martha, who is committed to a mental institution. It is Eva who characterizes Ruth as someone gifted in all languages but her own, and Ruth's startling discoveries about her personal history in Gmunden are due in no small part to the reflections on her Viennese experience that the distance, in time and space, Gmunden's vantage point provides. Reichart beautifully realizes this aspect in the constant changes in narrative register: first-, second-, and third-person are all used to describe Ruth and her experiences.

The Salzkammergut lake district has long been a beloved vacation destination for Austrians and foreign tourists alike. Its scenic beauty—snowcapped mountains, deep valleys, picturesque lakes, and well preserved hamlets—and historically strategic importance long made it a destination for the Monarchy's political and cultural elite: Franz Josef summered in Bad Ischl, writers and artists were drawn to the *Ausseerland*, hikers and skiers came to the imposing slopes. During the Nazi period in Austria, the Salzkammergut was of strategic importance to the rulers, who used it to store the ill-gotten gains of Aryanized property and to establish the concentration camp in Ebensee (at the opposite end of the Traunsee from Gmunden), among other things, but it was also the site of indigenous resistance to Nazi rule; the resisters' superior knowledge of the terrain allowed for some effective actions.

The gateway city to the Salzkammergut for travelers coming from Vienna is Gmunden. Upon her arrival, Ruth has a particularly troubling vision of what lies beneath the town's pleasant façade:

> 'To Ruth, Gmunden, this city that seemed so little of this time but still existed in time, was uncanny. She couldn't shake the feeling that it is a space, bathed in milk, and at any minute the facades may disintegrate, exposing the grimacing faces, the people going at each other, as so often here.'[10]

This vision, tantamount to second sight, contrasts the escapist fantasies to which such tourist destinations appeal with the underlying historical resonance of the place itself, the ghostly return of what has been excised from Austrian history. Gmunden does not honor or in any way ennoble those citizens who resisted the Nazis, but rather ostracizes the few who still live there. Ruth is inexorably drawn to one such citizen, Anna Zach, who lives in isolation from everyone else, including her own family, and yet whom Ruth comes to believe is intimately connected to her own personal history.

Anna lays out clearly how the conspiracy of silence works in Gmunden, as elsewhere in Austria—and how it was experienced by one deemed unacceptable—in her account of its history:

'Their [the Austrians'] long lasting effort to ignore whole genocides must have been similarly monstrous to the monstrosity itself. This effort had to have paid off. And it was rewarded. It was made state doctrine. Already in the summer of 1945 it was in the headlines of the Austrian press: 'Let's forget the last seven years! Together into the future!' With this 'together' the murdered were murdered yet again. The murderers are in power. They knew what they were doing. We don't exist in the reality of this country.'[11]

And yet in the novel the reality of the Salzkammergut's history keeps getting in the way of the escapist fantasies that the tourist industry produces. Ruth travels to the other end of the Traunsee, to Ebensee, where she patronizes a drugstore that had been Aryanized during the Nazi period and where a notorious concentration camp had been located. She travels to Gößl in the Ausseerland, where the nearby Toplitzsee is the site of storage of Nazi booty on a massive scale. The physical wonders of the area are rendered metaphorically in a recurring dream that Anna Zach recounts to Ruth:

'In the future we [the women of the resistance] will not have existed. We'll be like the caves inside the mountains, outside a vague knowledge that something was and is there, some will go into the caves, parts of us they will admire, the way they admire the waterfalls, huge amphitheaters, and stalagmites, they'll also find a lot they can admire, but they'll turn around in time, before their glances rest on the shimmering walls and their foot gets stuck in the slime, and who will dare to take them to task, these escapees from the conspiracy of forgetting, we'll

prepare them a feast, we'll be grateful, when the
lake is dried up, then a droplet is everything.'[12]

Ruth's training as a historian—the ones who follow the vague knowledge that these stories must be told—is depicted here visually in the image of the visitor who steps outside the norm, which in turn allows for the empathetic and original viewpoint that exposes the conspiracy of silence for what it is. This work is by its nature lonely, appropriately rendered in the image of a droplet against a vast sea of forgetting, but it is necessary to get beyond the façade.

Ruth's mother gave her that name so that the primal parental betrayals enacted in her formative years—when her name was Brigitta—might be erased. As Ruth, and well into her adult years, betrayal—of her and by her—is one of the overarching themes in her close relationships. While in Gmunden, Ruth reflects on these serial betrayals that had accompanied her life in Vienna, slowly coming to the realization that she was the one responsible for them, and something about her past prevented her from recognizing this. Her marriage to Walter runs aground on Ruth's accusation of hypocrisy: while he sees no contradiction in personal use of hashish at the same time that he, as a judge, sentences other users to harsh penalties, Ruth cannot get beyond this seeming contradiction between public and private behavior. Ruth abandons her college roommate Eva at a time of maximum need and vulnerability in order to begin her own career as a translator; Eva subsequently takes her own life. Ruth holds her freelance translator colleague Martha's descent into mental illness at arm's length, unable to find the words to help her friend. The name Ruth, of course, suggests the Biblical book, but the underlying qualities of loyalty and solidarity among women that animate Ruth and Naomi's journey find opposite expression in Ruth Berger's life in Vienna. Ruth is plagued by an inability to empathize with those in her immediate circle, but nevertheless is drawn to the academic topic of women's resistance to Nazi rule in Austria. It is only after departing from the comfort zone of Vienna that she develops the qualities of empathy and forgiveness that allow the human dimension of the resistance fighters to emerge, while at the same time she begins to understand its connection to her own identity.

Reichart artfully juxtaposes the metaphorical representation of the physical world of Gmunden with Ruth's extended narrated monologues. Her visions of Gmunden settling into the lake, what lies beneath its pleasant façade, and the account of Anna's subterranean dream are all meditations on the relationship between appearance and reality, the desire to transcend what is on the surface to pursue a different truth. The poem by Sarah Kirsch that gives the novel its name similarly expresses the call to transcend the known, to move across self-imposed boundaries to a deeper truth. That this pursuit need not be idealized, that it must embrace good, evil, and all their gradations, is exemplified by a scene on Gmunden's only tram, in which hazardous materials from a truck bring traffic to a standstill:

'A row of cars stopped in front of the tram, a truck was missing its rear door, from the inside a brown liquid was dripping, its drops fell hissing onto the pavement, changed color, and became shimmering blisters; Ruth couldn't look away from this metamorphosis, at once the most beautiful and ugliest sight.'[13]

Ruth's intense gaze at this seemingly contradictory image suggests what is going on in her personal and more public professional life: she begins to cast off the encumbrances which prevented a more humane inquiry into her scholarly subject and begins to embrace the contradictory aspects of her own identity.

Ruth's career as translator—and her seemingly well-intentioned recommendations to Eva to get on with her life and follow a similar path—represents assimilation into the dominant postwar Austrian cultural mode. She only leaves this job after realizing that the firm is involved in the production of armaments; her career path is one going in the direction from center to periphery, in that she becomes a teacher with no long-term job security, at the margins of that profession; such a vantage point allows for a more dispassionate look at the world around her, one less beholden to self-interest and compromise. Ruth's idealization of the women of the resistance—and the memory of her mother—yields, in her interview with Anna Zach, to a more nuanced approach to historical memory, and a more balanced view of her own personal history.

The prevailing gender dynamic is re-enforced in Gmunden, with its exclusively patriarchal institutional structures. How this dynamic contributes to the ultimate complexity of historical truth is exemplified in the subplot with the journalist Christian, with whom Ruth has a brief affair. Christian has uncovered a potentially incendiary story in Gmunden: a group led by a member of the city council but which also includes other leading politicians, lawyers, businessmen, and doctors annually celebrates "*Kristallnacht*," and openly so. When Christian presents his materials to the ORF, not only does the network fail to use them in production, but they mysteriously disappear. Christian does not pursue the matter further, in spite of Ruth's encouragement to do so, and in fact admits that he enjoyed the company of these men when he interviewed them for his piece. As Jennifer Michaels correctly points out in her analysis of this episode, "Reichart sharply criticizes how, in her view, politicians and media cooperate in trying to silence both the past and the fascist tendencies in the present."[14] One aspect of this continuity that the novel stresses is that the historical narrative, past and present, is controlled almost exclusively by men. Even the male-dominated accounts of the resistance itself do not allow a space for the role of women in its efforts, which make Anna Zach's story all the more revolutionary and necessary. Christian takes a cynical and resigned attitude when his story is censored. Ruth's approach is different: Anna Zach's story—as the reader finds out at the end of the novel—emerges direct and unmediated, beyond the reach of the patriarchal social machinery.

Still, it is worth noting here that Reichart's reference to the milk revolt of 1947 in the Salzkammergut—and Anna Zach's role as one of its leaders—leaves out much that is part of the historical record. Anna's involvement in the milk revolt, as recounted by the director of Ruth's school, bears a striking resemblance to that of the historical Maria Sams, one of its leaders. What Reichart's account omits is the leaders' instrumentalization of latent anti-Semitic attitudes that still prevailed in postwar Austria: a crucial element of the agitators' argument was that DPs [displaced persons] temporarily housed in the Salzkammergut—among them a high percentage of Jewish refugees from concentration camps—received preferential treatment from the U.S. occupation authorities with respect to the distribution of milk. According to Kurt Tweraser, 'the demonstrators' motives were probably a dangerous mixture of justified displeasure with the nutritional conditions, suspicion of the many DPs in the area, particularly the Jews among them, because of their perceived preferential treatment by the Americans, and finally a latent anti-Semitism that was activated by these events.'[15] Within the world of the text, the reader is pointed to the irony of Anna Zach's "criminal" past being tied to her designation as such by the American occupiers—whose motives the school director does not question—in turn providing a cover for the criminalization of her *anti-Fascist* activities. The role of latent and overt anti-Semitism does not fit neatly into the faintly hagiographical picture of Anna Zach drawn in the text, yet this added complexity provided by the historical record casts the events of the text in a new light, perhaps unintended by Reichart. The question is quite complex, as Ruth's colleague Susanne points out, particularly when Anna is being upheld to the students as a role model: 'The right wing is making more and more gains. Is everything supposed to begin again as before, just in different uniforms? That these women existed, here and everywhere, that's the most important thing!'[16] In the end, Ruth does not invite Anna to speak to her students, respecting her wishes to be left alone, yet the novel as a whole honors Anna's unique voice and perspective. The communication of individual to individual in an atmosphere of empathy and respect allows this to happen.

The focal point of Ruth's professional life in Gmunden remains the *Gymnasium*, but as Ruth soon finds out, it is not educating students to be critical thinkers about Austria's past, but rather is training them in the codes and manners of the conspiracy of silence that characterized postwar Austrian society. The school, indeed, represents continuity with respect to the Nazi past, seen, among other examples, in the director's unctuous praise for Ruth's birth father, a not atypical case of an artist swept along by the Nazi tide who suspends critical engagement in favor of career advancement. Such a workplace prompts Ruth to reflect on her ability to be a good teacher, how to emerge from all the incentives to conform to convey more eternal ideals to her students. Her doubts are strong: 'A different voice answered her: you'll lie to the students, betray them, penalize them, ignore them, grade them unfairly, and treat them unjustly, and you'll prefer some—all errors that teachers can commit in the daily course of events, you'll commit!'[17] Ruth is able to transcend such internal warnings by encouraging her students to question the conventional wisdom about the Salzkammergut and its history.

Conclusion

Coinciding with the 50-year anniversary of Austria's annexation by Nazi Germany, 'Come Across the Lake' (1988) did little to reinforce the comfortable history of Austria as a small land and Hitler's first victim. Rather, it holds up a mirror to Austrians and their accepted commonplaces of historical memory—their victim status, geopolitical insignificance, doing one's duty—that had dominated collective commemoration in the half-century after the war. How one creates or reawakens memory through an aesthetic experience is a central question in the debate over the appropriate commemoration of the past; 'Come Across the Lake' accomplishes such reawakening of memory both by overt emphasis on the nature of memory in the text, but also in the story's paradigmatic qualities: the particular historical resonance of Ruth's quest for knowledge about her own origins, things of which she is dimly and impressionistically aware, but has essentially repressed. Reichart's narrative suggests the intimate connections between individual memory and the spatial analog of relocation away from the "comfortable" center, here... Vienna.

Notes

[1] Elisabeth Reichart, *Komm über den See* (Wien: Franz Deuticke, 2001). All quotations from the Deuticke edition. The novel was originally published with S. Fischer in 1988.
[2] Elisabeth Reichart, *Februarschatten* (Wien: Edition Junges Österreich, 1984), also as *February Shadows*, translated by Donna L. Hoffmeister (Riverside, CA: Ariadne Press, 1989).
[3] "*Meine Entwicklung ist eigentlich die einer Befreiung. Das klingt vielleicht komisch, weil der Krieg immer geblieben ist. Aber ich hatte bei 'Februarschatten,' 'Komm über den See' noch das Gefühl, dass ich jemandem gerecht werden muss. Bei 'Februarschatten' waren es die getöteten Flüchtlinge und bei 'Komm über den See' die Widerstandskämpferinnen im Salzkammergut. Das war eigentlich eine große Belastung beim Schreiben, weil ich das Gefühl hatte, dass ich nicht nur schreiben kann, was ich schreiben will, sondern ich muss auch schauen, dass ich diesen Menschen gerecht werde.*" See Linda DeMeritt and Peter Ensberg, "'Für mich ist die Sprache eigentlich ein Schatz:' Interview mit Elisabeth Reichart," in *Modern Austrian Literature*, 29 (1996), 16-17. All translations within this essay, unless otherwise attributed, are my own.

[4] Heidemarie Uhl, "Zur Frage der Instrumentalisierung von 'Vergangenheitsbewältigung,'" in *Gestörte Identitäten? Eine Zwischenbilanz der Zweiten Republik,* Musner, Wunberg, Cescutti, eds. (Innsbruck: Studien Verlag, 2002), 10-26. Tina Walzer and Stefan Templ, *Unser Wien: Arisierung auf österreichisch* (Berlin: Aufbau, 2001).

[5] Robert Menasse, *Überbau und Underground: Die sozialpartnerschaftliche Ästhetik* (Vienna: Sonderzahl, 1996); Josef Haslinger, *Politik der Gefühle* (Darmstadt: Luchterhand, 1987).

[6] See Fatima Naqvi, "Dialectic at a Standstill: Victimhood in Thomas Bernhard's *Heldenplatz*," in *German Quarterly,* 75 (2002), 408-21.

[7] *"Das Argument der Vergangenheitsbewältigung bewegt sich heute in anderen Kontexten; es beschränkt sich nicht mehr allein auf den gesellschaftskritischen Diskurs, sondern ist vieldeutig und offen für unterschiedliche Instrumentalisierungen geworden. In der aktuellen österreichischen Situation lassen sich 'kritische' und 'affirmative' Verwendungszusammenhänge beobachten, die sich vor allem durch ihre Intentionen unterscheiden: Die Erinnerung an die dunklen Seiten der Vergangenheit kann sowohl den Appell an ein entscheidendes Vorgehen gegen Intoleranz, Fremdenfeindlichkeit und Antisemitismus intendieren als auch in image- und geschichtspolitische Strategien von Staat und Parteien integriert werden."* Uhl, 23.

[8] Simon Wiesenthal, ed., *Projekt: Judenplatz Wien* (Vienna: Zsolnay, 2000); Gerhard Milchram, ed., *Judenplatz: Place of Remembrance* (Vienna: Jewish Museum of the City of Vienna, 2000).

[9] *"Für einen Moment nur Freude, fast vergessene Eindeutigkeit der Gefühle. Dann mischte sich Enttäuschung in sie, gegen die sich Ruth wehrte, aber wie wehrt man sich gegen sich, wenn eine Stimme, die doch auch die eigene, einen an die verbotenen Hoffnungen erinnert und eine andere sich weigert, Wien zu verlassen und nach Gmunden, in diese Kleinstadt, zu*

gehen. Ruth versuchte, sich Gmunden vorzustellen. Suchte Hilfe bei Peter Altenberg, las: 'dieses geliebten Sees bewaldete Ufer mit meinen Augen tief freudig zu genießen!'—und sah den See und die Wälder, sah Gmunden, sah alles abgebildet auf vielen Ansichtskarten, die aus einer Schachtel herausgequollen waren, auf dem Boden lagen, aber wo sie diese Schachtel in den Händen gehalten hatte, wußte sie nicht mehr" – 45-46.

[10] "Ruth war Gmunden, die Stadt, die so wenig von dieser Zeit an sich hat und doch in der Zeit ist, unheimlich. Sie wurde das Gefühl nicht los, es ist ein Raum, mit Milch getüncht, und jeden Moment können die Fassaden abbröckeln, die Fratzen zum Vorschein kommen, die Menschen übereinander herfallen, wie schon öfter hier" – 54.

[11] "Ihre jahrelange Anstrengung, ganze Völkermorde nicht zu sehen, muss ähnlich ungeheuerlich gewesen sein wie das Ungeheuerliche selbst. Diese Anstrengung musste sich lohnen. Und sie wurde belohnt. Sie wurde zur Staatsideologie ernannt. Bereits im Sommer 1945 stand es groß in der österreichischen Presse zu lesen: 'Vergessen wir die letzten sieben Jahre! Gemeinsam in die Zukunft!' Mit diesem 'gemeinsam' wurden die Ermordeten noch einmal ermordet. Die Mörder sind an der Macht. Sie wussten, was sie taten. Es gibt uns nicht in der Realität dieses Landes" – 162.

[12] "Später wird es uns [Frauen im Widerstand—Anm. des Verfassers] nicht gegeben haben. Wir werden wie die Höhlen im Inneren der Berge sein, draußen ein dumpfes Wissen, dass da noch etwas war und ist, manche werden in die Höhlen gehen, manches an uns werden sie gerne sehen, wie sie die Wasserfälle, die riesigen Hallen und die Tropfsteingebilde bewundern, werden sie auch an uns vieles finden, das sie bewundern können, aber sie werden rechtzeitig umkehren, bevor ihr Blick die schimmelnden Wände streift und der Fuß im Schlamm steckenbleibt, und wer wird es wagen, ihnen daraus einen Vorwurf zu machen, diesen Heraustretenden aus

der Übereinkunft des Vergessens, ein Fest werden wir ihnen bereiten, dankbar werden wir sein, wenn der See ausgetrocknet ist, dann ist ein Tropfen alles" – 113.

[13] *"Eine Reihe von Autos hielt vor der Straßenbahn, einem Lastwagen fehlte die hintere Tür, aus dem Innenraum tropfte eine bräunliche Flüssigkeit, zischend fielen die Tropfen zu Boden, verfärbten sich, wurden zu schillernden Blasen, Ruth konnte sich nicht sattsehen an dieser Verwandlung, das Schönste und das Häßlichste in einem, dachte sie"* – 98.

[14] Jennifer E. Michaels, "Breaking the Silence: Elisabeth Reichart's Protest against the Denial of the Nazi Past in Austria," in *German Studies Review*, 19 (1996), 22.

[15] *"Die Motive der Demonstranten waren wahrscheinlich eine gefährliche Mischung aus berechtigtem Mißmut über die Ernährungslage, Mißstimmung gegen die vielen DPs in der Umgebung, besonders die Juden unter ihnen, sowie wegen ihrer bevorzugten Behandlung durch die Amerikaner und schließlich einem latenten Antisemitismus, der durch diesen Anlaß aktiviert wurde."*—Kurt Tweraser, *US-Militärregierung Oberösterreich* (Linz: Oberösterreichisches Landesarchiv, 1995), 284.

[16] *"Die Rechten breiten sich mehr und mehr aus. Soll alles wieder von vorne anfangen, nur in anderen Kleidern? Dass es diese Frauen gab, hier und überall, darauf kommt es doch an!"* – 173.

[17] *"Eine andere Stimme antwortete ihr: Du wirst die Schüler belügen und betrügen und bestrafen und übersehen und falsch benoten und ungerecht behandeln, und manche wirst du bevorzugen—alle Fehler, die Lehrer im Alltag nur machen können, wirst auch du machen!"* – 117.

230   *Beyond Vienna*

VLADIMIR VERTLIB
Courtesy of Deuticke Verlag

Vladimir Vertlib, a Global Intellectual: Exile, Migration, and Individualism in the Narratives of a Russian Jewish Author in Austria

by Dagmar C. G. Lorenz

I. Vertlib's Evolving Narrative Universe

Vladimir Vertlib's story *Abschiebung* ('Deportation,' 1995) and his novel *Zwischenstationen* ('Intermediate Stations,' 1999) introduce a reality shared by countless people worldwide in the second half of the twentieth century: migration, illegal immigration and exploitation by employers and, finally, deportation. Vertlib himself is familiar with the unprotected nomadic life resulting from an unwanted citizenship or no citizenship at all.[1] Vertlib's first two books revolve around the topic of migration, but they are not migrants' narratives. Before publishing them the author had already achieved a position of relative security in Austria. He had completed his studies at the University of Vienna, gained a masterful command of the German language, married an Austrian, and moved to Salzburg. An active participant in Austrian, notably Viennese, cultural life, he had access to the institutions available to the intellectual elite of which he soon became a member. It is important to note that Vertlib wrote about his and his parents' plight retrospectively from a vantage point that included reflection and creative work.[2]

Vertlib was born in 1966 in Leningrad, after the demise of the Soviet Union, St. Petersburg. He and his family had left the USSR already in 1971. They went to Israel, from there to Austria and returned to Israel. The stations on their futile odyssey in search of a country where Vertlib's parents would be able to live according to their expectations and abilities included the Federal Republic of Germany, the Netherlands, and Italy. In 1981, after a failed attempt to immigrate to the United States, the family returned to Austria, where Vertlib has lived ever since. He studied economics and business at the University of Vienna and moved to Salzburg for personal reasons. Since 1993 he has worked as a free-lance author, social scientist, and translator in Salzburg and Vienna. His writings have appeared in Austrian literary journals such as "*Mit der Ziehharmonika*" and "*Literatur und Kritik.*" The Salzburg publisher Otto Müller published his first book *Die Abschiebung* in 1995. Vertlib is a highly visible member of the Austrian cultural and literary scene and recipient of important prizes and awards including in 1999 the Austrian *Förderungspreis für Literatur*, and in 2001 the *Förderpreis zum Chamisso-Preis der Bayerischen Akademie der Schönen Künste* and the *Anton Wildgans Preis*.[3] Moving away from his early style of confrontation and dissociation, Vertlib, by his own admission, has adopted over the years aspects of what he considers the Austrian mentality: 'I have truly become an Austrian, or more precisely, Viennese. I have to leave Vienna in order to understand that, over the years, I have assumed all the prejudices of this city—the smugness, arrogance, egocentricity, narcissistic love-hate, contempt for the "provinces," an inferiority complex toward foreign countries, and a nostalgic transfiguration of our former significance as a metropolis.'[4] Vertlib's list contains some of the major themes of post-Shoah Austrian writing, Jewish and non-Jewish. However, he is particularly sensitive to what Matti Bunzl called "Austria's lackluster *Vergangenheitsbewältigung*" (or coming to terms with its past), and in his writing there is a clear association with the "contemporary Jewish practices of counter-memory" that evolved from the post-Shoah experience of Jews in Austria.[5] Bunzl observes that the "failed normalization of Austrian-Jewish relations" and the fact that anti-Semitic power structures remained effectively unchallenged in the wake of Austria's liberation" has continued to be a constant concern in post-Shoah Austrian writing to which it provides its oppositional structure.[6]

In Vertlib's writing several literary discourses and collective memories intersect. His writing also participates in Austria's post-Shoah literary tradition and the new Jewish intellectual culture that emerged during the Waldheim scandal and includes authors such as Robert Schindel, Ruth Beckermann, Anna Mitgutsch, and Doron Rabinovici. As is the case with these authors—perhaps mediated by their works—Vertlib's writing has become increasingly informed by the experience of Austrian and Central European prose writers of the fin-de-siècle and interwar periods such as Joseph Roth and Elias Canetti. His search for Jewish identity between tradition and secularization places him in the larger context of Jewish exiles worldwide who escaped from Nazi-controlled Europe, e.g. Isaac Bashevis Singer, Anna Seghers, and Jakov Lind.

In *Abschiebung* and *Zwischenstationen,* Vertlib's topic and motifs, exclusion and rejection, and the profoundly pessimistic and sarcastic tenor in *Abschiebung* and *Zwischenstationen* call to mind Holocaust survivor Edgar Hilsenrath's New York novels *Zibulski oder Antenne im Bauch* ('Zibulski, or Antennas in the Belly,' 1983) and *Bronskis Geständnis* ('Bronski's Confession,' 1980). The latter works are replete with grotesque elements bringing to light the protagonist's equally pathetic and hopeless situation. The deliberately fragmentary structure of the account of the narrator's migration experience in *Zwischenstationen* is reminiscent of the works of the Viennese Jewish exile Albert Drach, especially *Unsentimental Journey* (*Unsentimentale Reise,* 1966) and *Z.Z. das ist die Zwischenzeit* ('MT, That is the Meantime,' 1990), a master of grotesque ambivalence.[7] Like Drach, Vertlib reveals the disorientation and lack of understanding on the part of the exile as a result of being prevented by his insecure situation to position himself appropriately. The loss of social and political identity as a result of the unpredictability of the exile situation also bears similarity to Anna Segher's *Transit*.[8]

There is a noticeable shift in Vertlib's narrative style and focus in the following two works, the historical novel *Das besondere Gedächtnis der Rosa Masur* ('The Special Memory of Rosa Masur,' 2001), which spans the period from the late nineteenth to the late twentieth century, and *Letzter Wunsch* ('Last Wish,' 2003). Both of these works are based on a specific extraordinary event and are brought to closure, even if the endings are not entirely satisfactory. *Das besondere Gedächtnis der Rosa Masur* centers on the successful ruse on the part of the protagonist. Her assertion that she slept with Stalin to free her son, implying an intimate relationship that, as it turns out, never occurred, and later uses the story to win a contest. Vertlib's descriptions of Jewish *shetl* life, the nostalgic memory of a simpler albeit hard life in pre-revolutionary Russia and the transition of Eastern European Jews into modernity are reminiscent of Joseph Roth and Isaac Bashevis Singer. In addition the novel provides insights into the lives of contemporary Eastern European Jews moving west. As in Doron Rabinovici's novel *The Search for M*,[9] Vienna is the major, even though not the preferred site for several of Vertlib's protagonists, notably in *Zwischenstationen* and *Letzter Wunsch* (2003). Vienna is the history-rich place where past and future intersect and representatives of different groups of survivors and migrants meet and clash.[10] Vertlib's first language was Russian, and the narrator of *Zwischenstationen* stresses that he considers Leningrad, now St. Petersburg, rather than Vienna, his hometown or *Heimatstadt*.[11] Russian life before the fall of the Soviet Union, the Russian language, and classical and modern Russian literature had a decisive influence on Vertlib's literary writing.[12]

To reveal the erratic twists and turns that produce a sense of powerlessness and disorientation in his young protagonist in his first two books, Vertlib developed a disruptive narrative style of dissociation and confrontation. The repeated, even expected shocks caused by constant rejection and depersonalization prevent his narrator-protagonist—first as a young boy, later an adolescent—from forming a system of reference or network that provides him with a sense of stability. Older characters, including the narrator's parents, have master narratives available to them through which they integrate their repeated disappointments into already established interpretations of reality during their unsuccessful global quest. However, their master narratives fail to address the specific problems they face during their plight on a daily basis, even though they seemingly provide meaning.[13] But their inaccuracy also causes frustration that leads to rage and desperation as well as unproductive outbursts, especially on the part of the narrator's father.

The projection of familiar patterns onto new circumstances prevents the father from reacting in an appropriate manner to the problems the family encounters. The mother's acceptance of traditional gender roles keeps her from opposing his ill-conceived plans, even though her assessment of the situation at hand is usually more to the point than her husband's.[14] The narrator's father is a Russian academic deeply invested in traditional humanistic values. Already in his native Russia he had been out of touch with reality because of some of his personality traits and his exclusion from social and professional life. A scholar, journalist, and translator, he was unable to find work in Russia because of his Jewish background. He was a "Refjusnik" and became the object of political persecution until he was eventually incarcerated.[15] These negative experiences notwithstanding, the parents remained true to Socialist thought and the ideal of the collective: "The Communist education still exercised its hold on them."[16]

In contrast to his far more practical and employable wife, a mathematician and chemist, the father is also incapable of securing a job in his many countries of exile.[17] To explore the underlying conceptual problems with which the older generations of Russian Jewish immigrants must contend, Vertlib introduces several of the conflicting master narratives that inform their thinking. These include the Jewish history of suffering, the traumatic memory of the Second World War and the Stalinist persecution, the Zionist dream, and Socialist visions of a fair and equitable society, but also older notions of intellectual and class related privilege.[18] Vertlib's maturing protagonist/narrator in *Zwischenstationen* eventually does find his bearings and begins to overcome his disorientation by examining the processes that determined the course his life had taken. Ever more clearly the significance of the Jewish past, anti-Semitism, and changing patterns of Jewish identity emerge in his mind as defining elements in his development. Regardless where he and his parents end up, these issues eventually catch up with him and affect his life on all levels. In Israel he is not considered Jewish enough, because he comes from secular Russia, is not circumcised, has no Jewish education, and is not an observant Jew. In Germany, Austria, and the United States, on the other hand, he and his parents suffer abuse precisely because they are considered Jews and foreigners.[19]

The perspective of first-person narrators also dominates *Das besondere Gedächtnis der Rosa Masur* and *Letzter Wunsch*. In contrast to the earlier works, they are adults able to present a larger historical and generational panorama. The 92-year old Rosa Masur, the heroine of Vertlib's third book who makes a brief but decisive cameo appearance in *Letzter Wunsch* (254-259), represents a generation born in pre-revolution Russia. Her experience includes *shtetl* life described in a way that calls to mind traditional Yiddish and Jewish narratives from Leopold Kompert to Isaac Bashevis Singer and Esther Kreitman.[20] Furthermore, it includes the era of the Russian revolution, the increasing Stalinist oppression, the Shoah, the cold war period, and the changes of the 1970s and 1980s until, finally, her emigration to Germany in the company of her son Kostja and her daughter-in-law. The protagonist of *Letzter Wunsch*, Gabriel Salzinger, is closer to the author in terms of his age but not regarding his background and socialization. Salzinger lost his mother at a young age and grew up with his father in the fictional town of Gigricht. Parts of *Rosa Masur* were already set in this town, which, in the condensed milieu of a German *Kleinstadt,* reflects Vertlib's own highly ambivalent Munich experience.

After his wife's death, Salzinger's father remained without attachment except for regular visits to a prostitute named Elisabeth. The dual identity of David and Gabriel Salzinger, i.e., the dilemma of being a German and a Jew in post-Shoah Germany, is the central issue. In the novel Vertlib alludes to the best-selling German-Jewish author Jakob Wassermann, who had wrestled with the problem of being German and Jewish since the fin-de-siècle until his death in 1934. These allusions suggest that little or no progress has been made throughout the twentieth century regarding the "Jewish Problem."[21] Gabriel Salzinger records hostile incidents and invectives against him that are as humiliating and threatening as the insults and rejection recorded by Wassermann after the First World War: "The experience in my father's factory was the first humiliating highpoint in my life as a German and a Jew."[22] Through Salzinger and his father, Vertlib raises the issue of Jewish life in Germany after the Shoah in view of the debates between German Jews and segments of the international Jewish community. The former consider Jewish life in the country of the murderers an impossibility and a sacrilege; the latter regard it their right, even their duty, to live among the former perpetrators and their children as a constant reminder, and with the mission of continuing the Jewish tradition in Germany.[23] The differing points of view bring to light that there are also problems defining Jewish identity within a Jewish context. Within the dominant culture, torn between anti- and philo-Semitism, a major problem is the fact that Jews and Jewishness are still discussed in terms of the Nazi discourse on race and descent.

At the time Vertlib wrote *Letzter Wunsch,* he and his protagonist shared certain common traits. Like Vertlib, Salzinger lives in Austria, but he has close ties to Germany as well. Most important, both the author and his character are concerned with the same political and social issues. These issues had been addressed already in Vertlib's earlier works, but here they are taken up from the perspective of an adult male who is committed to living in a German-speaking society. In addition to the problems relating to the death of his father, Salzinger faces additional difficulties. He is recently divorced from his German wife and has learned that he is incapable of having children of his own, which makes him the last of his family. Standing at the end point of German or Austrian Jewish tradition is a frequent motif in the writing of Shoah survivors. In her 1982 memoir *Die Galizianerin* ('The Woman from Galicia'), the Polish survivor Eva Deutsch writes: "And so the broken branch grows old, sits in her apartment half-withered, and contemplates the purpose of her existence."[24] Through these and other fictional aspects of his Salzinger character, Vertlib positions himself within the context of Austrian and German post-Shoah literature.

Intertextualities can be noted between Vertlib and other Jewish writers, notably Jurek Becker and Doron Rabinovici. Vertlib's Salzinger is a man in his thirties. He faces a personal and legal crisis occasioned by his father's death. The motif of a younger man's coming face to face with his Jewish identity at the time his father dies calls to mind Becker's *Bronstein's*

Children.²⁵ The novel's protagonist, Hans, is forced to reconsider his status as a GDR citizen and a German when he realizes that his father never overcame the legacy of the Shoah and is ultimately not able to cope with the past. Like Becker's Hans Bronstein, Gabriel Salzinger has to face up to his marginality in the dominant society and his outsider status in the Jewish community. When he requests a grave for his father in the Jewish cemetery of Gigricht at his mother's burial site, it turns out that his father was Jewish by birth but his mother had been a convert to Judaism after the Nazi takeover.²⁶ Because Salzinger's grandmother was sponsored by a Reform rabbi whom the orthodox community in Gigricht does not recognize in accordance with Israeli practice, Salzinger's father is denied a proper Jewish burial at the very moment when the coffin is lowered into the ground. Along with this and other problems Salzinger faces around this time of crisis is the fact he is unable to have children of his own.

Figures such as Gabriel Salzinger, Rosa Masur, her son Kostja are elements in Vertlib's evolving literary universe. *Abschiebung* already recorded core events and character constellations that were developed more fully and from different points of view in Vertlib's later writings. While his first two books are strongly autobiographical, in *Das besondere Gedächtnis der Rosa Masur* and *Letzter Wunsch* Vertlib examines with empathy persons different from himself in terms of gender and age. These characters provide access roads into central issues and sites of twentieth-century Jewish culture. Beyond the global wanderings of the first two books, the more recent novels reconstruct German-and-Russian and German-and-Austrian Jewish memory, mediated through the subjective viewpoints of ordinary men and women. Their experiences reveal that the conditions and opportunities of the underprivileged have remained largely unaffected by even the most cataclysmic ideological and economic changes. As far as their quality of life is concerned, it matters little whether the family "Kogen / Masur / Schwarz" (*Masur* 28), lives in a sub-standard St. Petersburg apartment or in a German compound for asylum seekers. They are among the first to be affected by catastrophic events such as economic crises, wars, revolutions, and ethnic cleansing:

> 'In principle, it's the same wherever you go, my mother said. Whether in Russia, Israel, Germany or America. Everywhere the same kind of people are sitting at the controls. Are the people here supposed to be better than somebody else, just because some half-illiterate can learn to sign his 'x' by accident?'[27]

Central to Vertlib's writing is the day-to-day struggle for bare necessities of basically decent people. The author traces their thwarted professional and personal hopes, their defeats by institutions and the more privileged, and their distrust of one another. Regardless of the respective regime, social order, and geographic setting, the basic condition of the migrants in *Abschiebung* and *Zwischenstationen* and that of the characters around Rosa Masur and David and Gabriel Salzinger are quite similar—as if progress routinely passed them by. Their small victories are the results of disobedience and transgression: for example, Rosa Masur's story about her night with Josef Stalin; and the illegal burial at sea Gabriel Salzinger provides for his father after the Jews of Gigricht evict the dead body from their cemetery.

Vertlib is keenly aware of Vienna's disadvantages for Russian Jews, especially the legacy of the Nazi past,[28] but he also registers anti-Semitism in Russia during his visit to St. Petersburg in 1993. In Germany he encounters the boastful pride of veterans of Hitler's military, and in St. Petersburg accusations against the 'Jewish mafia' or *jüdische Mafia*, global Jewish crime, and American Jewry. Especially shocking, however, is the encounter of Vertlib's protagonists with the United States authorities. Here they face unprecedented intolerance, coupled with a pervasive brutality. While in school, the son is familiarized with a hierarchy of racisms. Instead of the democratic structures he and his parents dreamed of he finds a rigid social and economic stratification. Indeed, the problems he observes during his stay in the United States are reminiscent of those in the Soviet Union.

Abschiebung portrays the United States in such a way that this country seems even less of a refuge from prejudice and injustice than the former Nazi countries. With an eye on anti-Semitism as a presence in every society his protagonists experience, Vertlib paints an image of global prejudice and a panorama of oppression. His supranational perspective calls to mind Robert Menasse's historical novel *Vertreibung aus der Hölle* ('Expulsion from Hell,' 2001)[29] that links Sephardic history since the expulsion from Spain in 1492 to the Central and Eastern European Jewish experience of persecution and pogroms culminating in the Shoah. Menasse, like Vertlib, reveals the ubiquitousness of Jew-hatred throughout the ages and in different places.

In all of Vertlib's works there is a close relationship between personal experience, historical events, and the author's creative imagination that uncovers points of view other than his own. Vertlib comments on his approach in the afterword of *Das besondere Gedächtnis der Rosa Masur*: 'The contemporary historical background for this book is, by and large, authentic. However, individual historical events and details are subordinated to the dramaturgy of this novel.'[30] There is a noticeable shift, however, from the more direct autobiographical approach in *Abschiebung* and *Zwischenstationen* to the fictional story telling of the later works. In these two works, Vertlib develops a perspective that captures the unpredictability of migrant life in a highly effective manner. *Abschiebung* is written from the perspective of an adult who reviews his boyhood and adolescent experiences in conjunction with his parents' unsuccessful attempt to immigrate to the United States, an interlude that occurs in the second half of their 10-year long search described in *Zwischenstationen*.

In these two works, the boy is portrayed as he follows his parents on a hopeless journey through the antechambers of different nation-states. He is socialized in a situation of instability that allows for no attachment. He has never known a stable environment that could instill a sense of belonging, thus the young nomad does not miss home and homeland. He only regrets losing sight of short-term friends. He is never quite sure as to what his parents have planned as their next step, for example: 'At the platform, my suspicion was realized. My parents had lied to me. I wasn't aware of the train's destination: Amsterdam Central Station.'[31] The erratic expeditions undertaken to avoid staying in Russia, Israel, Germany, and Austria, end in non-admittance and rejection. In the case of Israel, where the family ends up twice for an extended period of time, they leave of their own accord, though they have difficulty gaining a foothold anywhere else. After the debacle with the United States Immigration and Naturalization Service they refuse to return to Germany as the least welcome option. It is nonetheless ironic that Germany and Austria, the countries most closely associated with the Nazi atrocities, are the most accessible fifty-some years after the Shoah. To make matters even more complicated, the narrator's father with his unrealistic dreams of a place where he can live in peace and dignity finds fault with almost every country and takes his rising disillusionment to every new station on his way.

Das besondere Gedächtnis der Rosa Masur is more indirectly informed by memories of the past and impressions gathered by the author as a migrant and asylum seeker. The events are filtered through the narrative of Rosa Masur, an old Jewish Russian woman, an expert on German philology, and mother of a sickly son, Kostik. The latter resembles the father in *Abschiebung* and *Zwischenstationen* in that he faces insurmountable obstacles in his pursuit of higher education and a career. In the Stalinist era he is considered a potential traitor unfit for university study because he is a Jew.[32] Rosa helps and supports him until his marriage to a competent realistic woman, Frieda. The couple calls to mind the constellation of the parents in *Abschiebung* and *Zwischenstationen*. Frieda's dedication to her husband and family resembles the mother in the two earlier books. The naïve Kostik, who is arrested because of supposed Zionist leanings but spared long-term incarceration, bears a resemblance to the father in the two earlier works. The personal fate and family history of these characters and those associated with them open a window into Russian Jewish history, Soviet anti-Semitism, and the corruption prevalent in the old and new Russia.

The narrative continuum in *Das besondere Gedächtnis der Rosa Masur* takes the readers from the orthodox East European Jewish *shtetl* culture to Jewish Socialism, Bundism, and Communism. The latter appealed to the Jewish minority because of its promise of social justice. The novel emphasizes the bitter disappointment of Jewish hopes for a better future under Stalin—the betrayal of the Socialist utopia—, notably the persecution of Jewish doctors and intellectuals in Stalinist Russia. The wave of emigration from Soviet Russia to Germany and other Western countries in the 1970s and 1980s is motivated economically and by the fear of a renewed anti-Semitic onslaught. The horrors of the Shoah loom large in the collective memory, but Vertlib's main focus is on the Russian experience and the betrayal of the Jews initiated by the pact between Hitler and Stalin. When Rosa Masur and her family are finally permitted to leave Soviet Russia in the 1980s, they wind up in Germany, a country still overshadowed by the Nazi past. They arrive at the threshold of a new era that will culminate in the fall of the wall and the restructuring of Europe. Already at the time of their arrival, anti-Semitism, coupled with xenophobia against migrants and asylum seekers from all over the world, has again become a public force. The Russian expatriates are aware of clashes between neo-conservatism and anti-Semitism with the officially condoned post-Shoah liberalism and the often uncritical and disingenuous philo-semitism.

II. The Narrative Mode of Confrontation and Dissociation

Beginning with the fragmentary narrative structure of *Abschiebung* and *Zwischenstationen,* Vertlib's prose texts constitute the log of a writer's development through languages and cultures. The focus in *Abschiebung* is narrow, concentrated on a key episode in the life of a young person who does not yet understand the full impact of the event. The perspective widens in *Zwischenstationen,* with the narrator gradually defining his existential base, and assumes comprehensive proportions in *Rosa Masur*. However, it is in the first two works that Vertlib establishes an unconventional narrative mode of confrontation and dissociation, and begins to define identity in terms of intellectual choice. As an illegal reader in the Boston Library, he turns to reading books that help him establish an identity independent of the chaos around him. Reading insulates him against constant conflicts with the outside world.[33]

This intellectual counterbalance is needed in view of the anonymity and the peripheral status of the narrator and his parents. They remain nameless throughout the narrative. The designations 'I' (*"ich"*), 'my mother' (*"meine Mutter"*), and 'my father' (*"mein Vater"*) signify the closeness of the small group as well as the universality of their fate. Other characters, even marginal ones, are referred to by name. *Abschiebung* also records the derogatory appellations by which others refer to the protagonists. They include 'pushy hooligans,' a term used by the U.S. immigration officer, Ms. Sea;[34] 'filthy Jews,' the insult used by a classmate of the narrator in Munich,[35] 'damn Jews... that Hitler forgot to gas,' the statement of a U.S. Immigration officer.[36] Also *Zwischenstationen* cites a wide range of demeaning terms directed at the narrator and his friends: 'stupid little shits' ("*Saubuam, depperte*") and 'foreigner from Eastern Europe' ("*Tschuschn*"), designations used by an older Viennese woman (35); 'stupid idiot' ("*bleder G'schropp*") by the supervisor of the cleaning crew in which the narrator's mother works (68); 'miserable rabble' ("*Bagage, elendigliche*") by a neighbor in a Vienna tenement (81). The Israeli teacher demeans the narrator by calling him "*ein Jored*," a traitor to the Zionist cause, when it becomes clear that he and his family are about to leave Israel (138). His fellow students in Israel, who suspect him of not being Jewish enough because of his Russian origin, call him a "*Goi*," a non-Jew (141). A Piroggi-seller in Ostia labels him an 'idiot' ("*Dummkopf*") (152) and a Viennese school director a 'foreigner' or 'immigrant' ("*Ausländer*") (162), an expression that in light of the Nazi past and contemporary rightwing politics has assumed a negative connotation. Fellow students in Vienna call him "*schwul*," homosexual; a Russian, since the Second World War a decidedly negative designation; and a "*Baustellenruss*" or 'building-site Russki' because of his fascination with construction zones (171). The intended viciousness of these appellations notwithstanding, the narrator's father worries out loud that things might become much worse once the others find out that his son is a Jew: 'Presently, for these children, he's just "the Russian," but when they eventually find out that he's a Jew....'[37] The ongoing abuse taints the perception the narrator and his parents, especially the father, have of other people. 'The whole world just walks all over me,' stammers the father, who is in tears when he enters Israel and has to fight off a pushy reporter who assumes the right to photograph any newcomer.[38] In Vertlib's first two narratives the only two roles available to the narrator and his family appear to be that of victim or aggressor. In most encounters they end up in the victim role. Worse yet, they are blamed for whatever it was that went wrong. The extreme frustration in such moments of helplessness results in resentment, obstinacy, and occasionally aggression.

The lack of access and social ties outside the family or an occasional transitional reference group of people in similar circumstances and of the same religious or ethnic background engenders paranoid group thinking. For example, a group of children, the narrator, and a boy named Viktor whom the narrator befriended get into a vicious brawl because their parents had a disagreement. Another instance is the narrator's resorting to violence in school during his second stay in Vienna because his fellow students bully him. His excessive response, kicking and violently beating his opponent, is described as an explosive release for pent-up pressure rather than an appropriate response to the situation at hand. The most desperate outburst on the part of the narrator and his family takes place in a deportation room and is initiated by a U.S. immigration officer who hits the son prior to the family's deportation and yells: 'Somebody ought to whip you bums into line.'[39] The father grabs a bronze figurine, ironically one representing the Statue of Liberty, and attacks the officer. He is quickly overpowered, beaten, and locked up. In his amateurish resistance, the father is no match for an American, the narrator observes. Based on his experience in a high security urban high school that resembles more a prison than a school, the young Russian Jew maintains that in the United States 'people of different races are brought up.'[40] The different level of brutality in the USA is immediately obvious to him, even though in Munich he had already been 'the favorite target of my schoolmates' attacks.'[41]

The universal experience of rejection engenders in the narrator and his parents the automatic anticipation of further rejection. Hence the family unit on its part meets new people with reservation and prejudice. Their harsh characterization of others mirrors their defensive attitude. A term of profound contempt, 'scum' ("*Abschaum*"), is reserved for the United States immigration officials. In another instance, the narrator's father—not entirely in error—refers to Mrs. Berger, an old woman who is kindly inclined toward his son as 'this old fascist woman' (*"diese alte Faschistin"*). Other derogatory terms reveal racism on the part of the exiles and attitudes adopted from the surrounding society even though it rejects them: for example 'these Turks' (*"diese Türken"*) applied in a demeaning manner to other immigrants. A similar mechanism is at work when in Israel the father is outraged about having to live next door to Jews from Central Asia whom he considers inferior to himself.[42] Disapproval without cause is signaled by terms such as 'this man, of all people' (*"dieser Mann ausgerechnet"*), applied by the father to a kindly but eccentric Dutchman the family meets on the train. The disparagement and belittling of others suggest sweeping biases that encompass the father's view of the world. For example he is afraid of going to Latin America because he suspects it to be a haven for Nazis, 'criminals who still today hunt down Jewish children,'[43] and he has adopted negative Turkish stereotypes in Germany who, like the 'black Jews' (*"die schwarzen Juden"*) in Israel are said to be lazy, dirty and criminal-minded. The narrator is by no means immune to such clichés. He is all too ready to join in his friend Ariel's hatred of 'the damned Arabs' (*"die verdammten Araber"*) and participates in an unwarranted attack on an old man.

After the dismal experience with the U.S. Immigration Service and life among the disenfranchised in different American cities, the United States are added to the objects of resentment. Only in retrospect years later is the narrator able to correct the perceptions of his younger years. His reflections reveal that perceptions and opinions are shaped in a subjective manner as part of a specific situation and context. The sightseeing tours the family takes between office visits in their attempt to secure immigration visas are a case in point. The fear of rejection overshadows all of the narrator's perceptions. During his first visit to Washington D.C. under the auspices of home- and statelessness he rages against the 'giganticism' (*"Gigantomanie"*) of American classicism, 'probably the most successful form of fascist bombasticism, admittedly created more than a century before the rise of fascism.'[44] After having made a home in Austria, his impressions change. He notes on a later visit that 'The White House and the Capitol were wonderful structures. The urban planning seemed impressive to me—that there were no skyscrapers was, for America, a great achievement.'[45]

The global-homeless people Vertlib writes about are rarely fore-grounded in literary writing. Migrants usually do not have the necessary mastery of the languages of their target countries and lack access to publishing venues. Like the family in *Abschiebung,* they usually are not tolerated long enough to find the peace of mind to reflect and write. From a narratological point of view, the wanderings of migrants and asylum seekers do not make for positive narratives. The protagonists hardly qualify as heroes; at best they are picaros. But they cannot be compared to a Tom Jones or even to an Oskar Matzerath since their stories consist of anti-climactic episodes moving from one failure to the next low point. The fate of Vertlib's family resembles a downward spiral. Contrary to the educational novel, there is no social integration, even if there may be a point where their wanderings come to an end. At the same time they lack the tragic dimensions that are often present in Holocaust fiction that would make for greatness of a different kind. Every chapter in *Zwischenstationen* ends with the disruption of what might have become a story.

Lasting relationships, the major elements in traditional plots, do not form, even when the family occasionally meets persons on the same path as theirs. ''What? You here, too?' he had called out to Lew Blau from Schitomir, whom I had gotten to know four years ago back in Ostia, and who also works in Liebmann's store.'[46] The narrator's tentative romance with a girl named Dora, a potential love interest, is purely imaginary.[47] With their initial decision to leave the Soviet Union, a decision made out of perceived necessity, the family is drawn into a vicious circle.

Every attempt to establish a "normal" life ends in disruption; every chapter is a new beginning. Vertlib's protagonists are caught up in a series of false starts because they have minimal control over their lives. When their wanderings finally come to an end in Vienna, it feels like a defeat, at least for the parents.

Two large segments of *Zwischenstationen* deal with the family's encounter with Vienna. The first stay is riddled with problematic interactions with non-Jews such as the mother's fellow cleaning women and an episode involving an old woman who introduces the Jewish boy to her stuffed pets and fond memories of the Nazi era. Then there are non-Jewish neighbors who verbally abuse the boy. The final sections in the novel also deal with Vienna, the narrator's final station before he relocates to Salzburg. Even though his parents felt they had to leave Israel for a second time because of the terrorist threat, the father did so with a sense of resignation:

> 'When you're grown up, you'll make a better life for yourself, father says. I'm convinced that you'll leave Austria. Your mother and I are just too tired, too old. We can't do it at our age. It won't be easy for you either to live in a country with the children and the cousins of Nazis, many of whom think exactly like their fathers and grandfathers.'[48]

On the surface, the second Vienna episode appears somewhat more optimistic. The narrator and his parents live in a Jewish enclave and associate almost exclusively with other Jews. Because of the length of their stay, closer bonds form with people of similar backgrounds and circumstances, including Holocaust survivors and their children. The older people are connected by common memories and personal ties, as is the case with Mendl, the father of the narrator's friend Rita, who turns out to be the girlhood friend of the narrator's grandmother, Rahil Solomonowna, a character with traits similar to those of Rosa

Masur. The protagonists and their new friends have trepidations about living in post-Shoah Austria, but also a certain affection for Vienna. The narrator's father characterizes Vienna as 'the only city in this god-forsaken little country where you can live, under the circumstances,' and his mother equates leaving Vienna with her son's throwing away his life 'for nothing, for absolutely nothing at all' (*"für nichts und wieder nichts"*).[49]

In these close-knit Jewish circles the narrator is an outsider. This becomes most evident when even his grandmother denies him information about the assault on Rita's father. When he suggests that the incident may have been a right-wing extremist's attack, Rita rebuffs him; she spells out that he does not belong to the inner circle, just as succinctly as Israeli fellow students had done. 'It's really tragic, Rita said, after she had sat back down. You're not allowed to be Russians, you're not real Jews anymore, but not goys either.'[50] The brief exchange with a Jewish woman who grew up among Holocaust survivors and questions secular Enlightenment categories in view of the rise of nationalism and the Holocaust, brings the narrator's dilemma to the point: 'There are human beings and then there are people, she said. There aren't many real human beings... You? You belong to the people. Most definitely to the people.'[51] The way Rita uses the term *"Mensch"* in her rebuff excludes the narrator from her world—*"Mensch"* in the Yiddish sense denotes a thoughtful and caring Jew, whereas for the narrator it is a universal concept, *Mensch, homo sapiens*. Rita's distinction represents yet another exclusion that results in further dissociation on the part of the narrator.

Rita's analysis leaves the narrator with 'diffuse' feelings and a 'bad conscience' (*"schlechtes Gewissen"*). Like other intellectuals of Jewish descent he realizes that he neither belongs to the dominant Austrian culture nor the orthodox Jewish community. In his exclusion he has no recourse but to his individual identity. Ironically, it is this painful realization that sets him free to move on, even to a place like Salzburg, even to become a yodeling Provinzler with a 'green hat with a feather' ("*grünen Hut mit Feder*").[52] In his autobiographical essay "*Jude, wie interessant*" ('A Jew, how interesting'), Vertlib comments: 'I had private reasons for making the move, so the positive aspects of this change of scenery were always foremost in my mind.'[53] Precisely because the provincial town was not 'Vienna; it wasn't even Graz, Czernowitz or Brünn' and 'has played virtually no role in Jewish history,' the author identifies it as a neutral space in which to construct a new identity.[54]

Abschiebung and the chapters of *Zwischenstationen* preclude the possibility of reconnecting or returning to an earlier mode of being, because the places themselves disappear, as is the case with the Soviet Union. In *Zwischenstationen,* the narrator's native Leningrad has become St. Petersburg by the time he visits his grandmother in 1993. The city is fast transforming itself: 'The 1950s were transformed into the 1990s. Posters advertised the computerization of small businesses, for video recorders and home appliances made by Siemens.'[55] People disappear as well. During his visit the narrator sees his grandmother for the last time. Her passing disconnects him from the world of his childhood, leaving only vague memories of poverty, persecution, and the father's imprisonment. The image of the grandmother's broken urn and her ashes strewn about on a bus—only part of her remains ever reach their final resting place—encapsulates the notion of perpetual homelessness that permeates the novel. Listening to xenophobic conversations on a train reinforces the narrator's sense of not belonging: 'What am I doing here?' ("*Was tu ich hier?*"). It seems little more than coincidence that the search for a place to live and work comes to an end, at least temporarily.

The process by which Austria becomes a possible final station results from an "exile" experience fundamentally different from that of earlier intellectuals—Thomas Mann,

Alfred Döblin, Bertolt Brecht, or Lion Feuchtwanger, who were prominent authors when they fled from National Socialism and active in exile presses and papers. In contrast to less-prominent refugees from Nazi Germany, Vertlib's migrants are not in immediate mortal danger—they are in search of a country where they can live productive lives free from discrimination. There is no exile community that would embrace Vertlib's protagonists except, possibly, for some relatives and passing acquaintances. The constant financial and visa problems call to mind Else Lasker-Schüler, who was left stranded in Palestine when Switzerland denied her reentry in 1936. However, she became part of the Germanophone exile community in Jerusalem. Most of these earlier exiles had a strong sense of identity and defined themselves through or against the German language, and some were eager to return to build a better Germany or Austria, e.g. Anna Seghers, Stefan Hermlin, and Hans Weigel.

The closest parallel to the desperate search of Vertlib's protagonists is the plight revealed by the Holocaust author Edgar Hilsenrath who, after an odyssey through Europe and Israel, ended up in New York. There he worked odd jobs and wrote his first novel in German. Although a US citizen, his aspiration was to become a German author and to live in Berlin. After the success of *The Nazi and the Barber* (*Der Nazi und der Friseur*, 1998),[56] he moved to the Federal Republic of Germany and eventually realized his dream. Hilsenrath's New York novels, 'Bronsky's Confession' (*Bronskys Geständnis*) and 'Zibulsky or Antenna in the Belly' (*Zibulski oder Antenne im Bauch*)[57] lead into the quagmire of below-standard housing, less than minimum-wage jobs, and poverty-stricken immigrants. He reveals the exclusion of immigrants from even the lowest social stratum of the dominant culture and thematicizes the unrequited emotional and sexual yearnings of young men shut out. Vertlib's young protagonist (who gains no foothold, regardless where his parents take him) calls to mind Hilsenrath's characters. Both authors, Hilsenrath and Vertlib, sketch a narrative universe of unwanted people at the mercy of xenophobes and gate-keeping agencies. *Abschiebung* culminates with a vision of aggression—the narrator bashes in the skull of a God who looks 'like Jesus in the religious texts,'[58] and God's blue blood splashes all over him. *Zwischenstationen* ends on a more hopeful note, if 'feeling at home' is a hopeful thing: 'I have truly become an Austrian, or more precisely, a Viennese.'[59] In the later text the discourse of exclusion and dissociation is already beginning to give way to a narrative of self-definition that opens an avenue to comprehensive processing of memory and identity formation, as is the case in *Das besondere Gedächtnis der Rosa Masur* and *Letzter Wunsch*.

Notes

[1] Vladimir Vertlib, *Abschiebung* (Salzburg: Otto Müller, 1995), a story (*"Erzählung"*), and his novel *Zwischenstationen* (Vienna: Deuticke, 1999).

[2] With Austrian authors and filmmakers of the same period as Vertlib, the fate of refugees and migrants from socially troubled and war-torn countries is a frequent topic, for example the novel by Doron Rabinovici, *Ohnehin* (Frankfurt: Suhrkamp, 2004) and the film directed by Barbara Albert about immigrants from the former Yugoslavia, *Nordrand,* Vienna, Lotus Film, 1999.

[3] In Wolfgang Malik, "Interview mit Vladimir Vertlib," *Ausblicke: Zeitschrift für österreichische Kultur und Sprache* 8/2 (2003), 21-24, Vertlib underscores his participation in Austrian cultural activities, even though he is familiar with the dark aspects of Austrian society. He considers it his obligation to live in Austria, because Hitler would have won another victory

if all Jews left Austria. Aware that he is generally perceived as a Jewish-Russian immigrant who writes in German, he maintained that he was at home in a "Zwischenwelt." Even though he has a better command of German than of Russian, the Russian language is emotionally closer to him. At the same time he notices that he has adopted aspects of the Austrian mentality, all the more since his wife is Austrian.

[4] *"Ich bin tatsächlich zum Österreicher geworden, besser gesagt, zum Wiener. Ich muß Wien verlassen, um zu begreifen, daß ich im Laufe der Zeit alle Vorurteile dieser Stadt übernommen habe—die Selbstgefälligkeit, Überheblichkeit, Egozentrik und narzißtische Haßliebe, die Verachtung der 'Provinz,' ein Minderwertigkeitsgefühl gegenüber dem Ausland und nostalgische Verklärung der einstigen Bedeutung als Metropole."* – Zwischenstationen, 291. All translations within the text have been rendered by myself and the editor.

[5] Matti Bunzl, "Counter-Memory and Modes of Resistance; the Uses of Fin-de-Siècle Vienna for Present-Day Austrian Jews," in *Transforming the Center, Eroding the Margins: Essays on Ethnic and Cultural Boundaries in German-Speaking Countries*, edited by Dagmar C.G. Lorenz and Renate Posthofen (Columbia, SC: Camden House, 1998), 169-184. Here: 172.

[6] Bunzl, 172.

[7] Consult Mary Cosgrove, *Grotesque Ambivalence: Melancholy and Mourning in the Prose Work of Albert Drach* (Tübingen: Niemeyer, 2004).

[8] Edgar Hilsenrath, *Zibulski oder Antenne im Bauch* (Düsseldorf: Claassen, 1983); *Bronskis Geständnis* (Munich: Langen-Müller, 1980); Albert Drach, *Unsentimental Journey*, translated by Harvey Dunkle (Riverside, CA: Ariadne Press, 1991), originally appearing as *Unsentimentale Reise* (Munich: dtv, 1988); *"Z.Z" das ist die Zwischenzeit* (Munich: dtv, 1990);

Anna Seghers, *Transit* (New York: Little, Brown, 1944), also in German as *Transit* (Amsterdam: Hafkamp, 1950).

[9] *Suche nach M.* (Frankfurt: Suhrkamp, 1997), translated by Francis Michael Sharp (Riverside, CA: Ariadne Press, 2000).

[10] Vladimir Vertlib, *Das besondere Gedächtnis der Rosa Masur* (Vienna: Deuticke, 2001); *Letzter Wunsch* (Vienna: Deuticke, 2003).

[11] *Zwischenstationen*, 8.

[12] In a discussion at the University of Illinois at Chicago on 16 November 2004, Vertlib emphasized this connection for his own writing.

[13] The narrator's father in *Abschiebung*, after having found Israel not to be the country he expected, refuses to consider Germany an option, either reiterating a common post-Shoah narrative according to which it is inappropriate for Jews to live in the country of the murderers: 'It was unacceptable for a Jew to live in Germany after the War or even to emigrate to Germany. Especially staunchly conservative Bavaria was the least favorable place imaginable to start a future....' *"Es sei für einen Juden untragbar, nach dem Krieg in Deutschland zu leben oder gar nach Deutschland einzuwandern. Besonders das stockkonservative Bayern war der denkbar ungünstigste Ort, um eine Zukunft aufzubauen..."* – 28.

[14] *Abschiebung*, 151. 'After we had settled in other western countries, my parents discovered that these places weren't much better than Israel, just wealthier and with a more glamorous façade, all the better to hide their darker sides.... But still, the disappointment over Israel remained, even after their reason had admitted its mistakes. Their injured and insulted feelings remained, nonetheless, if even unconsciously, as with a small child whom one had given a toy as a present that no longer was as bright and tempting as it had once been in the store window.' (*"Nachdem wir in andere westliche*

Länder übersiedelt waren, entdeckten meine Eltern, daß diese nicht viel besser waren als Israel, nur reicher und mit einer glänzenderen Fassade, die dunkle Seiten erfolgreicher verstecken konnten.... Die Enttäuschung über Israel blieb jedoch, auch nachdem der Verstand die Fehler eingestanden hatte. Das verletzte und beleidigte Gefühl blieb weiterhin, wenn auch unbewußt, wie bei einem kleinen Kind, dem man ein Spielzeug geschenkt hatte, das nicht so glänzte und nicht mehr so verlockend war wie einst in der Schaufensterauslage."–70-71).

[15] Cf. *Abschiebung*, 64-65; *Zwischenstationen*, 15.

[16] "*Die kommunistische Erziehung hatte sie noch fest im Griff.*"– *Abschiebung*, 66.

[17] Cf. *Abschiebung*, 28; 57-59.

[18] 'Sometimes you could escape a Jewish fate, but not the fate of being a Jew.' (*"Einem jüdischen Schicksal könnte man manchmal entgehen, aber dem Schicksal Jude zu sein?"–Abschiebung*, 60). 'So, he had now reached his goal. Finally free, finally in the land of his dreams, in Israel, finally at the Lod airport.' (*"Nun hatte er also sein Ziel erreicht. Endlich frei, endlich im Land seiner Träume, in Israel, endlich am Flughafen von Lod."–*62).

[19] See *Abschiebung*, 20, 182; *Zwischenstationen*, 103.

[20] Leopold Kompert, *Die Kinder des Randars*, ed. Primus-Heinz Kucher (Klagenfurt: Alekto, 1998), first published in 1848; Esther Singer Kreitman, *Deborah* (London: David Paul, 2004), first published 1936 in Yiddish; Isaac Bashevis Singer, *The Collected Stories by I.B. Singer* (New York: Library of America, 2004).

[21] Like Wassermann, who came from an old German Jewish family, Vertlib's Salzingers are cast as Jews whose families had lived in Gigricht for generations, the family of the father for three, that of the mother for four generations (*Letzter Wunsch*, 65). Jakob Wassermann, *Mein Weg als Deutscher und*

Jude (Berlin: S. Fischer, 1921). See also: Wassermann, *Die Juden von Zirndorf* (Berlin: Fischer, 1897).

[22] "*Das Erlebnis in Vaters Fabrik war der erste unrühmliche Höhepunkt in meinem Leben als Deutscher und Jude.*"– *Wunsch*, 230-231. Compare Wassermann's perspective: 'It is useless, to conjure up the people of poets and philosophers in the names of its poets and philosophers. Every prejudice one thinks to have overcome brings, like a corpse attracts worms, thousands of new ones... He is a Jew... What should the Jews do? There aren't enough sacrifices, courting sympathy is misunderstood.' ("*Es ist vergeblich, das Volk der Dichter und Denker im Namen seiner Dichter und Denker zu beschwören. Jedes Vorurteil, das man abgetan glaubt, bringt, wie Aas die Würmer, tausend neue zutage... Er ist ein Jude... Was sollen die Juden tun? Opfer sind nicht zureichend, Werbung wird mißdeutet."*–Wassermann, 103.

[23] As elucidated in *Wunsch*, 248.

[24] Eva Deutsch and Brigitte Schwaiger, *Die Galizianerin* (Vienna: Zsolnay, 1982): "*Und so ist der abgebrochene Zweig alt geworden, fast verdorrt sitzt sie in ihrer Wohnung und denkt nach am Zweck ihres Daseins.*"

[25] Translated by Leila Vennewitz (New York: Harcourt, 1988); in German as *Bronsteins Kinder*.

[26] 'As far as we're concerned, officially your grandmother is still a non-Jew and therefore your father is also not a Jew. "*Ihre Großmutter ist für uns offiziell immer noch Nichtjüdin, und somit ist auch Ihr Vater kein Jude.*"–*Wunsch*, 133.

[27] "'*Im Prinzip ist es doch überall dasselbe,*' sagte meine Mutter. '*Ob Rußland, Israel, Deutschland oder Amerika. Überall sitzt derselbe Menschenschlag an den Hebeln der Macht. Sollen die hier besser sein als drüben, nur weil irgendein Halbanalphabet einmal in vier Jahren sein Kreuz macht?*'"–*Abschiebung*, 147-148.

[28] See *Zwischenstationen*, 55-65; 286-287.
[29] Robert Menasse, *Die Vertreibung aus der Hölle* (Frankfurt: Suhrkamp, 2001).
[30] "*Der zeitgeschichtliche Hintergrund zu diesem Buch ist größteils authentisch. Einzelne historische Ereignisse und Details sind jedoch der Dramaturgie dies Romans untergeordnet.*"– *Masur*, 431.
[31] "*Am Bahnsteig wurde mein Verdacht zur Gewißheit. Die Eltern hatten mich belogen. Der Zielort des Zuges war mir unbekannt: Amsterdam CS.*"–*Zwischenstationen*, 79.
[32] *Masur*, 324-326.
[33] *Zwischenstationen*, 215-247. The construction of a "paper" identity is the central theme in the works of Doron Rabinovici as well. Like Vertlib, Rabinovici had to reshape his language and identity after his parents took him from Israel to Austria when he was still a boy. Doron Rabinovici, *Papirnik. Stories* (Frankfurt: Suhrkamp, 1994).
[34] "*aufdringliche Bande*"–*Abschiebung*, 12.
[35] "*dreckige Juden*"– *Abschiebung, 185.*
[36] "*Saujuden... Hitler [hat] vergessen zu vergasen*"– *Abschiebung, 182.*
[37] "*Vorläufig ist er für diese Kinder nur der Russe, aber wenn sie erst herausfinden, daß er Jude ist...*"–*Zwischenstationen*, 173.
[38] "*Die ganze Welt trampelt nur auf mir herum.*"–*Zwischenstationen*, 110-111.
[39] "*Euch Pack sollte man durchprügeln.*"–*Abschiebung*, 180.
[40] "*[werden] Menschen anderen Schlages großgezogen*"– *Abschiebung* 22.
[41] "*das Lieblingsobjekt der Angriffe meiner Mitschüler*"– *Abschiebung,* 20.
[42] *Zwischenstationen*, 103.

[43] *"Verbrecher, die auch heute noch Jagd auf jüdische Kinder machen"–Zwischenstationen*, 133.

[44] *"die wohl gelungenste Form faschistischer Bombastik, geschaffen, zugegebenermaßen mehr als ein Jahrhundert vor dem Aufkommen des Faschismus"–Abschiebung*, 130.

[45] *"Das Weiße Haus und das Kapitol waren wunderbare Bauwerke. Die Stadtplanung erschien mir beeindruckend, daß es keine Wolkenkratzer gab, war für Amerika eine große Leistung"–Abschiebung*, 131.

[46] *"'Was? Du auch hier?' hatte er [Lew Blau aus Schitomir] ausgerufen, den ich vier Jahre zuvor schon in Ostia kennengelernt habe und der ebenfalls in Liebmanns Laden jobbt."–Zwischenstationen*, 186.

[47] *Abschiebung*, 171-173.

[48] *"'Wenn du erwachsen bist, wirst du es besser machen,' sagt Vater. 'Ich bin überzeugt, daß du Österreich verlassen wirst. Ich und deine Mutter, wir sind einfach schon zu müde, zu alt. Wir schaffen es nicht mehr. Es wird auch für dich nicht leicht sein, in einem Land der Kinder und der Enkel von Nazis zu leben, von denen viele immer noch so denken wie die Väter und Großväter.'"–Zwischenstationen*, 251.

[49] *"die einzige Stadt in diesem gottverdammten Kleinstaat, wo man unter Umständen leben kann"–Zwischenstationen*. 283. The sentiment that Vienna is the only city in Austria where Jewish exiles and emigrants could really live is frequently expressed, see: Adi Wimmer, "Introduction," *Strangers at Home and Abroad: Recollections of Austrian Jews who Escaped Hitler*, transl. Ewald Osers (Jefferson, NC: McFarland, 2000), 1-22. Here: 22.

[50] *"'Es ist schon tragisch,' sagt Rita, nachdem sie sich wieder gesetzt hat. 'Russen durftet ihr nicht sein, richtige Juden seid ihr keine mehr, Gojim aber auch nicht.'"–Zwischenstationen*, 280.

51 "'*Es gibt Menschen und Leute,*' *sagt sie.* '*Richtige Menschen gibt es nur wenige... Du? Du gehörst zu den Leuten. In ganz besonderem Maße zu den Leuten.*'"–*Zwischenstationen*, 280.

52 Ruth Beckermann, in her autobiographical essay *Unzugehörig* ('Inappropriate') (Wien: Löcker, 1989), expresses a similar ambivalence as Vertlib. She is aware that in the dominant culture she is perceived as a Jew, especially when she is in the company of Jews less assimilated than herself, such as her parents. "I can disguise myself as an aristocrat, as a middle-class citizen, as a farmer or a proletarian. But no sooner does an 'unassimilated' person or someone who has assimilated differently show up then all is lost." *(Ich kann mich verkleiden wie ein Aristokrat, wie ein Bürger, wie ein Landwirt oder wie ein Proletarier. Doch kaum taucht ein 'Unverwandelter' oder anders 'Verwandelter' auf, ist alles hin...* 124).

53 Vladimir Vertlib, "'Jude, wie interessant' – 'A Jew, how interesting!'" *Juden in Salzburg*, ed. Helga Embacher (Salzburg: Anton Pustet, 2002) 104-111. Here: 105. A text excerpt from the novel *Zwischenstationen*, "Abfahrt," 282-292, appeared as the independent autobiographical prose piece in the essay collection *Juden in Salzburg*. See: FN 3.

54 "Jude," 105.

55 "*Die fünfziger Jahre gingen über in die neunziger. Plakate werben für die Computerisierung von Kleinbetrieben, für Videorecorder und Haushaltsgeräte der Firma Siemens.*"–*Zwischenstationen*, 6.

56 Edgar Hilsenrath, *The Nazi and the Barber*, transl. Andrew White (Garden City, NY: Doubleday, 1971), later *Der Nazi und der Friseur* (Köln: Literarischer Verlag Braun, 1977).

57 Edgar Hilsenrath, *Bronskys Geständnis* (München: Langen-Müller, 1980), re-released as *Fuck America* (Köln: DTV, 2005); and *Zibulsky oder Antenne im Bauch* (Düsseldorf: Classen Verlag, 1983).

[58] "*wie Jesus in den Religionsbüchern*"–*Abschiebung*, 191.
[59] "*Ich bin tatsächlich zum Österreicher geworden, besser gesagt zum Wiener.*"–*Zwischenstationen*, 291.

XAVER BAYER
Courtesy of Jung und Jung

Virtual Reality: The Internalization of External Reality in Xaver Bayer's Novel *Weiter*

by Renate Posthofen and Jörg Thunecke

> "Desire lets all thing flower,
> possession drags everything in the dust.
> It is better to dream your life than to live it..."
> Marcel Proust, *Pleasures and Days* (1896)[1]

Weiter ('Onward')[2] is Xaver Bayer's third major novel, following *Heute könnte ein glücklicher Tag sein* from 2001 ('This Could be a Happy Day')[3] and *Die Alaskastraße* of 2003 ('Alaska Road')[4]. However, the plot of this work—if one may call it that—by an author born, bred, and residing in Vienna[5]— does *not* take place in the Austrian capital, but outlines the unnamed first-person narrator's internalization of external reality during a road trip[6] through remote parts of Lower Austria— Asparn an der Zaya, Zwentendorf, Mistelbach, Helfers, Ladendorf, Poysdorf, Staatzer Klippen, Drasenhofen, Laa an der Thaya[7] on his way towards Brno in the Czech Republic and back home again. In Bayer's novels, however, as pointed out by Leopold Federmair, movement signifies inertia, i.e. anything but mobil-ity: 'For Bayer, movement more often indicates a lack of moti- vation, of lethargy.'[8] Not the provincial localities in Lower Austria *per se* matter, through which the protagonist passes on his way, but his reflections upon them in the light of a recent occurrence that fundamentally changed his life and which can be considered a kind of turning point in this brief piece of prose fiction.[9] 'Some time ago something happened to me, the reader is told, which I still cannot fully grasp, and, while sitting on this particular bench in Mistelbach... I tried to consciously reflect upon for the first time.'[10] In other words, the year before, normality still prevailed,[11] but then, one fine day, a change of consciousness occurred—though not immediately explained in the novel—which totally altered the narrator's life:

'What happened to me though, on this particular evening," he says, "took place in a flash of time. I do not know whether you are able to comprehend this, because I could not quite understand it myself; for on the one hand it is too complex, too big, and on the other hand so minuscule and tiny... I was strolling home alone this evening, following a visit to the movies, through narrow alleys, then along the Burggarten at the Ring.... I sauntered without a care, without real joy, just neutral sentiments... when all of a sudden, while walking along, something stopped inside me, causing me to stand still and, as if struck by lightning, made me realize with an immediacy I had never experienced before, that at that very moment something had happened to me after which I would never be the same person again, that something in me had ended, abruptly, and that something entirely different, new, unknown to me, had taken its place. And this new feeling was nothing at that moment but the brief fright of having lost something, once and for all, a feeling of pain, incredulity, and dismay, which at first I was merely able to counter with indignation and a gesture, close to panic, of wanting to offer compensation.... I had the feeling of someone who knows that he has gambled away his last chance, whose path is now blocked, and for whom there is no way forward but merely a dreary expanse lacking direction.'[12]

The objective of the ensuing narrative is to supply details[13]— and thus a possible explanation of the new situation—which basically amounts to a process of internalizing the protagonist's external reality during his trip to Brno and back to Austria. As Markus Hildenbrand put it in a review of *Weiter*: 'The author draws up a precise psychogram of a young man whose hitherto orderly life suddenly becomes empty, lacks direction.'[14]

The first of three stops on the narrator's itinerary through the northeastern part of Lower Austria is his deceased grandparent's house in Helfers, a small hamlet west of Mistelbach, where—to his surprise—he meets his younger brother, Veit. Following various conversations with his sibling in the kitchen and in a tree house, the narrator begins to explore the large garden where he used to spend a lot of time in his childhood. It is during this exploration of remote corners of the erstwhile farm that for the first time in Bayer's novel external parts of reality are being internalized:

'I didn't ask any more questions, but went across the farmyard, down a slight embankment that stretched as far as the pond. I fondly stroked the trunk of the old cherry tree. The arrangement of a couple of molehills, poking up from beneath the snow, looked like a stellar constellation. Hoping to get lost, I trod on, feeling the same kind of thrill that overcomes me when I first look at maps. But I still knew the area too well for this to happen. Down at the pond, surrounded by birch trees and weeping willows, I stopped briefly. The pond seemed to absorb the shadows of the trees on its bank. The water looked sated and inconsolable, and the snowflakes disappeared the moment they touched the surface of the water. I walked on until I reached a narrow passageway at the edge of the woods where my brother and I used to play as children. There is an old, uninhabited building, the whole front of which is scarred by a crack as if the area had been struck by an earthquake some time ago. I worked my way through the shrubbery toward the rear of the building, where there was nothing except a few boards and signs leaning against the wall. Noticing them, I suddenly felt an inclination to inspect everything more closely. I only wish I would have had a magnifying glass with me. Upon closer inspection the rear of the building cheered me up; like all places that are inaccessible and seemingly useless, it allowed me to breathe a sigh of relief. After a while of just standing there and looking, I walked back to the path and through the narrow passageway until I reached the edge of the woods again and the open fields. From that point forward, walking on and on, I felt relaxed and focused at the same time.'[15]

Reminders of the rural character of his grandparents' estate thus give rise to a highly critical comparison of provincial and urban areas,[16] a first instance of the narrator's internalization of external details of reality, which Markus Hildenbrand equates with the process of the narrator's unmasking his surroundings:[17]

'While I continued walking, I reflected upon the rear of the old house, and I kept thinking why interstices always made me feel so comfortable. I became aware that such interstices are increasingly rare. They are being extinguished, erased, eliminated in this world like something of which one feels ashamed. Materialization is everywhere. People can't bear emptiness, and space makes them feel uncomfortable. Everything has to be visible, come what may, and if need be without necessity, by means of surveillance cameras. Vastness is the foremost enemy, emptiness a horror vision, lack of visibility a nightmare, any interstice a blemish. Spaces are filled in and covered up with unsightly replacements, like mass graves or landfills, topped off with a layer of artificial idylls. Oases are institutionalized, sanctuaries are denied room, exit routes are blocked.'[18]

Thus by internalizing features of external reality, based on a comparison of town and countryside—regarding 'Alaska Road,' one critic spoke of an escape into nature, equally applicable to *Weiter*[19]—the narrator succeeds in subtly introducing a kind of cultural criticism or *"Kulturkritik"* into the novel—even the term "cultural pessimism" or *"Kulturpessimismus"*[20] crops up in the reviews—which gathers momentum during the course of the itinerary through Lower Austria and ultimately also proffers an explanation of the untoward experience that occurred to the protagonist some time before in Vienna. In other words, seemingly insignificant aspects of provincial reality give rise to a much more complex analysis of global problems, as can be gathered below.[21]

The narrator's next stop in Lower Austria is Ladendorf where, to all intents and purposes, he proposes to investigate an old derelict cinema that he used to frequent some twenty years prior. However, rummaging through the dilapidated building is once again merely an excuse for juxtaposing and superimposing internalized reminiscences on an external environment; for when the protagonist enters what was once the projection room, switches off his flashlight and is engulfed by total darkness, he recalls a similar experience he and some friends encountered when they entered a limestone cave somewhere in the Forest District, the *"Waldviertel*," a quasi-extension of virtual life to real life:

'The sudden darkness was so unbelievably intense that I almost sensed it like something tangible, this I remember very clearly. I didn't move.... And I remember how two friends and I some years ago descended into a cave. We climbed deeper and deeper on ladders and slippery rock faces until we finally reached what we thought was the lowest level of the cave. Here we rested. When all three of us switched off the lights on our helmets there was nothing but darkness, we were engulfed by the most intense darkness I have ever experienced. There was not a single sound, and I felt liberated as never before in my life. I had no desire to switch the lights on again, let alone return to the surface any time soon.... During the long minutes of silence I felt though as if I never ever had anything to say again. I felt like being immersed in a basin of warm water between the wet and loam-covered stones. The darkness seemed to be part of the rocks that surrounded us. When the light was extinguished, my friends and their very existence were extinguished. At that moment I felt as if I had been anaesthetized, enclosed in stone, with no need to breathe.... Never before had I experienced the present as unpolluted as then, and it seemed to me as if someone wanted to communicate to me that there was no past and no future, just one big, almighty, everlasting present.'[22]

Following this experience in the cave the narrator feels as if he were under the influence of narcotics. He has the decided feeling as if he has left something behind in that cave, the loss of which he would mourn for the rest of his life, a kind of longing the lack of which he would later identify as the cause of the attack on his consciousness way back in Vienna.

Next on his trip through Lower Austria is a stopover at a hotel in Poysdorf. However, this sojourn is relatively uneventful, and merely the description of the landscape during the following day's journey towards the Czech border offers, once again, an insight into the narrator's inner feelings and in the way nature is being internalized:

> 'For quite some time during the subsequent drive hardly any colorful features entered my vision, only the greyish white sky, the snow, the black trees and vines, and the huge pylons of the wind farm, and involuntarily I imagined a universal switch that someone had flipped so that I would see everything just in black and white. But after a while I noticed that the colors were merely hidden, and as soon as I had realized that, the landscape seemed almost more colorful than in summer, the variations and transitions by the side of the road and at the edge of the fields were so diverse. The turquoise colors of misty woods, which seemed to hover across the horizon, in addition to dark violet, bruise-colored shrubs along its borders. The bright yellow of the mistletoe in many trees was almost like neon. The brick-red and lichen-brown shades of the roofs, the ochre-like shine of many bare spots in the snow and across the stubble fields, the silver haze between the defoliated bushes. And the intestine-red of a run-over rabbit in the snow by the roadside.'[23]

At the same time, nature's genuine emanations contrast sharply with man-made features, like the 'universally visible rhythm of the vineyards and furrows… the trees of monocultures planted at regular intervals.'[24]

On arrival in Brno—the second largest city in the Czech Republic, the capital of the province of Moravia during the heyday of the Austro-Hungarian Empire—the narrator checks into a hotel near the main train station, and since the interview with Kroupa,[25] a local software developer, is delayed by a couple of hours, he goes for a stroll. This inner city walk is of key importance to our understanding of the plot of the novel, since it helps explain the protagonist's strange experience back in Vienna.

'As I passed a group of Asian tourists and heard their voices, I was momentarily happy to be in a foreign city and not in Vienna.... But while walking along I noticed that my surroundings did not satisfy my desire to truly feel like a stranger. I still believe to this day that the inability to feel like a stranger in Brno was connected to what had happened to me some time ago in front of the *Burggarten* fence, that is, it was linked to the change that took place in me, my loss of longing.'[26]

The reasons for the narrator's inability to be able to truly yearn—already intimated in the cultural criticism at an earlier stage of the narrative during the visit to his grandparents' farm in Helfers—are explained in an ongoing critique of adverse developments in Western society which had already gained some prominence in Bayer's previous novel, 'Alaska Road,' where the protagonist states at one point:

'It seemed to me as if, with the disappearance of all things considered rundown or unprofitable and their replacement with flashy, transparent and chromeplated items, all human aspects were retreating from public life, or rather: as if such human features were deliberately stifled.'[27]

In other words, reference is being made to the so-called "leveling effects" imported from the United States, which quite obviously were also beginning to affect towns like Brno, only recently liberated from Communism:

'I thus had to admit to myself that I did not feel nearly as much a stranger as I would have liked. That also had to do with the fact that the inner city of Brno basically looked like any other central-European town, the same stores, banks, supermarkets as in Vienna or Munich. The majority of the people wore the exact same clothes and had the same wretched looking expression in their eyes.'[28]

And the narrator's incapability of feeling like a genuine stranger in any of today's Western cities seems to have been aggravated by the repetitiveness of modern life—contrary to life in the provinces not so long ago—the monotony and uniformity of modern existence, eliminating the possibility of any element of surprise strangers might have experienced in days gone by:
'Even in Brno, everything happened according to archaic laws of nature, never questioned.... Because of that I suddenly felt aggrieved by this eternal repetitiveness of all those things that surrounded me.'[29]

The consequence of such negative experiences was self-deception, an attempt to artificially create a feeling of being a stranger in a foreign town, which—according to Thomas Ballhausen—amounts to the long-coveted wish for extinction of one's own personality:[30]
'When this feeling sunk in, my environment suddenly began to trouble me again. I felt tempted to assume that events surrounding me were mere deception.'[31]

When the narrator eventually returns to his hotel room, he lays in the empty bathtub, allowing his thoughts to wander. In the course of these musings further evidence emerges that the real world all around him is singularly deficient and that the virtual reality offered by many computer games, 'the new utopia of virtual infinity,'[32] is highly preferable:
'I was mentally occupied again with computer games.... The external world was shut out for a time, as if it didn't exist. I saw jungle land-

scapes, the corridors of haunted castles, ghostly factory halls, and French villages through which I ran as a British soldier, killing Nazis during World War Two. The graphics of some of these games were extraordinarily beautiful, for example, when a nightly breeze ruffled the leaves of trees. The circles that arose when one shot into the water. The plodding walk of game-figures, sounds in the distance, dogs barking and shouts, and, quite breath-taking, moments of intense silence.'[33]

Therefore it is not really surprising that the narrator not only considers this virtual reality of computer games superior to the real world that surrounds him in everyday life, but equates and compares it with the lost provincial reality of his childhood, which he quite obviously also deems vastly preferable to the contemporary countryside:

'Retrospectively it occurred to me that I had experienced the same feeling of suspense and freedom when I entered the old barns and buildings, dilapidated brickworks and closed-down factories in the surrounding area, roaming the overgrown debris of past lives, during stays with my grandparents in the countryside as a boy.'[34]

But that is not the end of it. For at the conclusion of a marathon computer game,

'it occurred to me then, in addition to my previous thoughts, what it was like when my friends and I, following such a marathon session of computer games, returned to the real world.... Suddenly one was ejected from the artificial world. Though sobered up, one was still under its influence. On those occasions, when I said goodbye and headed home from the apartment of one of my friends, my perceptions functioned totally according to the inveterate and internalized standards of the game.... The game wasn't over yet, and I knew that in my dreams during the coming nights I would have to continue my missions in enemy territory. Until one fine day, when I would wake up and re-establish contact with reality.'[35]

In fact, the narrator's estrangement from reality usually does not disturb his equilibrium for as long as he is either actively engaged in playing a computer game or, to a lesser degree, when he expertly discusses such a game in his capacity as a journalist.[36] However, the very moment everyday life reasserts itself, as in Teri's—Kroupa's sister's—question how he liked Brno, a feeling of *"Fremdlosigkeit"*—a concept of alienation difficult to render into English, the double negative suggesting familiarity—immediately begins to torture him again:

'Teri then asked me how I liked Brno, and I told her that I regretted the fact that, by now, the town looked just like any other in central Europe; that I could barely discern any regional differences; that, all in all, fewer and fewer places existed in the world where I could feel like a stranger; and that I yearned for a place like Antarctica, as a kind of antidote to my estrangement. I became quite loquacious and confessed to her that I considered what was happening to the world to be ridiculous and deadly....'[37]

Corroborating the narrator's own views, Teri is also of the opinion that current trends can only gain momentum; for 'in the future, people would venture more and more into virtual spaces, because they gave them a good feeling, and developments in this direction were already more advanced and virtually existent than conceivable.'[38]

The protagonist's mistrust of everyday reality is aroused again during his return trip to Austria. Once he has crossed the border, he pulls into a rest area and deliberates whether to drive straight back to Vienna or spend another night in a local hotel. However, these deliberations in due course give rise to yet another departure into an unreal, virtual world:

> 'I still had a yearning for something novel, unknown, something which would completely unsettle me. Furthermore I have always been a person who could not just quit. I always had to go one step further. I sensed, in a way, that last night I had reached the end of a stage in my life and that I had to do one more thing to advance to the next level, that I simply had to be daring and see what would happen.'[39]

Eventually he decides not to return to Vienna by the shortest possible route and instead pays a visit to the "*Staatzer Klippen*," a rock formation topped by the ruins of an old fortress. After the ascent to this dilapidated castle, the narrator is overcome by yet another, even more violent attack of unreality:

> 'Suddenly I felt violently ill and deliberated whether I should throw up.... I closed my eyes and breathed deeply. When I opened them again, everything suddenly looked yellow, like sulphurous lights.... There was a droning in my ears that grew louder and louder. It sounded a bit like the rising applause of a gigantic audience. I briefly recalled the system of satellites which had been set up around the earth during the past couple years.... And the idea that soon there would be no place on earth where one could not be detected, had an eerie ring, especially on such an exposed spot as on the upper level of the cliffs of Staatz....'[40]

Ultimately the narrator crawls, rather than walks, down the cliff side, gets into his car and drives to the branch office of a nearby bank, where he collapses in a chair in the anteroom. On entering this room, for a few seconds he has 'the impression that he was getting into a spaceship.'[41] And the virtual reality, which had afflicted him on the cliff, continues unabated:

> '...I increasingly felt as if I were in a cave painted yellow. Every time I looked at the yellow wall of the anteroom I was unsure whether it was actually white or whether it was merely a fiction of my imagination that it seemed yellow. On the other hand, the wall behind me seemed so intensely red that I was afraid to look around. I had the impression that it radiated heat. The black screen of the computer, too, frightened me; it might explode without warning.'[42]

Eventually he grabs the hatchet that he had stolen a day earlier in a museum in Asparn and begins attacking the menacing wall. 'I cannot remember what happened exactly, he informs the reader retrospectively, but if you are interested, you can always consult the shots taken by the security camera.'[43] In fact, this fit of rage lasts until the hatchet ultimately breaks into two pieces:

> 'After that I put the two fragments of the hatchet on the table, lifted the receiver of the phone, but the only number that occurred to me was that of the automated time-of-day. And while I was sitting in the armchair, listening to the recorded message, a deadly sadness overcame me, and I lay down on the floor in front of the statement printer, and after I lay there a while, staring at the ceiling, my head suddenly cleared, and with a pain in my chest I recalled once again the loss of my ability to feel any yearning, and that most likely this feeling would never return.'[44]

The narrator's ruminations, however, ultimately give rise to a lifesaving idea, namely that to yearn for yearning also amounts to some kind of longing.[45] And this very idea brings him peace of mind until the local police arrive.

Basically, that is the end of the story, as the narrator himself explains, except to say that, from this point onward, things improve again, at least so it appears in the protagonist's retrospective outlook upon his life following these events. 'I now know, he maintained, that it is impossible to get lost in this world.'[46] The picture of the world that he subsequently paints and in which he feels comfortable is *not* that of our modern urban environment, but that of a rural provincial landscape, that is to say, by and large an imaginary location, a virtual world unobtainable in the real world:

> 'I'm closing my eyes, longing to walk through the snow, listening to my plodding footsteps and the grinding noise of the frozen snow covering the ground, as well as my being out of breath. If I were to turn around and backtrack, I would like to see my footprints on the path. I would like to see the clouds hovering across the land, casting shadows on the earth. I want to slide on the ice of the frozen river.'[47]

The narrator concludes that he has nothing else to say—except, however, to refer to a note composed by his brother (a writer, whose first novel caused quite a stir in literary quarters in Austria), which he had pocketed during his visit in Helfers. The contents of this note are now presented to the reader as a kind of key for a possible interpretation of the novel:

> *'I grew up in a palace of curtains, surrounded by walls, with wild animals like those in a jungle, encompassed by a moat that has since been drained and filled in, a drawbridge and an open staircase that nowadays is overgrown: over the years the whole thing has become frayed and threadbare like an old tapestry: like in a foxhole, my dreams have dug escape passages*

into the walls. Gradually the interior fittings were stripped down, most passages between the rooms caved in and became impassable. The curtains have been taken down and turned into covers for upholstery that now gather dust in second-hand shops. From the outside one can barely recognize anything anymore; only in winter, when the leaves of the trees and the bushes have disappeared, is one able to see, if one happens to look closely enough, that there are cracks in the outside walls behind the boughs and branches. The ruined and desolate rooms are nowadays covered with shards and debris, with pigeon wings and fragments of stucco. Children's drawings and words scratched on the walls, occasionally there are still remnants of frescoes, most of them covered with slogans, each one of them a gateway to another world."[48]

Although messages from the first-person narrator—of which this slim novel abounds—have to be taken with a grain of salt, the reader can only ignore the hint preceding the final passage at his or her peril. For obviously the story of such a magical palace, in which the narrator spent his childhood and that, over the years, fell apart, amounts to an allegory of the protagonist's mental and emotional development, an allegory of a virtual world that—in confrontation with the real world—gradually fell apart. Such a reading of the final passage also helps to explain the one that immediately precedes it:

'I am longing for the jungle. In the maze of computer programs, I shall hide behind a tree for as long as I like and shall not re-emerge until curiosity gets the better of me. I shall walk across forest glades and medieval market squares or drive a car along mountain ridges. I once again feel yearning, and consequently everything is quite easy now.'[49]

In fact, one could interpret Xaver Bayer's novel *Weiter* as the narrator's ongoing longing for virtual worlds offered by computer programs, although it must at once be added that such yearnings do not aim at just any kind of virtual world, but one echoing a rural, provincial environment (cf. the tail end of his previous novel 'Alaska Road'), an environment undamaged and not yet affected by so-called "progress" of modern civilization, a surrounding—as has been stressed *ad nauseum*—which allows a person to still feel like a stranger, where yearning—for whatever—is still possible. Overall therefore—as in his previous novels—a kind of nihilistic, self-destructive atmosphere prevails in *Weiter*, neatly expressed in 'Alaska Road' in the metaphor of an empty escalator, which—similar to the ancient Greek myth of Sisyphus—is condemned to eternal futility.[50] Xaver Bayer's *Die Alaskastraße*, and even more so *Weiter*, reminds one of Christian Kracht's novel *Faserland* ('Threadbare'), which caused a stir in Germany in 1995;[51] for the theme of aimless escapism (also prominent in Daniel Kehlmann's *Die Vermessung der Welt*[52]) is prescient.[53] Thus *Weiter* is fundamentally a protocol of self-estrangement (*"Protokol einer Entfremdung"*[54]) that takes place against the backdrop of provincial Austria; it could, however, have happened almost anywhere else. Consequently, it is quite fitting that the novel ends with a colon—and not a period; for as Federmair maintains, such a colon permits the reader to imagine or dream of any kind of ending he sees proper.[55] As Marcel Proust wrote more than a hundred years ago in *Pleasures and Days*: "We dream it [life], and we love it in its dream-state. We don't have to try to live it."[56]

Notes

[1] "*Le désir fleurit, la possession flétrit toutes choses; il vaut mieux rêver sa vie que la vivre...*" in Marcel Proust, *Les Plaisirs et les Jours* (Paris: Gallimard, 1962; 1895).

[2] Xaver Bayer: *Weiter* (Salzburg, Wien: Jung und Jung, 2006). Since none of Bayer's works has appeared in English to date, the authors have provided working titles to correspond to the German originals. Moreover, all textual translations are those of the authors as well.

[3] *Heute könnte ein glücklicher Tag sein* (Salzburg, Wien: Jung und Jung, 2001) is a city novel, a "*Großstadtroman*," which takes place primarily in Vienna, but also in Munich and Amsterdam; see Petra Nachbaur, "Ich fühle mich kitschig," in *Der Standard* (Wien: 8 March 2002), Supplement, 9.

[4] Xaver Bayer, *Die Alaskastrasse: Roman* (Salzburg: Jung und Jung, 2003).

[5] Born in 1977, Xaver Bayer grew up in a Viennese medical familiy, 'well protected, almost under a type of belljar' ("*gut behütet, fast unter einer Art Glasglocke*"): see Stefan Ender's "Dreck muss es geben," in *Falter* (Wien: September 2006), Nr. 40, 14-15. Bayer studied German and philosophy at the University of Vienna where he obtained a Ph.D. before becoming a professional writer. He was initiator of the "Österreichische Autorenseite" *Die Flut* (2000/01); cf. Cornelia Niedertmeier, "'Geistige Welpen' im Internet," in *Der Standard* (Wien: 8 February 2001), 16. In 2002 Bayer was granted the *Hermann Lenz Stipendium* as well as the *Autorenprämie der Republik Österreich*; in 2004 he was awarded the *Reinhard-Priessnitz-Preis*, and in 2005 the *Förderpreis für Literatur*. He currently lives and works in Vienna.

[6] See Stephan Hilpold's "Aus der Fremde," in *Der Standard* (Wien: 17 May 2003), Supplement, A6: 'Bayer chose the form of a road movie' ("*Bayer wählte die Form eines Road-Movies*"); also Helmut Sturm, "Verloren im Kosmos," in

Salzburger Nachrichten, (Salzburg: 31 May 2003), Supplement, VII.

[7] One reviewer, Peter Landerl, comments: 'The narrator drifts aimlessly through northern Lower Austria' (*"Ziellos treibt es den Erzähler... durch das nördliche Niederösterreich"*); see "Inkompatibel mit der Welt," in *Wiener Zeitung* (Wien: 14 October 2006), Supplement, 11.

[8] See Leopold Federmair "Nach den Utopien," in *Neue Zürcher Zeitung* (Zürich: 24 November 2006), 27: *"Die Fortbewegung ist bei Bayer eher ein Zeichen von Antriebsschwäche, von Trägheit."*

[9] The plot unfolds similarly in 'Alaska Road' (*Alaskastraße*), where the first-person narrator states near the beginning of the novel that some change must occur in his life (*"Ich muß etwas ändern in meinem Leben,"* 33), and concludes at the very end that his mission has been accomplished (*"Ich hatte meine Mission erfüllt,"* 150); *Alaskastraße*, by the way, has no connection whatsoever with the U.S. state, but is the name of a street in provincial Austria.

[10] *"Es ist vor einiger Zeit etwas mit mir passiert, das ich noch immer nicht ganz begreifen kann, und damals, auf dieser Bank in Mistelbach sitzend..., habe ich zum ersten Mal versucht, mit vollem Bewusstsein darüber nachzudenken"* – 22-23.

[11] *"Vor einem Jahr war alles noch ganz normal"*– 23.

[12] *"Was jedoch dann, an diesem gewissen Abend, mit mir passierte, geschah von einem Moment zum anderen. Ich weiß nicht, ob Sie es begreifen werden, denn ich selbst habe es nicht begreifen können, weil es zum einen zu umfassend, zu groß und zum anderen so verschwindend winzig ist... Ich bin an diesem Abend nach einem Kinobesuch allein nach Hause spaziert, durch die Gassen, dann entlang des Burggartens am Ring.... Ich bin so dahingeschlendert ohne Kümmernis, ohne rechte Freude, neutral mein Empfinden..., als auf einmal, mitten im Dahingehen, etwas in mir stehenblieb, das auch mich zum Stehenbleiben veranlasste und mich, wie vom Blitz getroffen, mit einer zuvor so noch nie erlebten Plötzlichkeit*

wissen ließ, dass gerade etwas mit mir geschehen war, etwas, wonach ich nie wieder derselbe sein würde, dass etwas in mir zu Ende war, jäh, und dass etwas anderes, Neues, mir Unbekanntes an die Stelle gerückt war, und dieses neue Gefühl ist in diesem Moment nichts anderes gewesen, als das rasche Erschrecken darüber, etwas ein für allemal verloren zu haben, ein Gefühl von Schmerz und Ungläubigkeit und Entsetzen, dem ich als erste Reaktion nur meinen Unwillen und eine fast panische Geste des Wiedergutmachenwollens entgegensetzen konnte.... Ich hatte das Gefühl wie jemand, der seine letzte Chance verspielt weiß und dem von nun an der Weg zurück versperrt und der Weg nach vorne kein Weg, sondern nur eine sich trist ausdehnende Ebene ohne Richtung ist" – 23-24.

[13] See hkk, "Digitale Romantik," in *Salzburger Nachrichten*, (Salzburg: 23 September 2006), Supplement, VII: 'Bayer creates a wonderful mixture of precision, wealth of detail, and poetry.' (*"Bayer schafft die wunderbare Mischung aus Präzision, Detailreichtum und Poesie."*)

[14] Markus Hildebrand, "Mensch als Spielfigur?", in *Die Furche* (Wien: 16 November 2006), Nr. 46, Supplement, II: *"Der Autor entwirft das präzise Psychogramm eines jungen Menschen, dessen geregeltes Leben plötzlich schal und der jeder Gewissheit verlustig geworden ist."*

[15] *"Ich habe nicht weiter gefragt, sondern bin quer durch den Hof bis zum hinteren Gartentor, wo sich eine leichte Böschung hinab bis zum Teich erstreckt. Dem alten Kirchbaum habe ich gutmütig über den Stamm gestrichen. Ein paar Maulwurfshügel, die aus der Schneedecke geragt haben, haben in ihrer Anordnung wie ein Sternbild ausgesehen. Ich bin mit der Lust, mich zu verlaufen, losgestapft, mit derselben Lust, mit der ich beim ersten Betrachten von Landkarten in diesen verloren gehe. Aber ich habe freilich die Gegend noch zu gut gekannt, als dass es hätte passieren können. Unten, beim Teich, der von Birken und Trauerweiden umgeben ist, bin ich kurz stehen geblieben. Der Teich schien die Schatten seiner Uferbäume in sich aufzusaugen. Das Wasser hat satt und untröstlich ausge-*

sehen, und die Schneekristalle sind, sobald sie auf die Wasseroberfläche auftrafen, verschwunden. Ich bin weitergegangen, bis ich in den Wald, zum Anfang des Hohlwegs, gekommen bin, in dem mein Bruder und ich als Kinder gespielt hatten. Dort steht auch ein altes, unbewohntes Haus, über dessen gesamte Vorderfront ein großer Riss zackt, als hätte es da einmal ein Erdbeben gegeben. Ich habe mir einen Weg durch das Gebüsch zur Hinterseite gesucht, wo nur ein paar Bretter und alte Schilder gelehnt sind. Bei ihrem Anblick bin ich plötzlich ganz darauf bedacht gewesen, alles aus nächster Nähe anzusehen. Am liebsten hätte ich eine Lupe dabei gehabt. Dieses ausführliche Betrachten der Rückseite des verlassenen Hauses hat etwas Tröstliches gehabt, so wie mich jeder Ort, der schwer einsehbar und vordergründig nutzlos ist... innerlich aufatmen lässt. Nach einer Weile des Nur-still-Dastehens-und-Schauens bin ich zurück auf den Weg und weiter durch den Hohlweg marschiert, bis ich wieder an den Waldrand und auf die Felder gekommen bin. Von da an habe ich mich im Weiter-und-immer-weiter-Gehen entspannt und konzentriert zugleich gefühlt" – 45-47.

[16] Anton Thuswaldner, "Der brutale Sturz ins Ego-Land," in Die Presse (Wien: 7 June 2003), Suppl., VI: 'Like some figure by Handke, a character in Bayer's work also turns his home into a gigantic ego-land beyond civilization and culture.' (*"Wie eine Handke-Figur baut sich auch bei Bayer einer im großen Ego-Land abseits von Zivilisation und Kultur sein Heim."*)

[17] Hildenbrand II: 'Parallels impose themselves that reveal the intended environment as an illusion.' (*"Parallelen... drängen sich auf... welche die vermeintliche Umwelt als Illusion entlarven."*)

[18] *"Während ich so dahingegangen bin, bin ich im Geist noch bei der Rückseite des alten Hauses gewesen, und ich habe darüber nachgedacht, warum ich mich in Zwischenräumen immer so wohl fühle. Und ich bin mir bewusst geworden, dass Zwischenräume ja eigentlich mehr und mehr verschwinden. Sie werden getilgt, ausgelöscht, aus der Welt geschaffen wie*

etwas, wofür man sich schämt. Überall Materialisation. Die Menschen halten keine Leere mehr aus, Lücken sind ihnen unangenehm. Alles muss einsehbar sein, auf Teufelkommraus, notfalls und nicht nur notfalls durch Überwachungskameras. Die Weite der Staatsfeind Nr. 1, die Leere allein schon eine Horrorvorstellung, die Uneinsehbarkeit ein Schreckgespenst, eine jegliche Lücke der Makel schlechthin. Die Zwischenräume werden zugeschüttet und aufgefüllt mit dem Unansehnlichen wie ein Massengrab oder eine Mülldeponie, darüber kommt eine Schicht künstlicher Idylle. Oasen werden institutionalisiert, Zufluchtsorten wird der Platz genommen, Auswegen wird der Weg abgeschnitten" – 47-48.

[19] See Thomas Ballhausen, "Schädel unterm Arm," in *Wiener Zeitung* (Wien: 4 July 2003), Supplement, 11: 'His flight leads him back to nature.' (*"Die... Fluchtbewegung führt ihn in die Natur...."*)

[20] Eberhard Falcke, "Einfach raus und weg!" in *Die Zeit* (Frankfurt: 9 October 2003), Supplement No. 4, 1.

[21] Hildenbrand II refers to the narrator's 'diffuse discomfort in the midst of everyday places and situations' (*"diffuse Unbehagen... inmitten ganz alltäglicher Orte und Situationen"*).

[22] *"Die plötzliche Dunkelheit ist so unfassbar dicht gewesen, dass ich sie fast als etwas Gegenständliches empfunden habe, dessen erinnere ich mich genau. Ich habe mich nicht bewegt... und es ist mir ins Gedächtnis gekommen, wie ich vor Jahren mit zwei Freunden in eine Höhle gestiegen war. Wir waren über Leitern und glitschige Felswände immer tiefer geklettert, bis wir am vermeintlich untersten Niveau der Höhle angelangt waren. An dieser Stelle hatten wir Rast gemacht. Als wir dann dort alle drei unsere Kopfleuchten ausgeschaltet hatten, gab es nur noch das Dunkel, das vollkommenste Dunkel, das ich je erlebt hatte. Kein Laut war zu hören, und ich fühlte mich befreit wie noch nie. Ich hatte kein Verlangen, bald wieder die Lampe einzuschalten oder gar schnell wieder zurück ins Tageslicht zu kommen.... Während der langen Minuten des Schweigens aber war mir, als gäbe es nie wieder etwas zu*

sagen. Ich fühlte mich zwischen den lehmnassen Steinen wie in einem Becken aus warmem Wasser. Die Finsternis schien eins zu sein mit dem Fels, der uns alle umschloss. Mit dem Auslöschen des Lichts hatte ich auch meine Gefährten ausgelöscht, ihre Existenz. Ich war wie narkotisiert in diesen Minuten damals, wie eingeschlossen in den Stein, fast unnötig, Luft zu holen.... Noch nie hatte ich die Gegenwart so pur erlebt, und mir schien jemand mitteilen zu wollen, dass es keine Vergangenheit und keine Zukunft gebe, sondern nur eine sehr große, hoch und heilig andauernde Gegenwart" – 58-60.

[23] "Einige Zeit ist mir im darauffolgenden Unterwegs-Sein gar nichts Farbiges ins Blickfeld gekommen, nur grauweiße Himmel, der Schnee, die schwarzen Bäume und Reben und die riesigen Propellersäulen der Windparks, und ich habe unwillkürlich an einen universalen Schalter gedacht, den jemand umgelegt hatte, um mich alles in Schwarz-Weiß sehen zu lassen. Aber dann habe ich bemerkt, dass sich die Farben nur versteckt hielten, und sobald ich das durchschaut hatte, ist mir die Landschaft fast bunter als je im Sommer vorgekommen, so vielfältig sind die farbigen Abstufungen und Übergänge gewesen, am Straßenrand und an den Feldrändern. Der türkisdiesige Wald, wie über dem Horizont schwebend, dazu dunkelviolett, blauerfleckblau das Gesträuch an seinen Säumen. Die Farben der Misteln in manchen Bäumen, ein Leuchtgelb, fast neonfarben. Das Ziegelrot und Flechtenbraun der Dächer, der Ockerglanz über mancher kahlen Erdstelle im Schnee und über den Stoppelfeldern, der Silberdunst zwischen entlaubtem Gebüsch. Und das Eingeweiderot eines überfahrenen Hasen im Schnee am Straßenrand" – 73.

[24] "[der] allerorts sichtbare Rhythmus der Weinlüssen und Ackerfurchen... die in regelmäßigem Abstand gepflanzten Bäume der Monokulturen" – 74.

[25] "Kroupas Spieleschmiede" – 79.

[26] "Als ich an einer Gruppe von asiatischen Touristen vorbeigekommen bin und ihre Stimmen gehört habe, bin ich momentan beglückt gewesen, mich in einer fremden Stadt auf-

zuhalten, nicht in Wien sein zu müssen.... Aber im Weitergehen habe ich bemerkt, dass mein Verlangen, mich wirklich fremd zu fühlen, von der Wirklichkeit nicht gesättigt wurde. Ich glaube auch heute noch, dass dieses Unvermögen, mich fremd zu fühlen, damals in Brno, mit dem zu tun hatte, was mir damals vor dem Zaun des Burggartens widerfahren war, mit meiner Verwandlung, meinem Sehnsuchtsverlust" – 80-81.

[27] "Mir schien, als würde sich mit dem Verschwinden des Vergammelten und Unrentablen und dem An-die-Stelle-Treten des Glitzernden und Transparenten, des Verchromten auch das Menschliche aus der Öffentlichkeit zurückziehen, oder eher noch: Als würde es wissentlich abgewürgt werden" – Die Alaskastraße, 21.

[28] "Ich habe mir also eingestehen müssen, dass ich mich bei weitem nicht so fremd fühlte, wie ich es gerne gehabt hätte. Das ist auch daran gelegen, dass es in der Innenstadt Brnos im Grunde so ausgesehen hat wie in jeder anderen x-beliebigen mitteleuropäischen Stadt, dieselben Geschäfte, Banken, Supermärkte wie in Wien oder München. Die Mehrzahl der Leute in derselben einfallslosen Einheitskleidung und mit demselben unseligen Ausdruck in den Augen" – 81.

[29] "Auch da, in Brno, ist alles nach archaischen, nicht hinterfragbaren Naturgesetzen abgelaufen.... In dieser Hinsicht bin ich plötzlich gekränkt gewesen von der ewigen Wiederholung all dessen, was ich vor mir gesehen habe" – 81.

[30] Ballhausen 11: "die Auslöschung des Subjekts."

[31] "Die Realität hat dann, mit dieser Erkenntnis, plötzlich wieder begonnen, mir zu schaffen zu machen. Ich habe gefühlt, wie mir die Versuchung, dem Geschehen um mich herum ein Mich-täuschen-Wollen unterstellen zu müssen, durch den Körper gerieselt ist" – 82.

[32] Federmair 27: "die neue Utopie der virtuellen Unendlichkeit."

[33] "Meine Gedanken haben erneut angefangen, sich mit Computerspielen zu beschäftigen.... Die Außenwelt war für diese Zeitspanne ausgeblendet, wie nicht vorhanden. Ich habe die Augen geschlossen und mir die Spiele, die ich gespielt

hatte, vergegenwärtigt. Ich habe die Dschungellandschaften vor mir sehen können, die Korridore der Spukschlösser und die gespenstischen Fabrikhallen und die französischen Dörfer, durch die ich als englischer Soldat im Zweiten Weltkrieg gelaufen bin, um Nazis abzuknallen. Wie unmenschlich schön war manchmal die Grafik bei diesen Spielen. Wenn da der Wind in der Nacht die Blätter der Bäume kräuselte. Die Ringe, die entstanden, wenn man ins Wasser feuerte. Die Stapfgeräusche der Spielfigur, die Laute aus der Ferne, Hundegebell und Rufe, und, am atemberaubendsten, die Momente der Stille" – 102-103.

[34] *"Im Nachhinein gesehen war dieses Gefühl von Spannung und Freiheit dasselbe, das mich überkommen hatte, als ich als Kind auf dem Lande bei meinen Großeltern in die alten Scheunen und Häuser und verfallenen Ziegelwerke und stillgelegten Fabriken in der Umgebung eingestiegen war, um allein zwischen den überwachsenen Trümmern vergangener Existenzen umherzugehen"* – 104.

[35] *"Dann ist mir, wie als Ergänzung zu meinen vorhergehenden Gedanken, noch eingefallen, wie es war, wenn meine Freunde und ich nach solchen Computerspielmarathons wieder in die Außenwelt gewechselt waren.... Schlagartig war man aus der künstlichen Welt gestoßen. Man war zwar ernüchtert, aber immer noch unter ihrem Einfluss. Wenn ich mich damals verabschiedete und mich von der Wohnung eines meiner Freunde auf den Heimweg machte, funktionierte meine Wahrnehmung ganz nach den eingefleischten und verinnerlichten Maßstäben des Spiels.... Das Spiel war noch nicht zu Ende, und ich wusste, dass ich auch in den Träumen der kommenden Nächte meine Missionen im Feindgebiet durchführen würde müssen. Bis ich eines Tages aufwachte und wieder einen Konnex zur Wirklichkeit fände"* – 104-105.

[36] *"Ich habe mich, während meine Blicke ihren Fingerbewegungen beim Hantieren mit den Zutaten [fürs Essen] gefolgt sind, angestrengt, möglichst normal zu denken und mich nicht automatisch an irgendein Computerspiel erinnert zu fühlen, und*

das hat auch eine Weile ganz gut funktioniert, bis Teri dann von sich aus über ihre Lieblingsspiele geredet hat, aber selbst da hat die Wirklichkeitsentfremdung, die mich manchmal quält, nicht überhand genommen, gerade, als wäre man solange davor gefeit, solange man nur darüber spricht" – 124-125.

[37] "Teri hat mich dann gefragt, wie mir Brno gefalle, und ich habe gesagt, ich würde bedauern, dass die Stadt mittlerweile so aussehe wie jede andere Stadt in Mitteleuropa, dass kaum noch eine regionale Besonderheit zu erkennen sei, und im weiteren habe ich gemeint, dass überhaupt für mich immer weniger Orte auf der Welt existieren würden, an denen ich mich fremd fühlen könne, und dass ich mich nach einem Ort wie Antarktis sehnen würde wie nach einem Gegengift gegen die Fremdlosigkeit. Ich habe mich in meinen Redefluss hineingesteigert und ihr gestanden, dass ich für lächerlich und tödlich hielte, was mit der Welt geschehe" – 126.

[38] "dass sich die Menschen in Zukunft immer mehr in virtuelle Räume begeben würden, weil man sich dort noch wohlfühlen könne, und dass die Entwicklung in diese Richtung schon umfassender und virtueller sei, als man denke" – 138.

[39] "Ich habe nach wie vor in mir das Verlangen nach etwas Neuem, Unbekanntem gehabt, nach etwas, das mich vielleicht richtig über den Haufen werfen würde. Außerdem bin ich seit jeher einer gewesen, der nie aufhören hat können. Immer schon habe ich noch eins draufsetzen müssen. Ich habe auch in gewisser Weise geahnt, mit dieser Nacht am Ende eines Levels in meinem Leben angelangt zu sein, und das Letzte, was ich zu tun hatte, um weiterzukommen, um einen neuen Abschnitt zu betreten, war, noch etwas zu wagen und zu sehen, was dabei passiert" – 142-143.

[40] "Mir ist auf einmal furchtbar übel gewesen, und ich habe mir überlegt, ob ich mich übergeben sollte.... Ich habe die Augen geschlossen und tief durchgeatmet. Als ich die Augen aufgeschlagen habe, habe ich mit einem Mal alles gelb gesehen, wie in einem Schwefellicht.... Ein Dröhnen in meinen Ohren ist immer lauter geworden. Es hat ein bisschen geklungen wie

der anschwellende Applaus einer riesigen Zuhörerschaft. Kurz habe ich an das Netz von Satelliten denken müssen, das man in den letzten Jahren um die Erde aufgebaut hat... und der Gedanke, dass es bald nirgendwo einen Platz unter freiem Himmel geben würde, in dem man nicht aufgespürt werden könnte, hatte gerade dort, an diesem exponierten Fleck am obersten Plateau der Staatzer Klippen, etwas besonders Unheimliches" – 148.

[41] "*Beim Eintreten bin ich einige Sekunden lang an der Vorstellung hängengeblieben, in ein Raumschiff einzusteigen*" – 152.

[42] "*...ich bin mir mehr und mehr wie in einer gelbgestrichenen Höhle vorgekommen. Jedes Mal, wenn ich auf die gelbgestrichene Foyerwand rechts vom Eingang geschaut habe, war ich nicht sicher, ob die Wand nicht vielleicht doch weiß war und sie mir nur jetzt, in meinem Zustand, gelb erschien. Die Wand hinter mir ist dagegen so rot gewesen, dass ich mich davor gefürchtet habe, mich zu ihr hinzudrehen. Es ist mir vorgekommen, als würde sie Hitze ausstrahlen. Auch die schwarze Mattscheibe des Computers hat mir Angst eingejagt, sie könnte ohne Vorwarnung explodieren*" – 152-153.

[43] "*An den genauen Ablauf kann ich mich nicht erinnern, aber Sie können sich ja die Bilder der Überwachungskamera ansehen*" – 153.

[44] "*Ich habe anschließend die beiden Faustkeilfragmente vor mir auf den Tisch gelegt, den Hörer von dem Telefon abgehoben... und die einzige Nummer, die mir eingefallen ist, ist die der Zeitansage gewesen, und wie ich da in dem Sessel gesessen bin und die Stimme vom Tonband mir die aktuelle Zeit ins Ohr gesprochen hat, hat mich eine knöcherne Traurigkeit überwältigt, und ich habe mich auf den Boden vor dem Kontoauszugautomaten gelegt, und nach einer Weile, in der ich dagelegen bin und an die Decke des Raumes gestarrt habe, sind meine Gedanken plötzlich wieder sehr klar gewesen, und ich habe mit einem Schmerz in der Brust wieder an meine*

verlorengegangene Sehnsucht denken müssen, und dass es wahrscheinlich nie mehr anders werden würde" – 154-155.

[45] *"[da] ist mir eine lebensrettende Idee in den Sinn gekommen, dass es doch auch eine Sehnsucht ist, wenn man sich nach der Sehnsucht sehnt, und dass die Sehnsucht also vielleicht doch noch da ist, dass sie sich vielleicht die ganze Zeit über nur bedeckt und versteckt gehalten hat"* – 155.

[46] *"Ich weiß jetzt, dass man nicht verloren gehen kann in der Welt"* – 155.

[47] *"Ich schließe die Augen und sehne mich danach, durch den Schnee zu laufen, das Stapfen meiner Schritte zu hören und das Knirschen der eisigen Schneedecke und mein Außer-Atem-Sein. Wenn ich mich umdrehe und zurücklaufe, möchte ich meine Spuren am Wege sehen. Ich möchte auch die Wolken sehen, die über die Landschaft schweben und ihre Schatten über die Erde ziehen. Ich will auf dem gefrorenen Fluss dahinschlittern"* – 155-156.

[48] *"Aufgewachsen bin ich in einem Schloss aus Vorhängen, umgeben von Mauern, mit wilden Tieren wie im Dschungel, rundherum ein Wassergraben, der mittlerweile trockengelegt und zugeschüttet wurde, mit einer Zugbrücke und einer Freitreppe, die heute zugewachsen ist: der Anblick all dessen ist mit den Jahren faserig und durchscheinend geworden wie ein alter Gobelin. Wie in einem Fuchsbau haben meine Träume Fluchtwege ins Mauerwerk gegraben. Mit der Zeit wurde das Interieur geplündert, die meisten Gänge zwischen den Zimmern sind eingestürzt und unpassierbar. Die Vorhänge sind abgenommen und zu Polsterüberzügen verarbeitet worden, die in Secondhandläden verstauben. Von außen ist kaum mehr etwas zu erkennen, nur im Winter, wenn die Blätter von Bäumen und Gestrüpp verschwunden sind, kann man, wenn man zu sehen versteht, hinter den Ästen und Zweigen die Risse in der Bausubstanz erkennen. In den ruinösen, desolaten Räumen sind heute allein Scherben und Schutt zu Hause, Taubenflügel und Fragmente vom Stuck. An den Wänden Kinderzeichnungen und Wörter eingeritzt,*

manchmal noch Überreste von Fresken, der Großteil von ihnen mit Slogans übermalt, ein jeder von ihnen ein Tor in eine andere Welt" – 157 [italics in the original].

[49] *"Ich habe Sehnsucht nach dem Urwald. Ich werde mich hinter einem Baum verstecken, im Dickicht des Programms, solange ich möchte, und ich werde mich hinauswagen, sobald meine Neugier mir das vorschreibt. Ich werde über die Waldlichtung und den mittelalterlichen Dorfplatz gehen oder mit dem Auto auf dem Kamm eines Berges entlangfahren. Ich fühle wieder Sehnsucht, und deswegen ist alles sehr leicht"* – 156.

[50] *"Die Rolltreppen... sahen aus, als würden sie wie Sisyphos Sinnloses heraufschaufeln"* (*Die Alaskastraße*, 144).

[51] See Stephanie Würster, "Verschwinden in Posen," in *die tageszeitung* (Berlin: 15 July 2003); Würster calls Bayer, with some justification, a *"Wiedergänger"* of Christian Kracht, who started the cult of 'Pop-Literatur' in the mid-90s, i.e. a reincarnation of sorts of the German author, the only difference being that *Faserland* (Köln: Kiepenheuer & Witsch, 1995) contains far more social criticism and is also much funnier than Bayer's novels.

[52] Daniel Kehlmann, *Die Vermessung der Welt: Roman* (Reinbek: Rowohlt, 2005), and translated into English by Carol Brown Janeway as *Measuring the World* (New York: Pantheon Books, 2006).

[53] Susanne Messmer, "Stille Tage im Wienerwald," in *die tageszeitung* (Berlin: 24 January 2002).

[54] Hilpold A 6.

[55] Federmair 27: 'Logically, "Onward" ends with a colon, beyond which you can think or dream whatever you want' (*"Konsequenterweise endet 'Weiter' mit einem Doppelpunkt, hinter dem Sie sich denken oder träumen können, was Sie wollen."*)

[56] Marcel Proust, *Les Plaisirs et les Jours* (Paris: Gallimard, 1962; 1895): *"Nous la [vie] songeons, et nous l'aimons de la songer. Il ne faut pas essayer de la vivre"* – 181.

Contributors

Kathleen Condray (Ph.D., University of Illinois at Urbana-Champaign) is an Associate Professor of German and Director of German Graduate Studies at the University of Arkansas at Fayetteville. Her research and teaching interests include minority and women writers of the 20th and 21st centuries, and her book *Women Writers of the Journal Jugend from 1919-1940: "Das Gehirn unsrer lieben Schwestern"* appeared in 2003. She was the recipient of a Fulbright German Studies Seminar award in 2002, an NEH German Studies Institute award in 2005, and a Fulbright College Master Teacher Award in 2007.

Donald G. Daviau, Emeritus Professor of Austrian and German Literature at the University of California, Riverside, has been president of the International Arthur Schnitzler Research Association, editor of the journal *Modern Austrian Literature*, president of the American Council for the Study of Austrian Literature, organizer of the Annual Austrian Symposium, as well as co-founder and editor of Ariadne Press. Daviau is the author of numerous books and articles on Bahr, Hofmannsthal, Schnitzler, Kraus, Zweig, Auernheimer, Lothar, Bernhard, Frischmuth, Musil, Turrini, Mitgutsch, Zech, Sutter, Trenker, Austrian Identity, Biedermeier, Censorship in the Vormärz, The Austrian Postwar Revival, and Major Figures of Austrian Literature.

Paul F. Dvorak is Professor and coordinator of the German program at Virginia Commonwealth University, where he has been teaching language, literature, and culture courses since 1974. Recently he taught a course on Vienna for the University Honors Program. He is also program coordinator for the six residential components of the Virginia Governor's Foreign Language Academies. His research interests encompass modern German literature, especially Austrian literature of the turn of the century and the contemporary Austrian scene. He is the translator of literary and secondary works, editor of *Modern Austrian Prose: Interpretations and Insights*, and a member of the editorial board of Ariadne Press.

Todd C. Hanlin, Emeritus Professor of German at the University of Arkansas, has authored a book on Franz Kafka and edited Charles

Sealsfield's *Austria as It Is*. He has written on Peter Henisch, Paulus Hochgatterer, Hugo von Hofmannsthal, Arthur Schnitzler, and Peter Turrini, translated novels by Gustav Ernst, Anton Fuchs, Hochgatterer, Georg Potyka, Peter Steiner, and Gerald Szyszkowitz, several plays by Fritz Hochwälder, Felix Mitterer, and Szyszkowitz, as well as a volume on *The Best of Austrian Science Fiction*.

Geoffrey C. Howes (Ph.D. University of Michigan, 1985) is Professor of German at Bowling Green State University in Ohio. From 2000 to 2005 he was co-editor with Jacqueline Vansant of *Modern Austrian Literature*. He has published on a variety of topics in Austrian studies including Robert Musil, Joseph Roth, Ingeborg Bachmann, Peter Rosei, Lilian Faschinger, Thomas Bernhard, Michael Scharang, and recent Austrian essays, and is working on a book about the representation of madness in Austrian fiction. His translations into English include texts by Rosei, Faschinger, Margret Kreidl, Gerhard Kofler, and Doron Rabinovici.

Dagmar C. G. Lorenz is Professor of Germanic Studies and Director of Jewish Studies at the University of Illinois, Chicago. Her book publications include *Keepers of the Motherland: German Texts by Jewish Women Writers* (1997) and *Verfolgung bis zum Massenmord. Diskurse zum Holocaust in deutscher Sprache* (1992). She has served as editor of the *German Quarterly* and has edited or co-edited five books, including monographs on Ilse Aichinger and Franz Grillparzer, and companion volumes to Elias Canetti and Arthur Schnitzler.

Renate S. Posthofen received her Ph.D. in German from the State University of New York at Albany, and is currently Associate Professor of German at Utah State University in Logan. She is the author of numerous articles dealing with contemporary Austrian and German literature and culture, including such authors as Robert Schindel, Robert Menasse, Ruth Beckermann, Claire Goll, and György Sebestyén. Dr. Posthofen authored *Treibgut: Das vergessene Werk George Saikos* (1995), coedited *Transforming the Center, Eroding the Margins: Essays on Ethnic and Cultural Boundaries in German-Speaking Countries* (1998), and edited a volume of critical essays on *Barbara Frischmuth in Contemporary Context* (1999).

Contributors 293

Gerlinde Ulm Sanford, is currently Professor in the Department of Languages, Literatures & Linguistics at Syracuse University. Her scholarly publications include *Wörterbuch von Berufsbezeichnungen* (1975), a new text edition and commentary of Andreas Gryphius' *Aemilius Paulus Papinianus* (1977), a *Konkordanz zu Schillers philosophischen und aesthetischen Schriften* (1980), *Goethes Briefwechsel mit seinem Sohn August* (2005), as well as numerous essays on modern Austrian writers such as Alois Brandstetter, Barbara Frischmuth, Michael Köhlmeier, Felix Mitterer, Robert Schindel, Werner Schwab, Peter Turrini, and Josef Weinheber.

Jörg Thunecke, was Senior Lecturer at Nottingham Trent University in England from 1970 to1997, and since 1998 has been a wissenschaftlicher Mitarbeiter at the Westdeutsche Akademie für Kommunikation (Cologne). His scholarly publications on 20th-century German literature include books on Exile- and NS-Literatur: *Leid der Worte: Panorama des literarischen Nationalsozialismus* (ed., 1987); *Deutschsprachige Exillyrik von 1933 bis zur Nachkriegszeit* (ed., 1998), *Theodor Kramer: Chronist seiner Zeit* (co-ed., 2000); *126, Westbourne Terrace: Erich Fried im Londoner Exil* (co-ed., 2001); *Hitler im Visier: Literarische Satiren und Karikaturen als Waffe gegen den Nationalsozialismus* (co-ed., 2005); *Das Echo des Exils* (ed., 2006); *Preserving the Memory of Exile: Festschrift for John M. Spalek* (co-ed., 2008).

Felix Tweraser is Associate Professor of German at Utah State University (Logan). He is the recipient of Fulbright and NEH fellowships and served as Book Review Editor for *German Quarterly* from 2001-2004. His research spans contemporary Austrian literature and politics and the works of Arthur Schnitzler; publications include: "Paris Calling Vienna: The Congress for Cultural Freedom and Friedrich Torberg's Editorship of *Forum*"; "Imagining Jörg Haider: Artistic Responses to the Rise of the FPÖ and the Democratization of the Austrian Public Sphere"; "Schnitzler's Turn to Prose Fiction: The Depiction of Consciousness in Selected Narratives;" and *Political Dimensions of Arthur Schnitzler's Late Fiction*.

Beyond Vienna: Contemporary Literature from the Austrian Provinces

For centuries, Vienna had been the imperial residence and capital of the great multilingual, multinational Habsburg Empire, and thus a magnet for the accumulation of power, prestige, wealth, and beauty. However, it is self-evident that not everyone could or should reside in the capital, that many talented authors, whether by choice or by chance, lived outside that glamorous city, in Kafka's words, far from "the Imperial sun."

At the outset of the twenty-first century, with technological advancements in transportation and communication—with international publishing houses and chain bookstores, with e-mail and the Internet, for example—is there any social, political, economic, or professional advantage to residing in Vienna, or has it become irrelevant today where artists live? Are their life experiences notably different, whether they reside in the capitol or in any other city, large or small? Are authors' choices of language or themes influenced by their provincial backgrounds? Thus the idea of "Beyond Vienna"— a compelling and timely topic.

This volume will attempt to address these questions, while serving as an introduction to nine authors—poets, novelists, and dramatists— and their relationships to the capital: Xaver Bayer, Alois Brandstetter, Gloria Kaiser, Christine Lavant, Anna Mitgutsch, Felix Mitterer, Elisabeth Reichart, Vladimir Vertlib, and Friedrich Ch. Zauner. The contributors are respected scholars who were personally invited to join this project and who ultimately determined which authors would be included.

Todd C. Hanlin, professor emeritus of German at the University of Arkansas, has published a monograph on Franz Kafka and edited Charles Sealsfield's *Austria As It Is*. He has written on Hofmannsthal, Schnitzler, Peter Turrini, Peter Henisch, Paulus Hochgatterer, and translated novels by Anton Fuchs, Gustav Ernst, Gerald Szyszkowitz, Georg Potyka, and Peter Steiner, plays by Szyszkowitz, Felix Mitterer, and Fritz Hochwälder, as well as a volume on *The Best of Austrian Science Fiction*.